RIP HAYWIRE

AND THE CURSE OF TANGAROA!

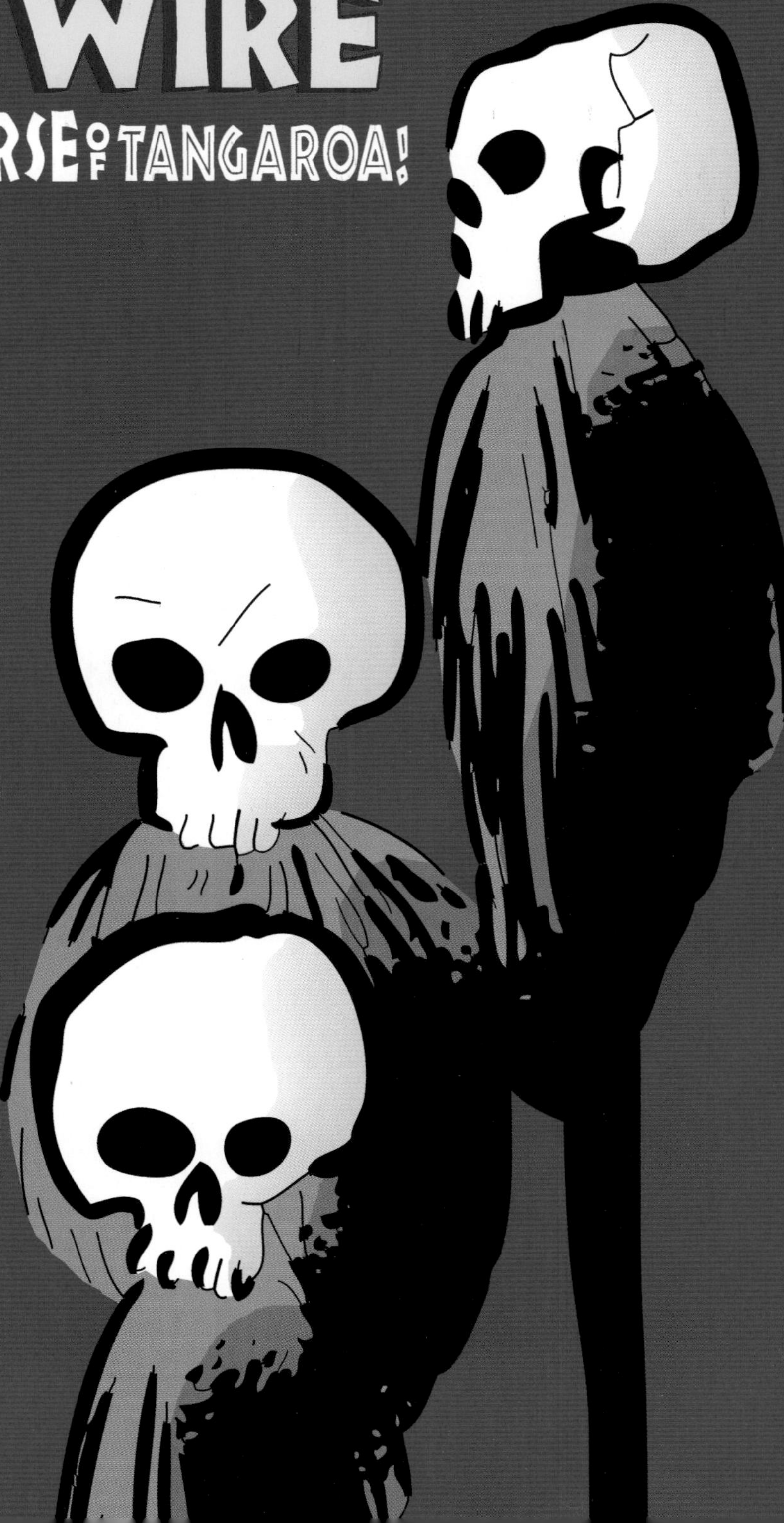

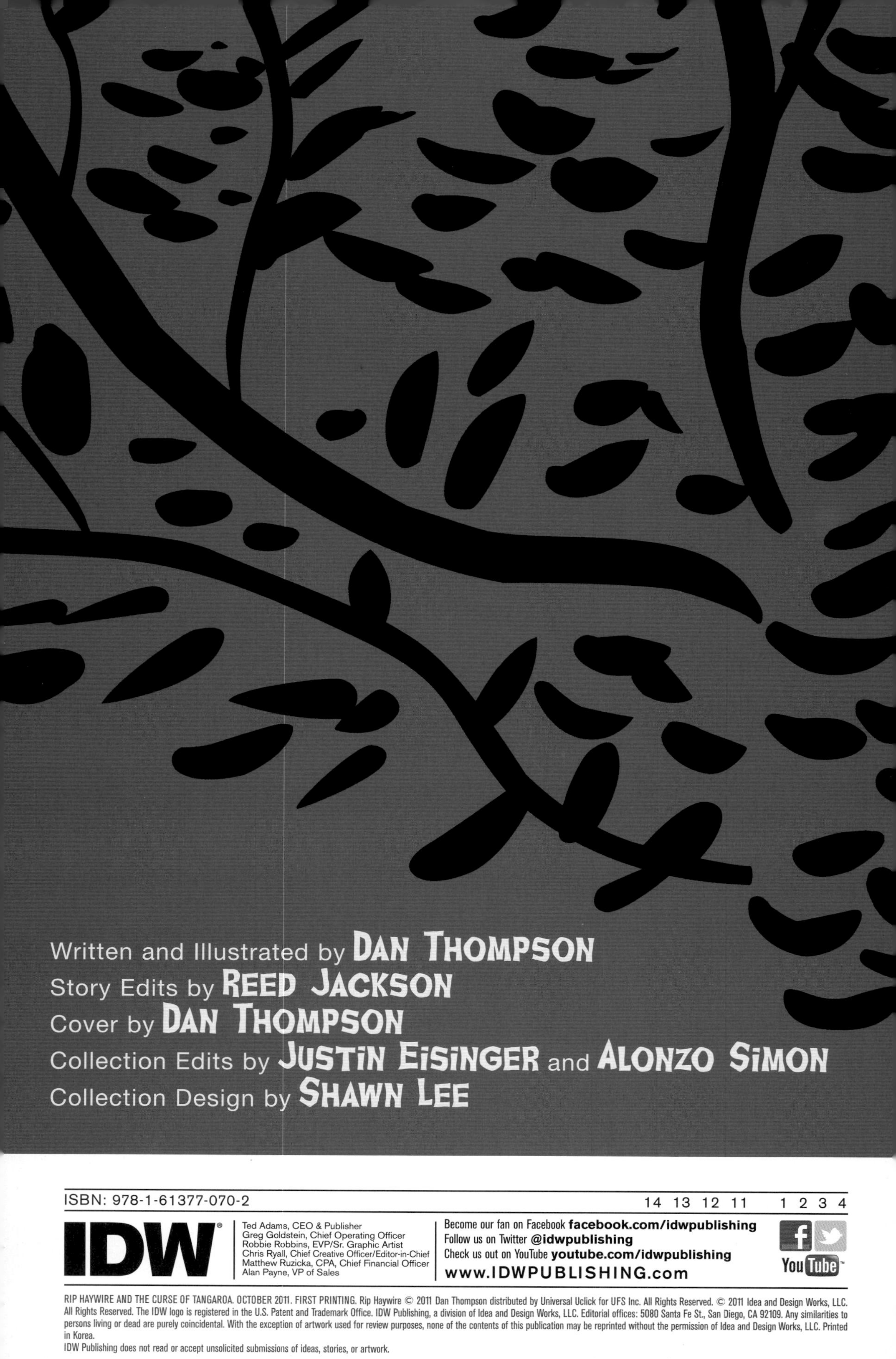

Written and Illustrated by **DAN THOMPSON**
Story Edits by **REED JACKSON**
Cover by **DAN THOMPSON**
Collection Edits by **JUSTIN EISINGER** and **ALONZO SIMON**
Collection Design by **SHAWN LEE**

ISBN: 978-1-61377-070-2

14 13 12 11 1 2 3 4

IDW®

Ted Adams, CEO & Publisher
Greg Goldstein, Chief Operating Officer
Robbie Robbins, EVP/Sr. Graphic Artist
Chris Ryall, Chief Creative Officer/Editor-in-Chief
Matthew Ruzicka, CPA, Chief Financial Officer
Alan Payne, VP of Sales

Become our fan on Facebook **facebook.com/idwpublishing**
Follow us on Twitter **@idwpublishing**
Check us out on YouTube **youtube.com/idwpublishing**
www.IDWPUBLISHING.com

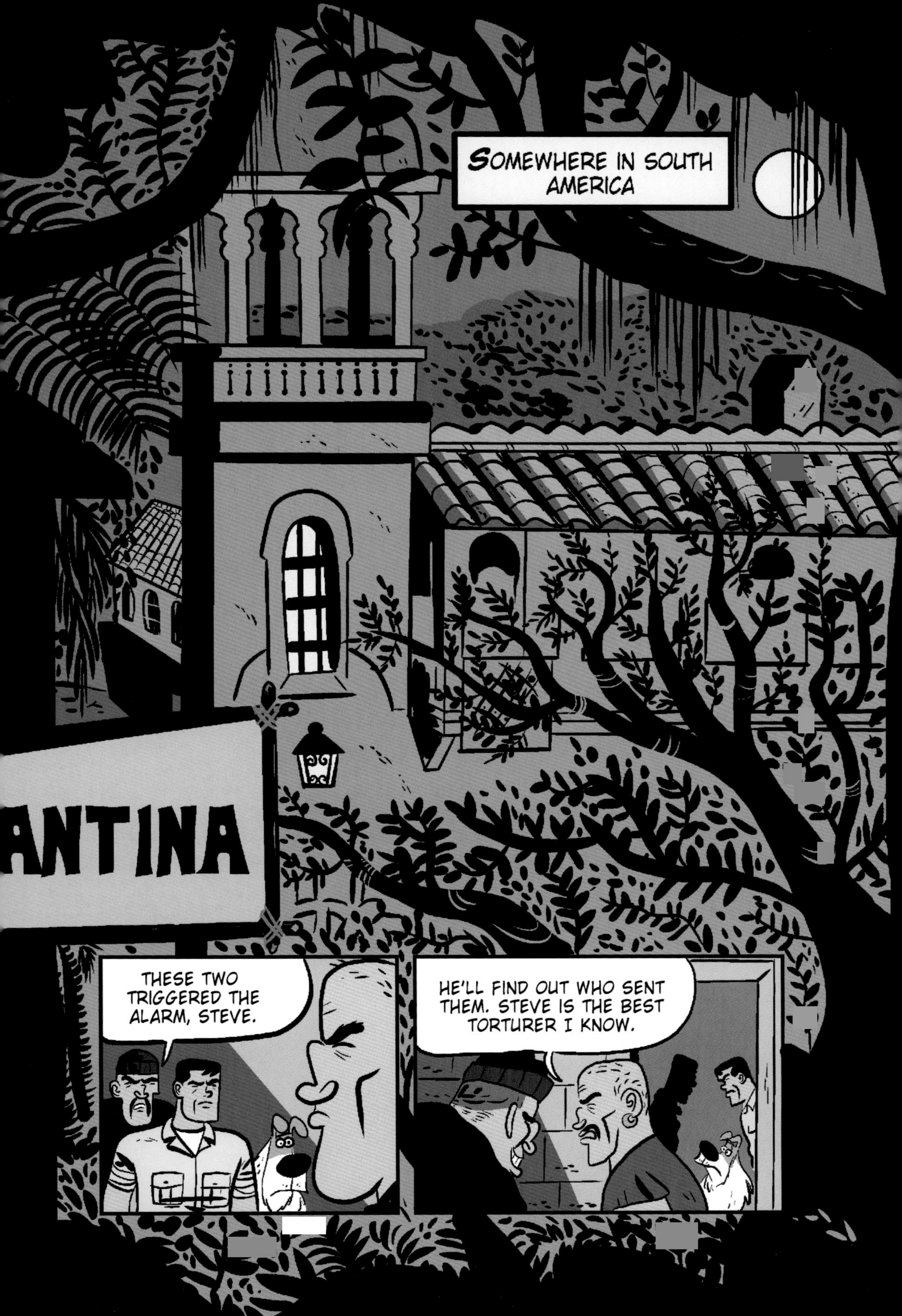
SOMEWHERE IN SOUTH AMERICA
ANTINA
THESE TWO TRIGGERED THE ALARM, STEVE.
HE'LL FIND OUT WHO SENT THEM. STEVE IS THE BEST TORTURER I KNOW.

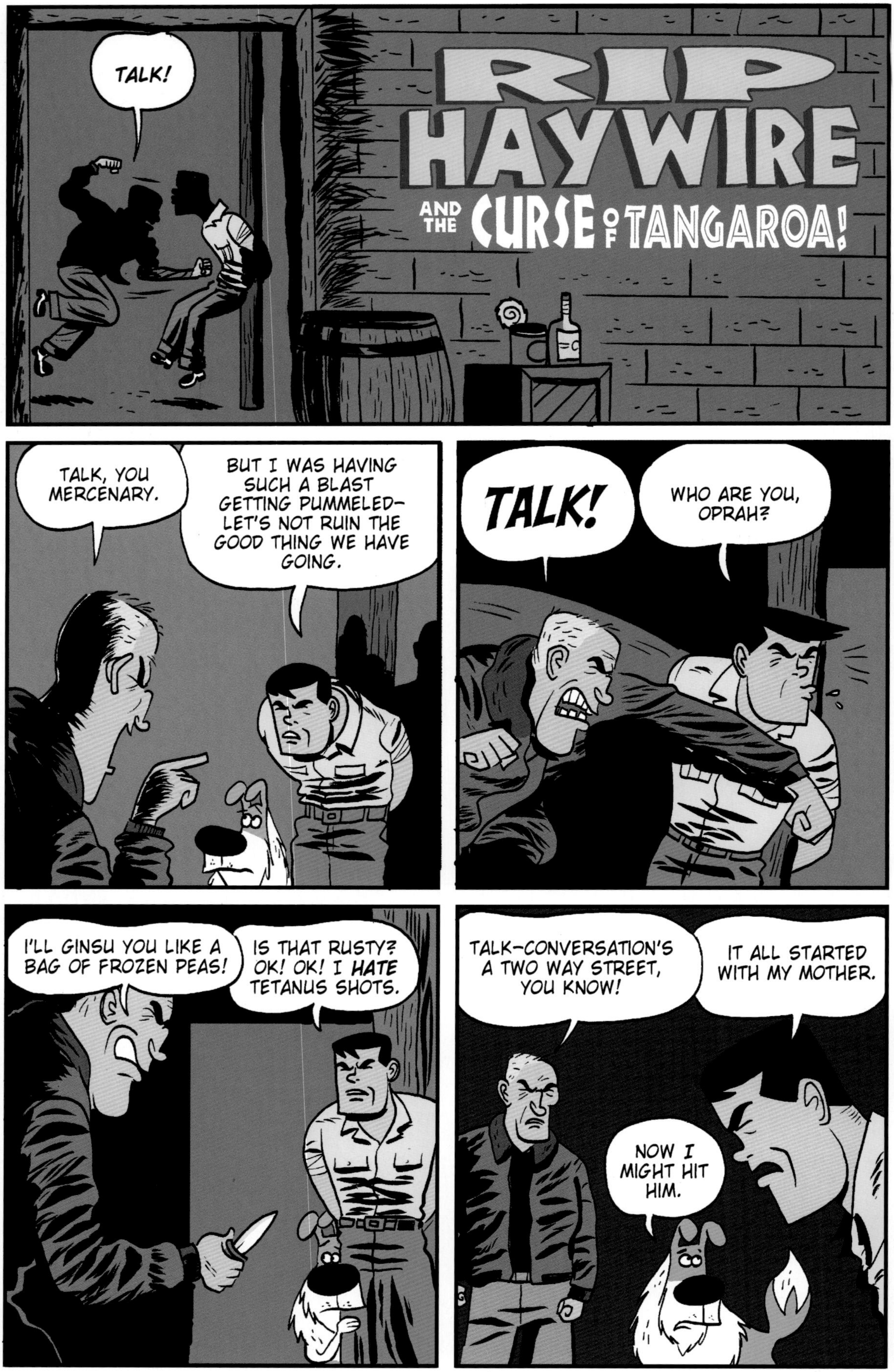
TALK!
RIP HAYWIRE AND THE CURSE OF TANGAROA!
TALK, YOU MERCENARY.
BUT I WAS HAVING SUCH A BLAST GETTING PUMMELED— LET'S NOT RUIN THE GOOD THING WE HAVE GOING.
TALK!
WHO ARE YOU, OPRAH?
I'LL GINSU YOU LIKE A BAG OF FROZEN PEAS!
IS THAT RUSTY? OK! OK! I *HATE* TETANUS SHOTS.
TALK—CONVERSATION'S A TWO WAY STREET, YOU KNOW!
IT ALL STARTED WITH MY MOTHER.
NOW *I* MIGHT HIT HIM.

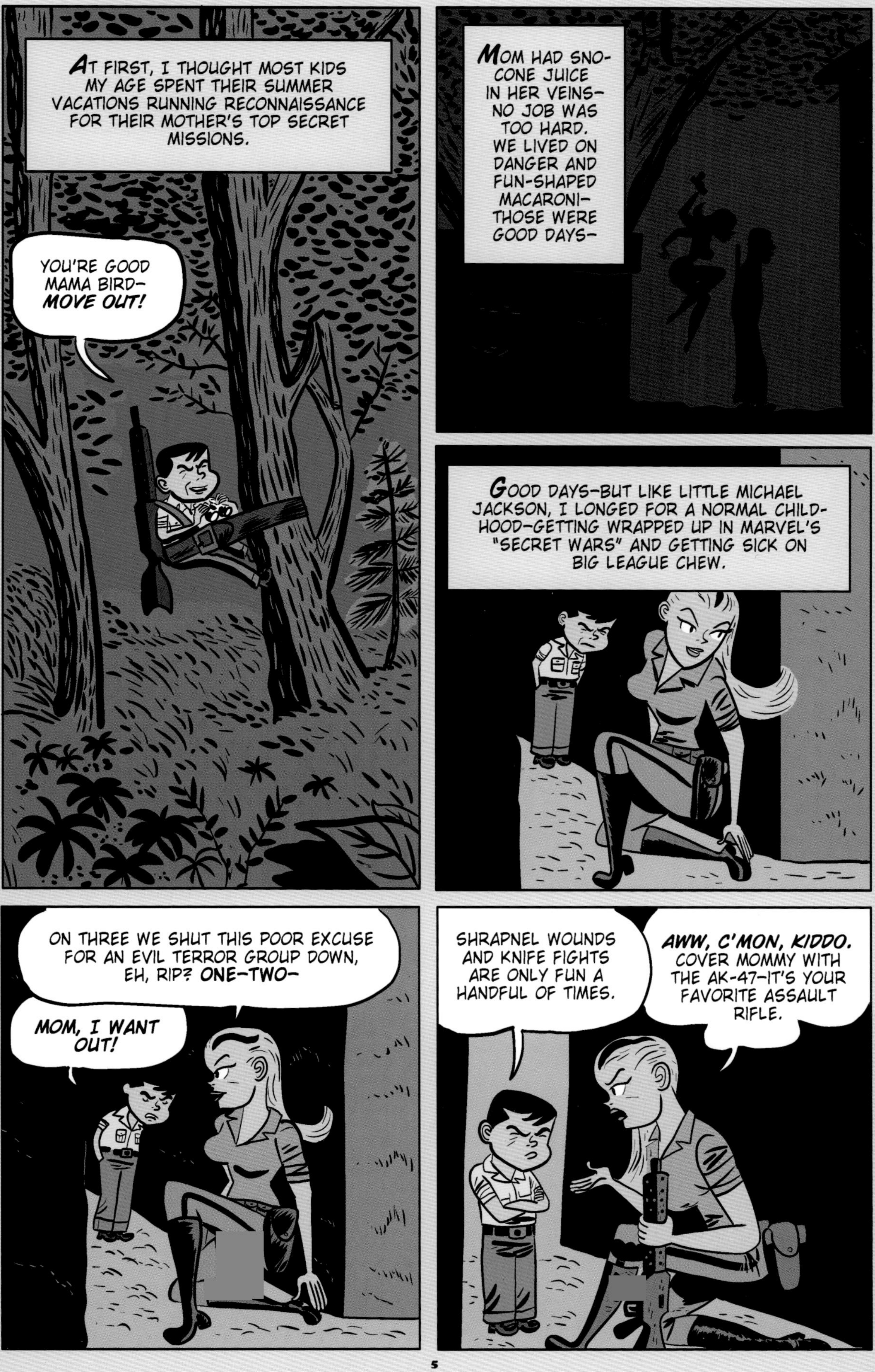
AT FIRST, I THOUGHT MOST KIDS MY AGE SPENT THEIR SUMMER VACATIONS RUNNING RECONNAISSANCE FOR THEIR MOTHER'S TOP SECRET MISSIONS.
YOU'RE GOOD MAMA BIRD– MOVE OUT!
MOM HAD SNO-CONE JUICE IN HER VEINS– NO JOB WAS TOO HARD. WE LIVED ON DANGER AND FUN-SHAPED MACARONI– THOSE WERE GOOD DAYS–
GOOD DAYS–BUT LIKE LITTLE MICHAEL JACKSON, I LONGED FOR A NORMAL CHILD-HOOD–GETTING WRAPPED UP IN MARVEL'S "SECRET WARS" AND GETTING SICK ON BIG LEAGUE CHEW.
ON THREE WE SHUT THIS POOR EXCUSE FOR AN EVIL TERROR GROUP DOWN, EH, RIP? ONE–TWO–
MOM, I WANT OUT!
SHRAPNEL WOUNDS AND KNIFE FIGHTS ARE ONLY FUN A HANDFUL OF TIMES.
AWW, C'MON, KIDDO. COVER MOMMY WITH THE AK-47–IT'S YOUR FAVORITE ASSAULT RIFLE.

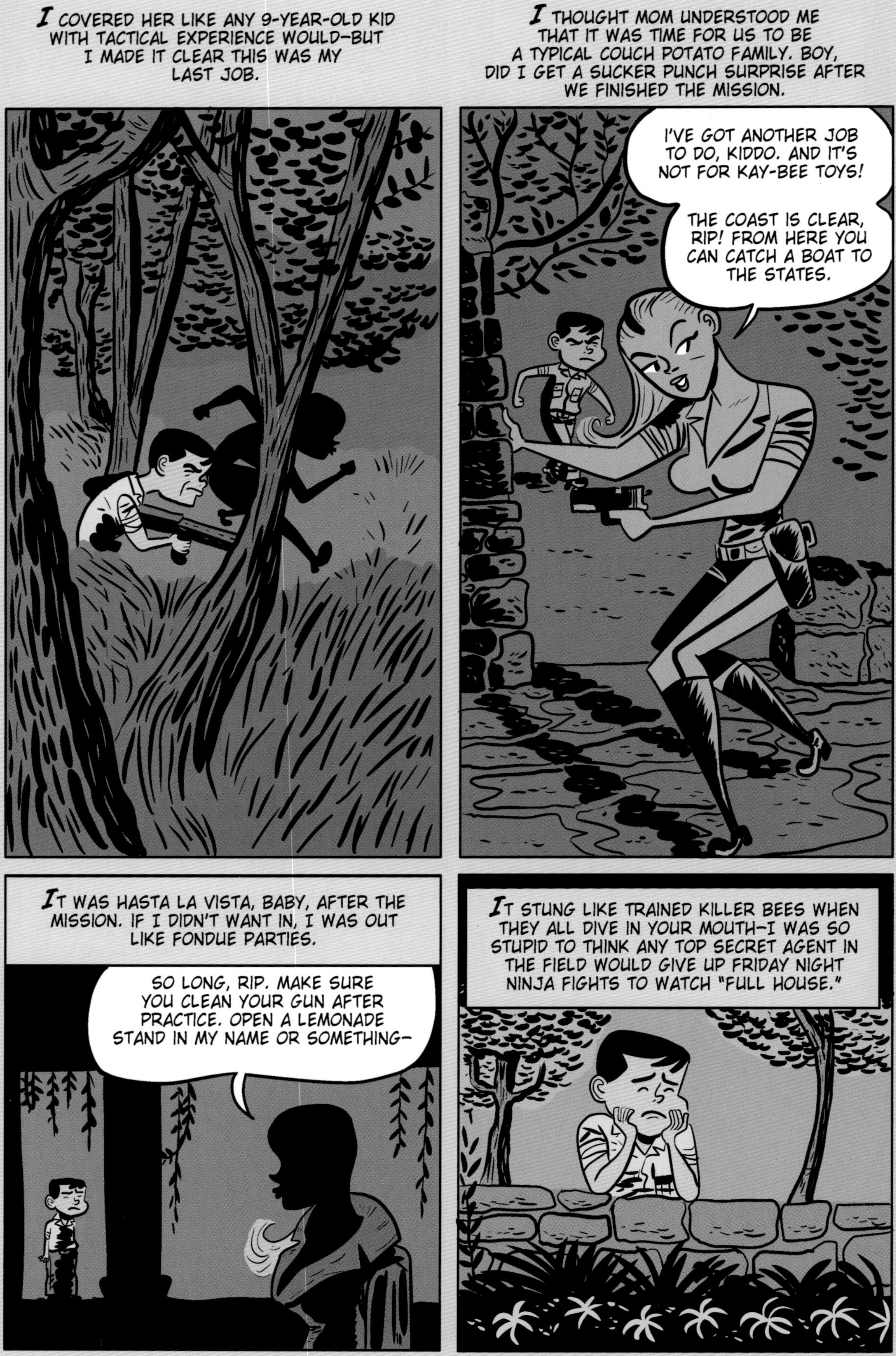
I COVERED HER LIKE ANY 9-YEAR-OLD KID WITH TACTICAL EXPERIENCE WOULD—BUT I MADE IT CLEAR THIS WAS MY LAST JOB.
I THOUGHT MOM UNDERSTOOD ME THAT IT WAS TIME FOR US TO BE A TYPICAL COUCH POTATO FAMILY. BOY, DID I GET A SUCKER PUNCH SURPRISE AFTER WE FINISHED THE MISSION.
I'VE GOT ANOTHER JOB TO DO, KIDDO. AND IT'S NOT FOR KAY-BEE TOYS!
THE COAST IS CLEAR, RIP! FROM HERE YOU CAN CATCH A BOAT TO THE STATES.
IT WAS HASTA LA VISTA, BABY, AFTER THE MISSION. IF I DIDN'T WANT IN, I WAS OUT LIKE FONDUE PARTIES.
SO LONG, RIP. MAKE SURE YOU CLEAN YOUR GUN AFTER PRACTICE. OPEN A LEMONADE STAND IN MY NAME OR SOMETHING—
IT STUNG LIKE TRAINED KILLER BEES WHEN THEY ALL DIVE IN YOUR MOUTH—I WAS SO STUPID TO THINK ANY TOP SECRET AGENT IN THE FIELD WOULD GIVE UP FRIDAY NIGHT NINJA FIGHTS TO WATCH "FULL HOUSE."

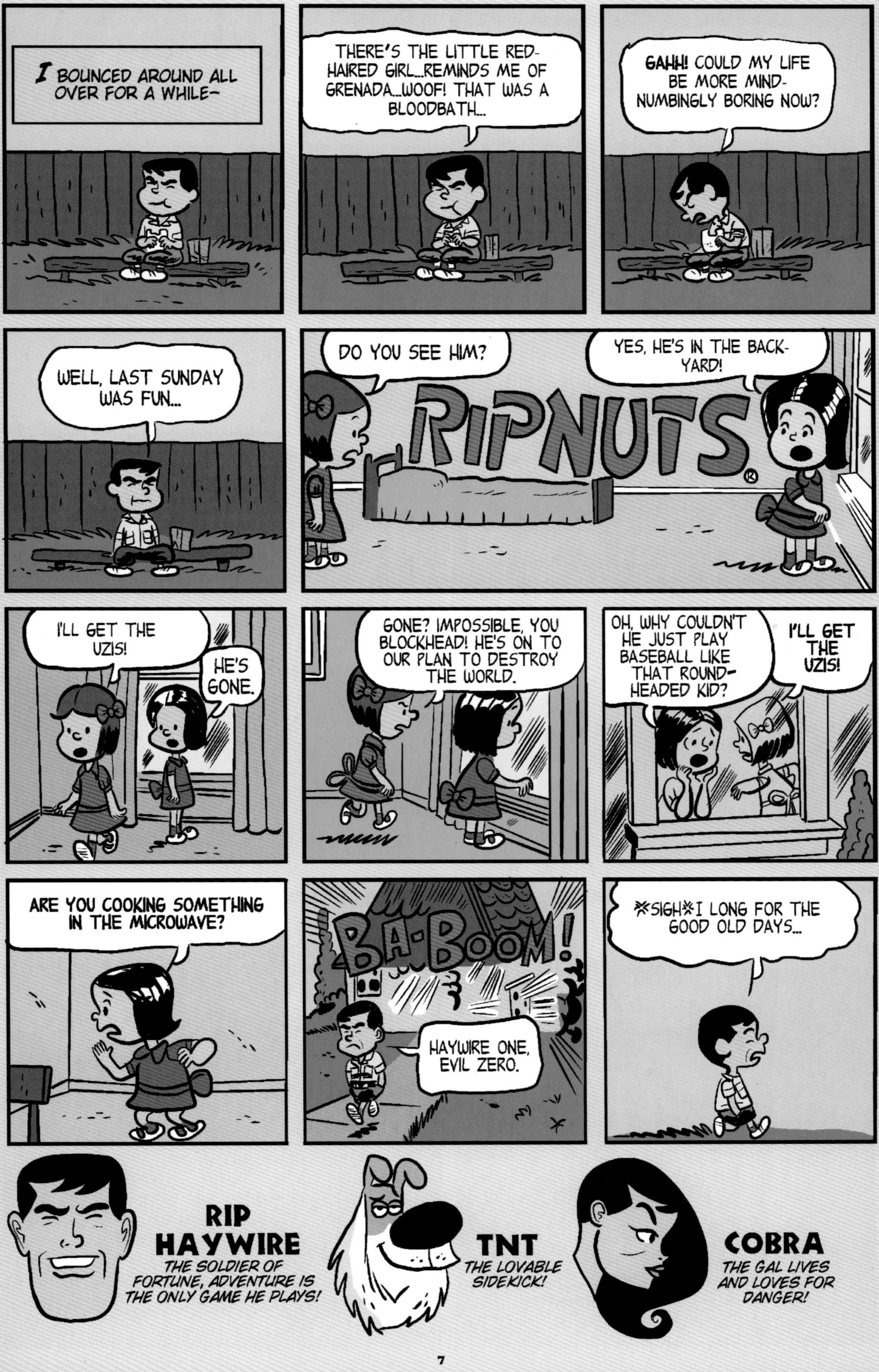
I BOUNCED AROUND ALL OVER FOR A WHILE–
THERE'S THE LITTLE RED-HAIRED GIRL...REMINDS ME OF GRENADA...WOOF! THAT WAS A BLOODBATH...
GAHH! COULD MY LIFE BE MORE MIND-NUMBINGLY BORING NOW?
WELL, LAST SUNDAY WAS FUN...
DO YOU SEE HIM?
RIPNUTS®
YES, HE'S IN THE BACK-YARD!
I'LL GET THE UZIS!
HE'S GONE.
GONE? IMPOSSIBLE, YOU BLOCKHEAD! HE'S ON TO OUR PLAN TO DESTROY THE WORLD.
OH, WHY COULDN'T HE JUST PLAY BASEBALL LIKE THAT ROUND-HEADED KID?
I'LL GET THE UZIS!
ARE YOU COOKING SOMETHING IN THE MICROWAVE?
BA-BOOM!
HAYWIRE ONE, EVIL ZERO.
SIGH I LONG FOR THE GOOD OLD DAYS...
RIP HAYWIRE
THE SOLDIER OF FORTUNE, ADVENTURE IS THE ONLY GAME HE PLAYS!
TNT
THE LOVABLE SIDEKICK!
COBRA
THE GAL LIVES AND LOVES FOR DANGER!

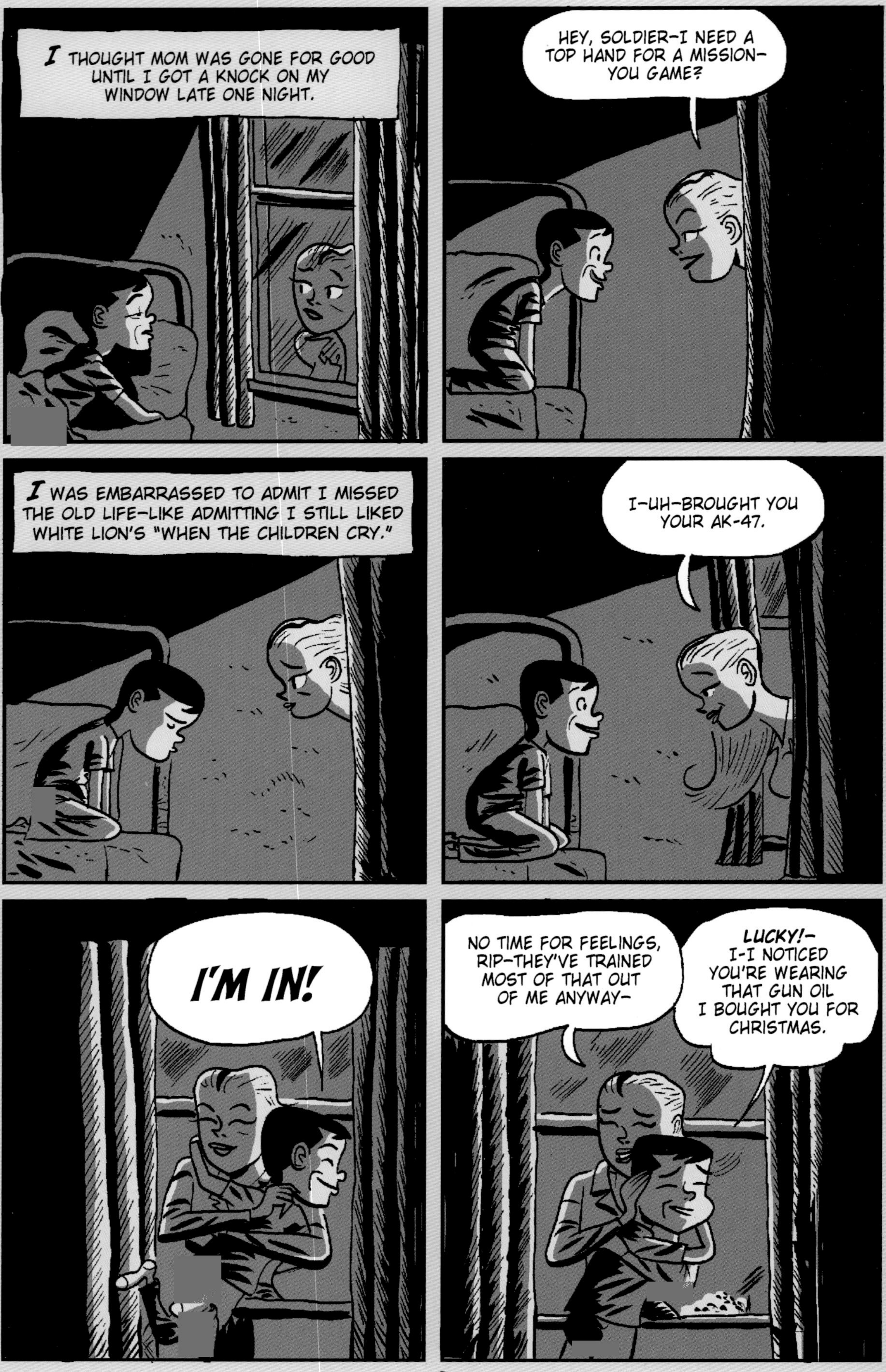
I THOUGHT MOM WAS GONE FOR GOOD UNTIL I GOT A KNOCK ON MY WINDOW LATE ONE NIGHT.
HEY, SOLDIER–I NEED A TOP HAND FOR A MISSION–YOU GAME?
I WAS EMBARRASSED TO ADMIT I MISSED THE OLD LIFE–LIKE ADMITTING I STILL LIKED WHITE LION'S "WHEN THE CHILDREN CRY."
I–UH–BROUGHT YOU YOUR AK-47.
I'M IN!
NO TIME FOR FEELINGS, RIP–THEY'VE TRAINED MOST OF THAT OUT OF ME ANYWAY–
LUCKY!– I-I NOTICED YOU'RE WEARING THAT GUN OIL I BOUGHT YOU FOR CHRISTMAS.

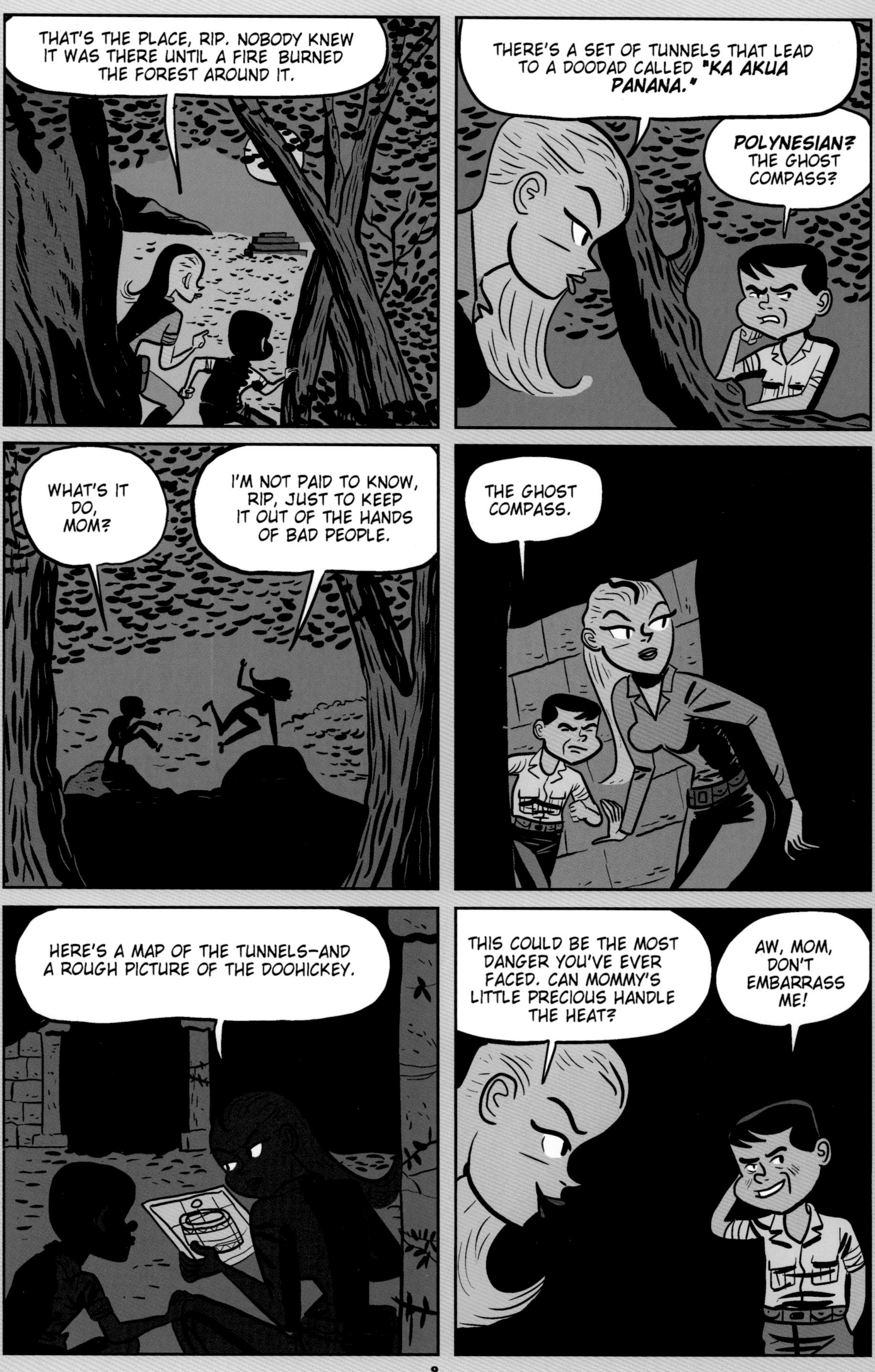
THAT'S THE PLACE, RIP. NOBODY KNEW IT WAS THERE UNTIL A FIRE BURNED THE FOREST AROUND IT.
THERE'S A SET OF TUNNELS THAT LEAD TO A DOODAD CALLED "KA AKUA PANANA."
POLYNESIAN? THE GHOST COMPASS?
WHAT'S IT DO, MOM?
I'M NOT PAID TO KNOW, RIP, JUST TO KEEP IT OUT OF THE HANDS OF BAD PEOPLE.
THE GHOST COMPASS.
HERE'S A MAP OF THE TUNNELS—AND A ROUGH PICTURE OF THE DOOHICKEY.
THIS COULD BE THE MOST DANGER YOU'VE EVER FACED. CAN MOMMY'S LITTLE PRECIOUS HANDLE THE HEAT?
AW, MOM, DON'T EMBARRASS ME!

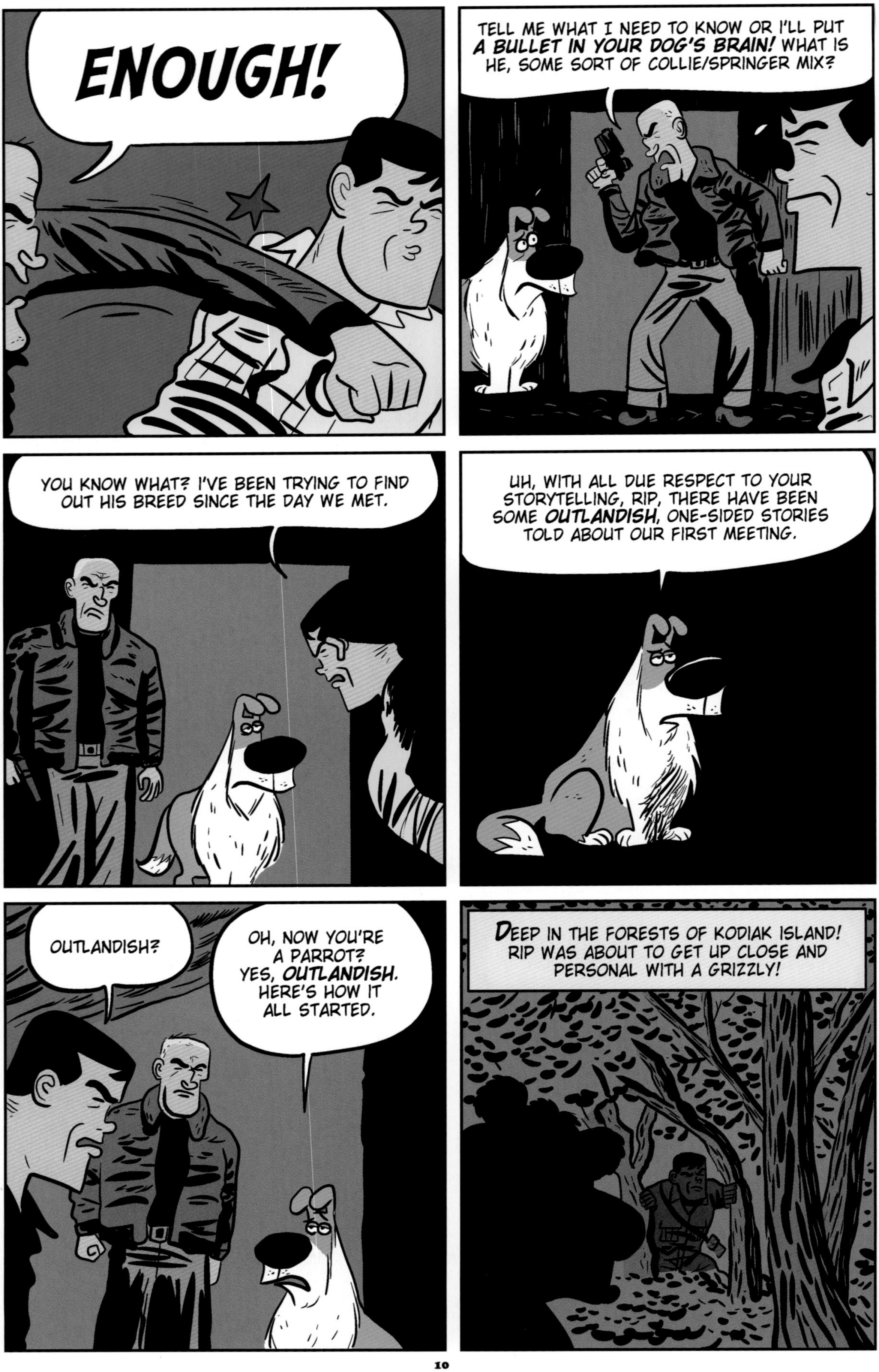
ENOUGH!
TELL ME WHAT I NEED TO KNOW OR I'LL PUT A BULLET IN YOUR DOG'S BRAIN! WHAT IS HE, SOME SORT OF COLLIE/SPRINGER MIX?
YOU KNOW WHAT? I'VE BEEN TRYING TO FIND OUT HIS BREED SINCE THE DAY WE MET.
UH, WITH ALL DUE RESPECT TO YOUR STORYTELLING, RIP, THERE HAVE BEEN SOME OUTLANDISH, ONE-SIDED STORIES TOLD ABOUT OUR FIRST MEETING.
OUTLANDISH?
OH, NOW YOU'RE A PARROT? YES, OUTLANDISH. HERE'S HOW IT ALL STARTED.
DEEP IN THE FORESTS OF KODIAK ISLAND! RIP WAS ABOUT TO GET UP CLOSE AND PERSONAL WITH A GRIZZLY!

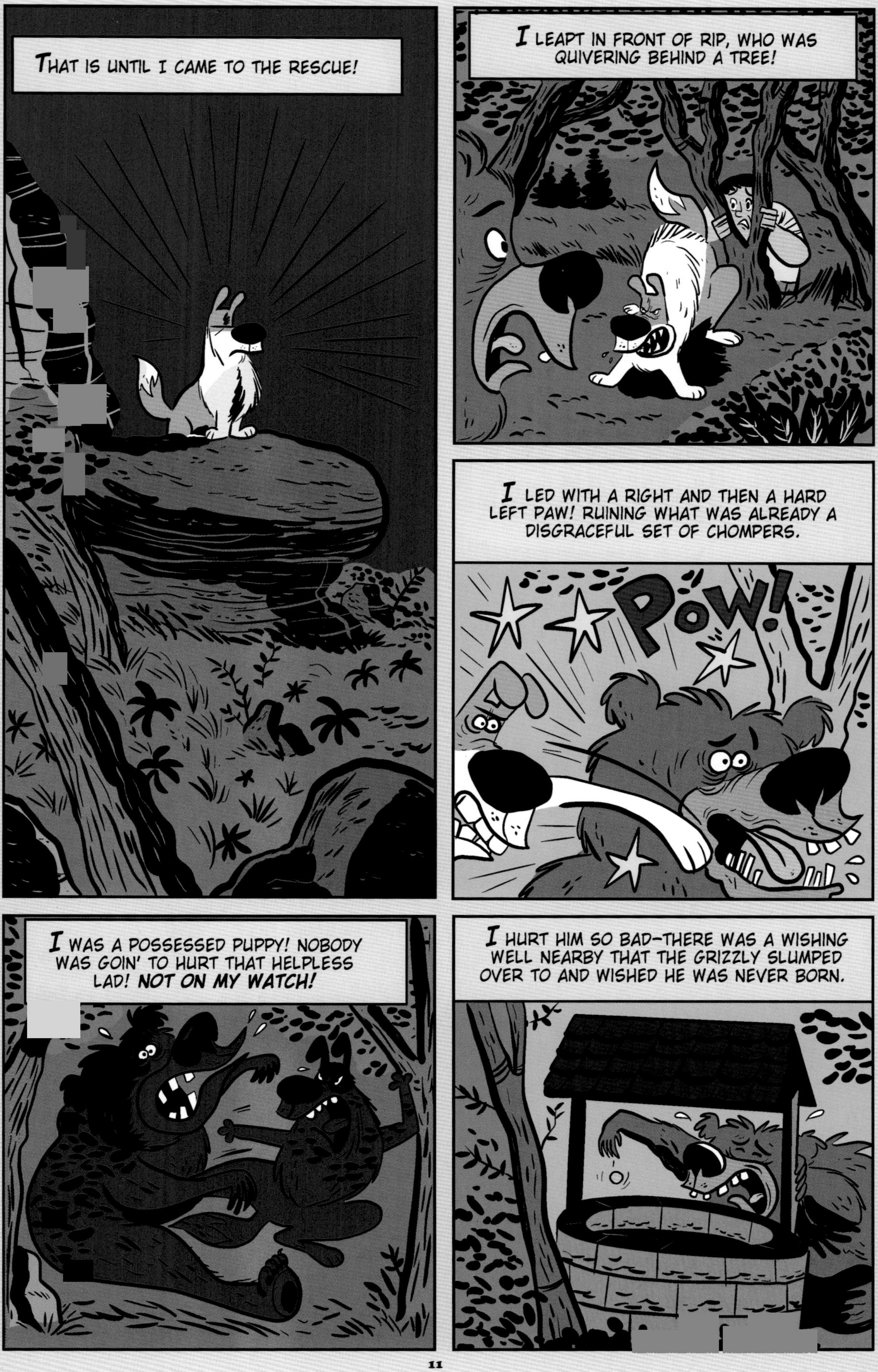
THAT IS UNTIL I CAME TO THE RESCUE!
I LEAPT IN FRONT OF RIP, WHO WAS QUIVERING BEHIND A TREE!
I LED WITH A RIGHT AND THEN A HARD LEFT PAW! RUINING WHAT WAS ALREADY A DISGRACEFUL SET OF CHOMPERS.
POW!
I WAS A POSSESSED PUPPY! NOBODY WAS GOIN' TO HURT THAT HELPLESS LAD! NOT ON MY WATCH!
I HURT HIM SO BAD—THERE WAS A WISHING WELL NEARBY THAT THE GRIZZLY SLUMPED OVER TO AND WISHED HE WAS NEVER BORN.

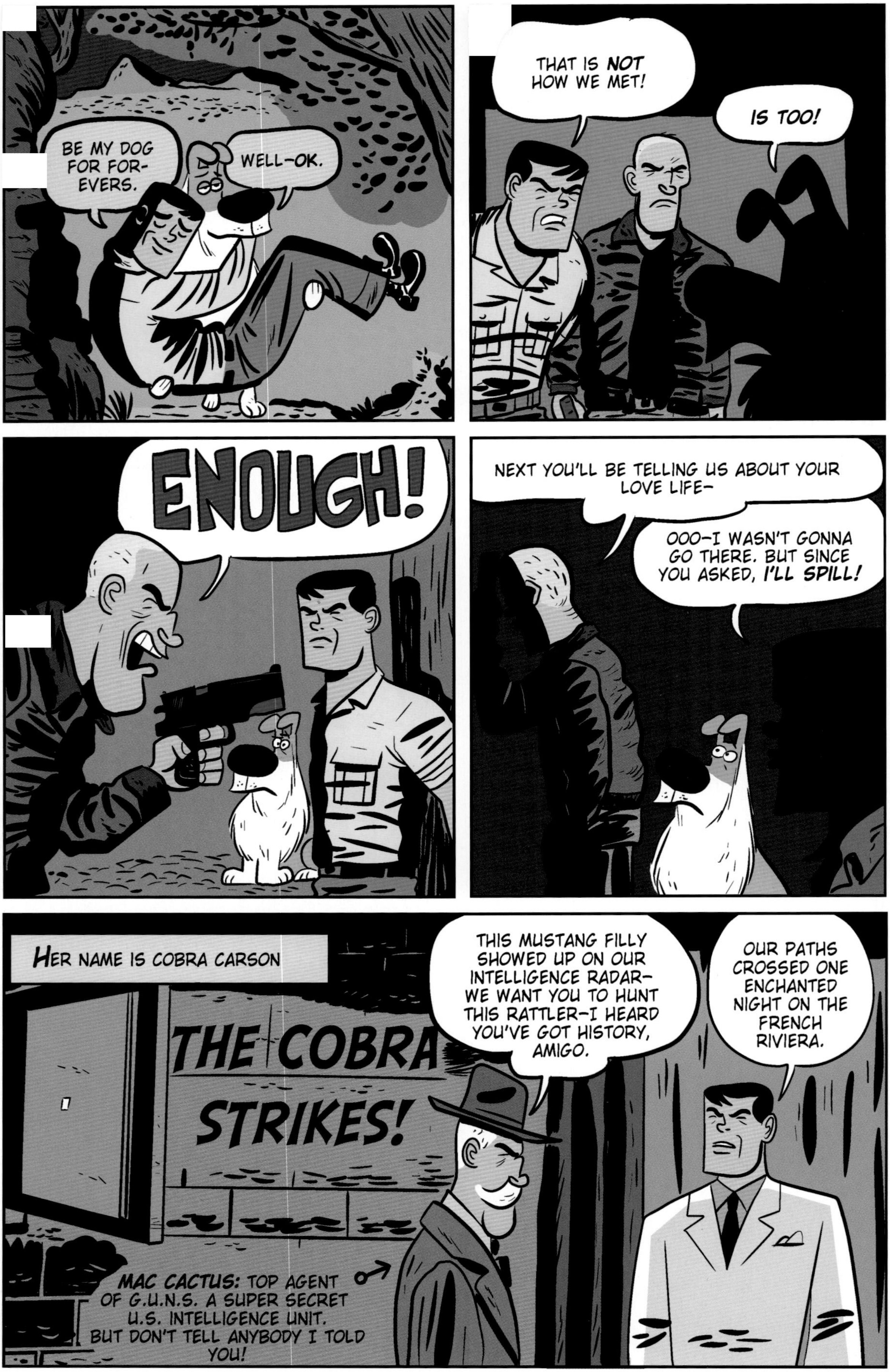
BE MY DOG FOR FOR-EVERS.
WELL-OK.
THAT IS NOT HOW WE MET!
IS TOO!
ENOUGH!
NEXT YOU'LL BE TELLING US ABOUT YOUR LOVE LIFE-
OOO-I WASN'T GONNA GO THERE. BUT SINCE YOU ASKED, I'LL SPILL!
HER NAME IS COBRA CARSON
THE COBRA STRIKES!
THIS MUSTANG FILLY SHOWED UP ON OUR INTELLIGENCE RADAR- WE WANT YOU TO HUNT THIS RATTLER-I HEARD YOU'VE GOT HISTORY, AMIGO.
OUR PATHS CROSSED ONE ENCHANTED NIGHT ON THE FRENCH RIVIERA.
MAC CACTUS: TOP AGENT OF G.U.N.S. A SUPER SECRET U.S. INTELLIGENCE UNIT. BUT DON'T TELL ANYBODY I TOLD YOU!

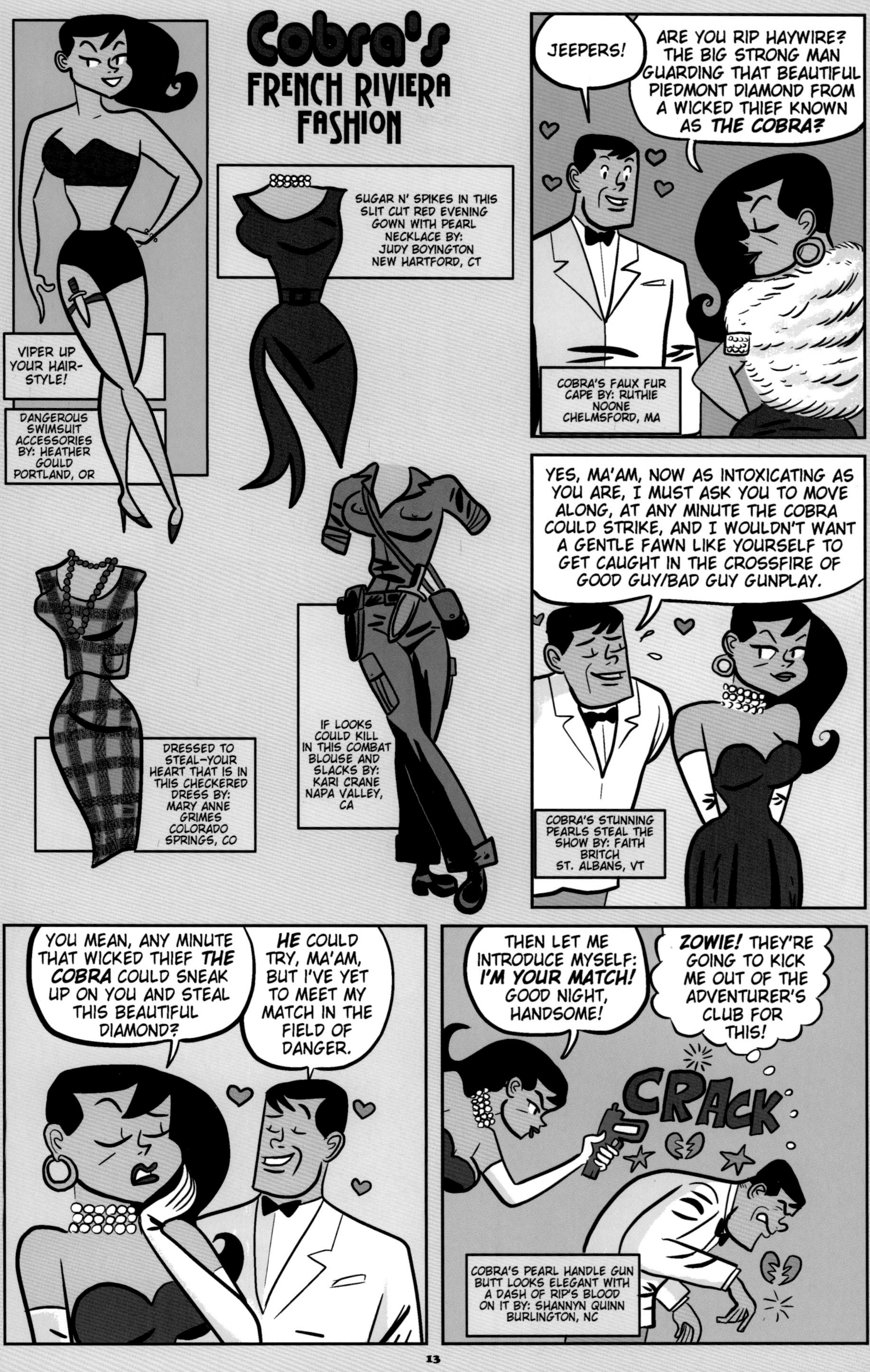
Cobra's FRENCH RIVIERA FASHION
VIPER UP YOUR HAIR-STYLE!
DANGEROUS SWIMSUIT ACCESSORIES BY: HEATHER GOULD PORTLAND, OR
SUGAR N' SPIKES IN THIS SLIT CUT RED EVENING GOWN WITH PEARL NECKLACE BY: JUDY BOYINGTON NEW HARTFORD, CT
DRESSED TO STEAL—YOUR HEART THAT IS IN THIS CHECKERED DRESS BY: MARY ANNE GRIMES COLORADO SPRINGS, CO
IF LOOKS COULD KILL IN THIS COMBAT BLOUSE AND SLACKS BY: KARI CRANE NAPA VALLEY, CA
JEEPERS!
ARE YOU RIP HAYWIRE? THE BIG STRONG MAN GUARDING THAT BEAUTIFUL PIEDMONT DIAMOND FROM A WICKED THIEF KNOWN AS THE COBRA?
COBRA'S FAUX FUR CAPE BY: RUTHIE NOONE CHELMSFORD, MA
YES, MA'AM, NOW AS INTOXICATING AS YOU ARE, I MUST ASK YOU TO MOVE ALONG, AT ANY MINUTE THE COBRA COULD STRIKE, AND I WOULDN'T WANT A GENTLE FAWN LIKE YOURSELF TO GET CAUGHT IN THE CROSSFIRE OF GOOD GUY/BAD GUY GUNPLAY.
COBRA'S STUNNING PEARLS STEAL THE SHOW BY: FAITH BRITCH ST. ALBANS, VT
YOU MEAN, ANY MINUTE THAT WICKED THIEF THE COBRA COULD SNEAK UP ON YOU AND STEAL THIS BEAUTIFUL DIAMOND?
HE COULD TRY, MA'AM, BUT I'VE YET TO MEET MY MATCH IN THE FIELD OF DANGER.
THEN LET ME INTRODUCE MYSELF: I'M YOUR MATCH! GOOD NIGHT, HANDSOME!
ZOWIE! THEY'RE GOING TO KICK ME OUT OF THE ADVENTURER'S CLUB FOR THIS!
CRACK
COBRA'S PEARL HANDLE GUN BUTT LOOKS ELEGANT WITH A DASH OF RIP'S BLOOD ON IT BY: SHANNYN QUINN BURLINGTON, NC

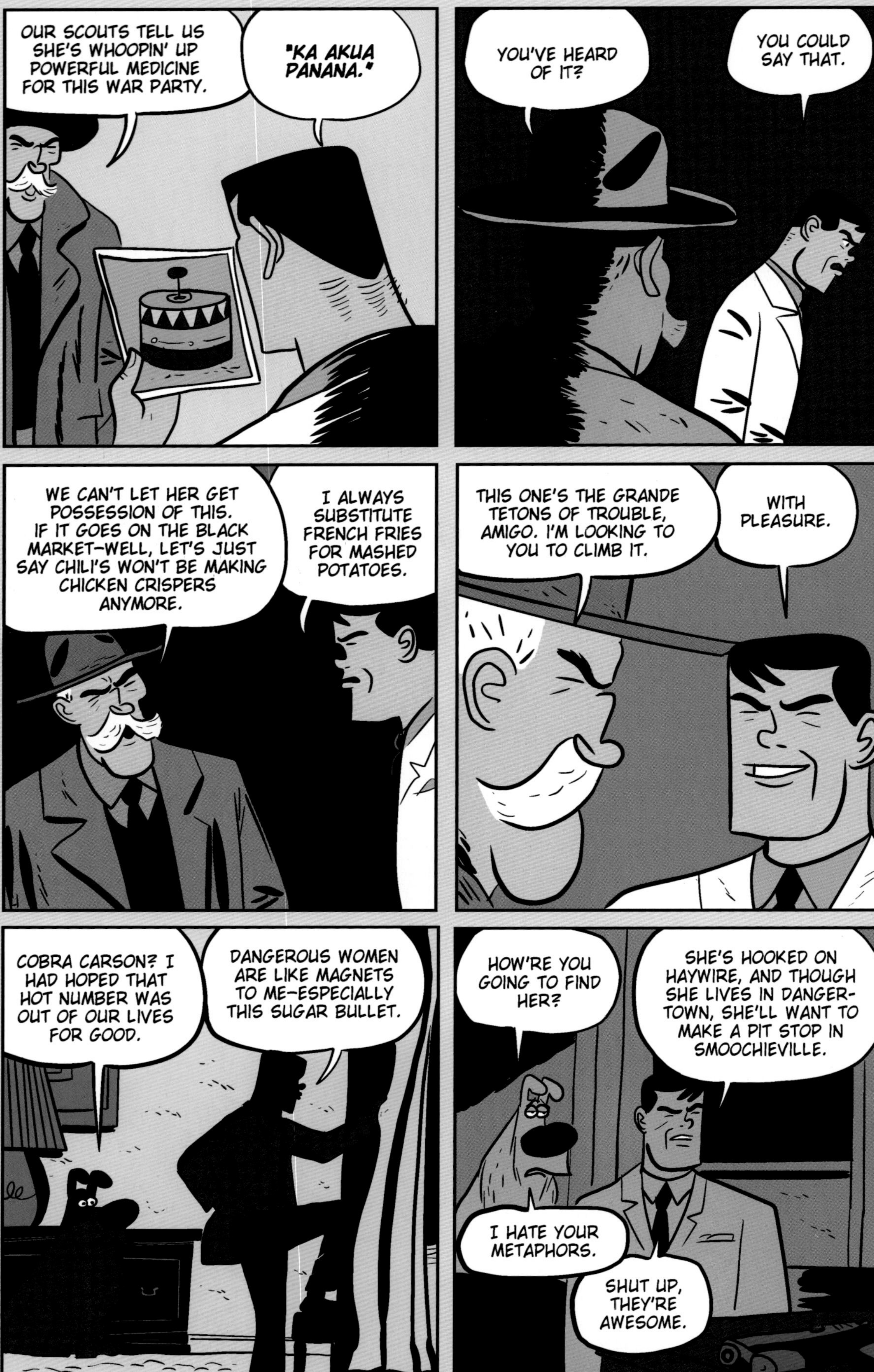
OUR SCOUTS TELL US SHE'S WHOOPIN' UP POWERFUL MEDICINE FOR THIS WAR PARTY.
"KA AKUA PANANA."
YOU'VE HEARD OF IT?
YOU COULD SAY THAT.
WE CAN'T LET HER GET POSSESSION OF THIS. IF IT GOES ON THE BLACK MARKET—WELL, LET'S JUST SAY CHILI'S WON'T BE MAKING CHICKEN CRISPERS ANYMORE.
I ALWAYS SUBSTITUTE FRENCH FRIES FOR MASHED POTATOES.
THIS ONE'S THE GRANDE TETONS OF TROUBLE, AMIGO. I'M LOOKING TO YOU TO CLIMB IT.
WITH PLEASURE.
COBRA CARSON? I HAD HOPED THAT HOT NUMBER WAS OUT OF OUR LIVES FOR GOOD.
DANGEROUS WOMEN ARE LIKE MAGNETS TO ME—ESPECIALLY THIS SUGAR BULLET.
HOW'RE YOU GOING TO FIND HER?
SHE'S HOOKED ON HAYWIRE, AND THOUGH SHE LIVES IN DANGER-TOWN, SHE'LL WANT TO MAKE A PIT STOP IN SMOOCHIEVILLE.
I HATE YOUR METAPHORS.
SHUT UP, THEY'RE AWESOME.

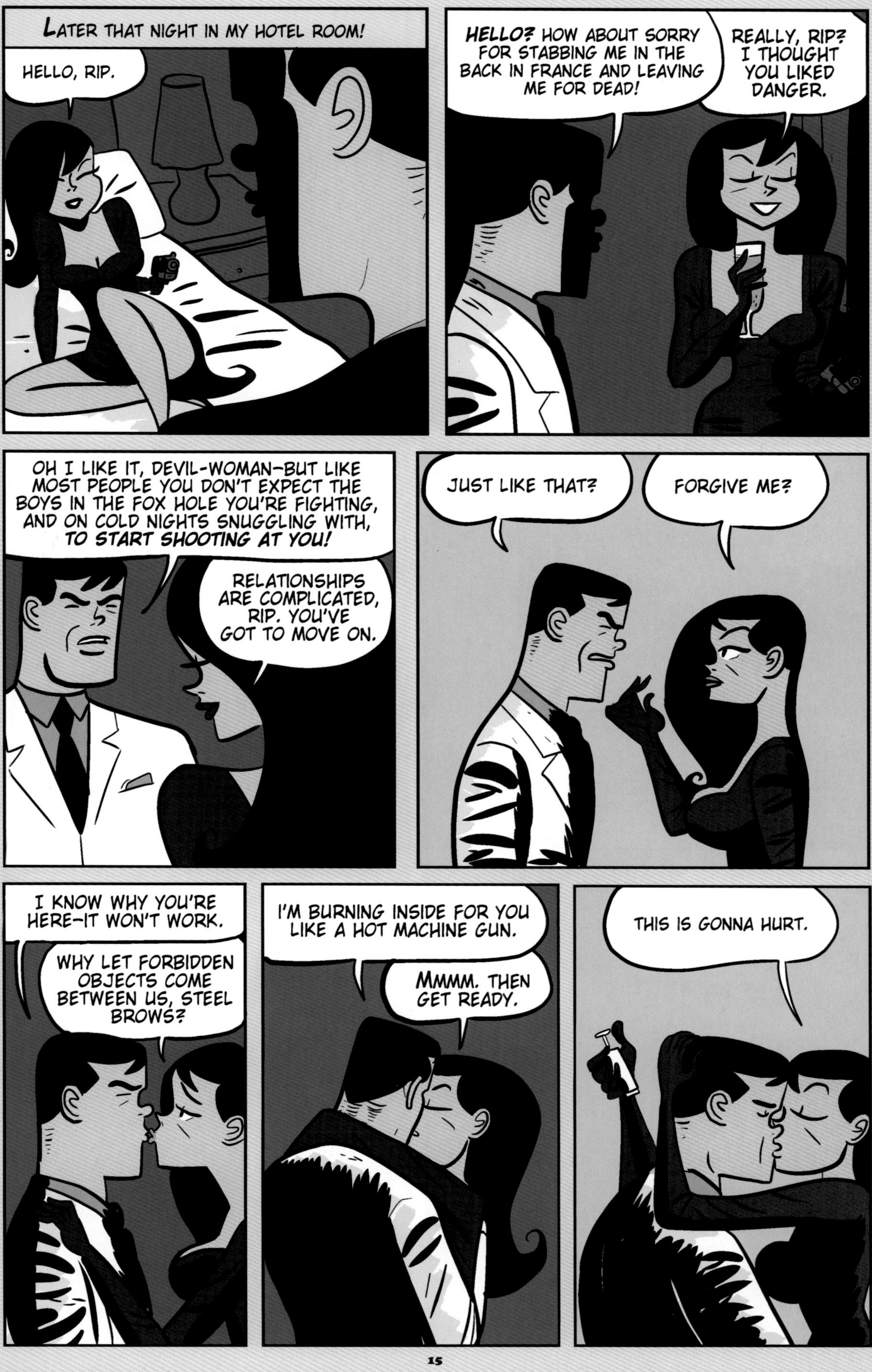
LATER THAT NIGHT IN MY HOTEL ROOM!
HELLO, RIP.
HELLO? HOW ABOUT SORRY FOR STABBING ME IN THE BACK IN FRANCE AND LEAVING ME FOR DEAD!
REALLY, RIP? I THOUGHT YOU LIKED DANGER.
OH I LIKE IT, DEVIL-WOMAN—BUT LIKE MOST PEOPLE YOU DON'T EXPECT THE BOYS IN THE FOX HOLE YOU'RE FIGHTING, AND ON COLD NIGHTS SNUGGLING WITH, TO START SHOOTING AT YOU!
RELATIONSHIPS ARE COMPLICATED, RIP. YOU'VE GOT TO MOVE ON.
JUST LIKE THAT?
FORGIVE ME?
I KNOW WHY YOU'RE HERE—IT WON'T WORK.
WHY LET FORBIDDEN OBJECTS COME BETWEEN US, STEEL BROWS?
I'M BURNING INSIDE FOR YOU LIKE A HOT MACHINE GUN.
MMMM. THEN GET READY.
THIS IS GONNA HURT.

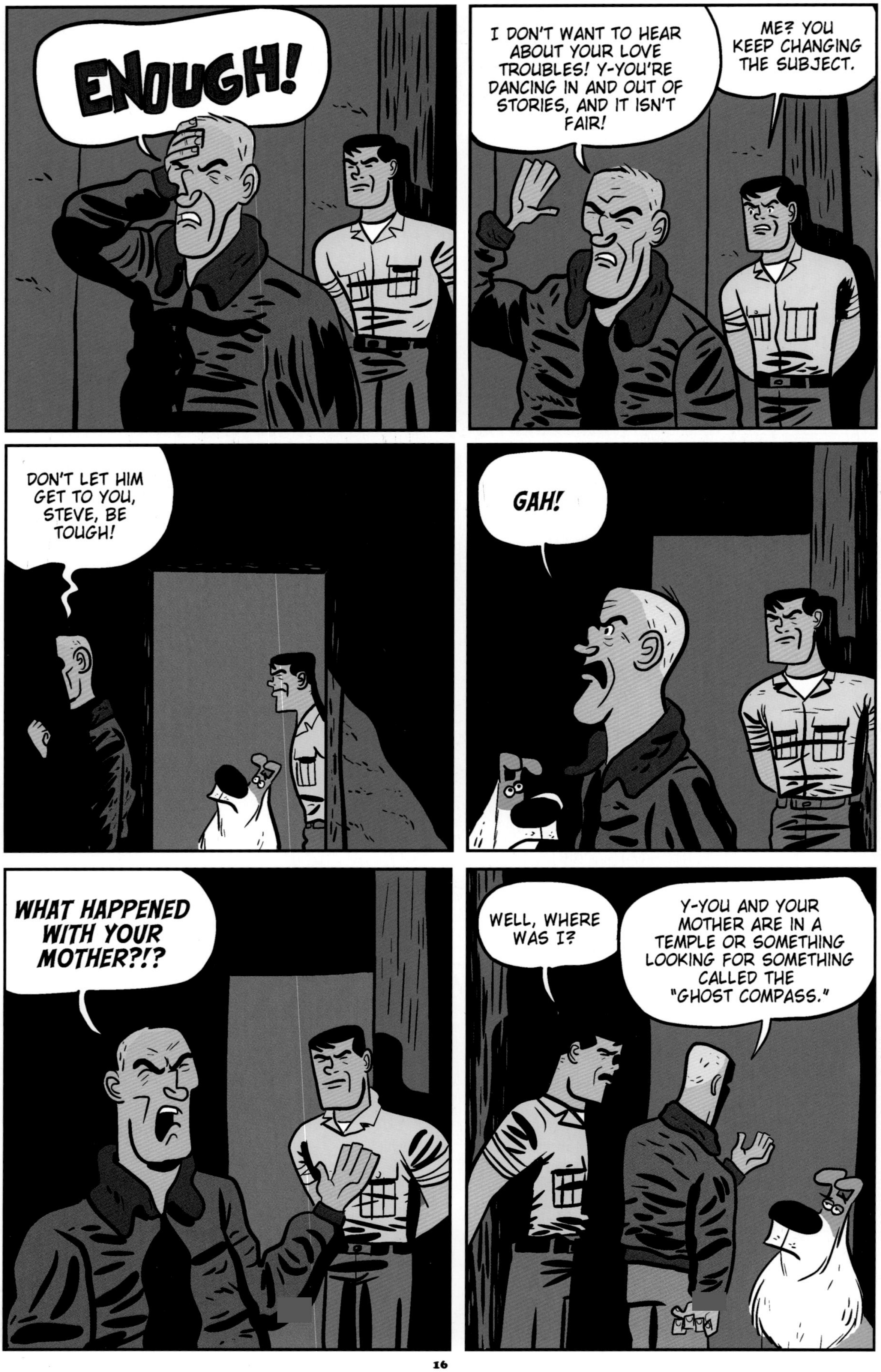
ENOUGH!
I DON'T WANT TO HEAR ABOUT YOUR LOVE TROUBLES! Y-YOU'RE DANCING IN AND OUT OF STORIES, AND IT ISN'T FAIR!
ME? YOU KEEP CHANGING THE SUBJECT.
DON'T LET HIM GET TO YOU, STEVE, BE TOUGH!
GAH!
WHAT HAPPENED WITH YOUR MOTHER?!?
WELL, WHERE WAS I?
Y-YOU AND YOUR MOTHER ARE IN A TEMPLE OR SOMETHING LOOKING FOR SOMETHING CALLED THE "GHOST COMPASS."

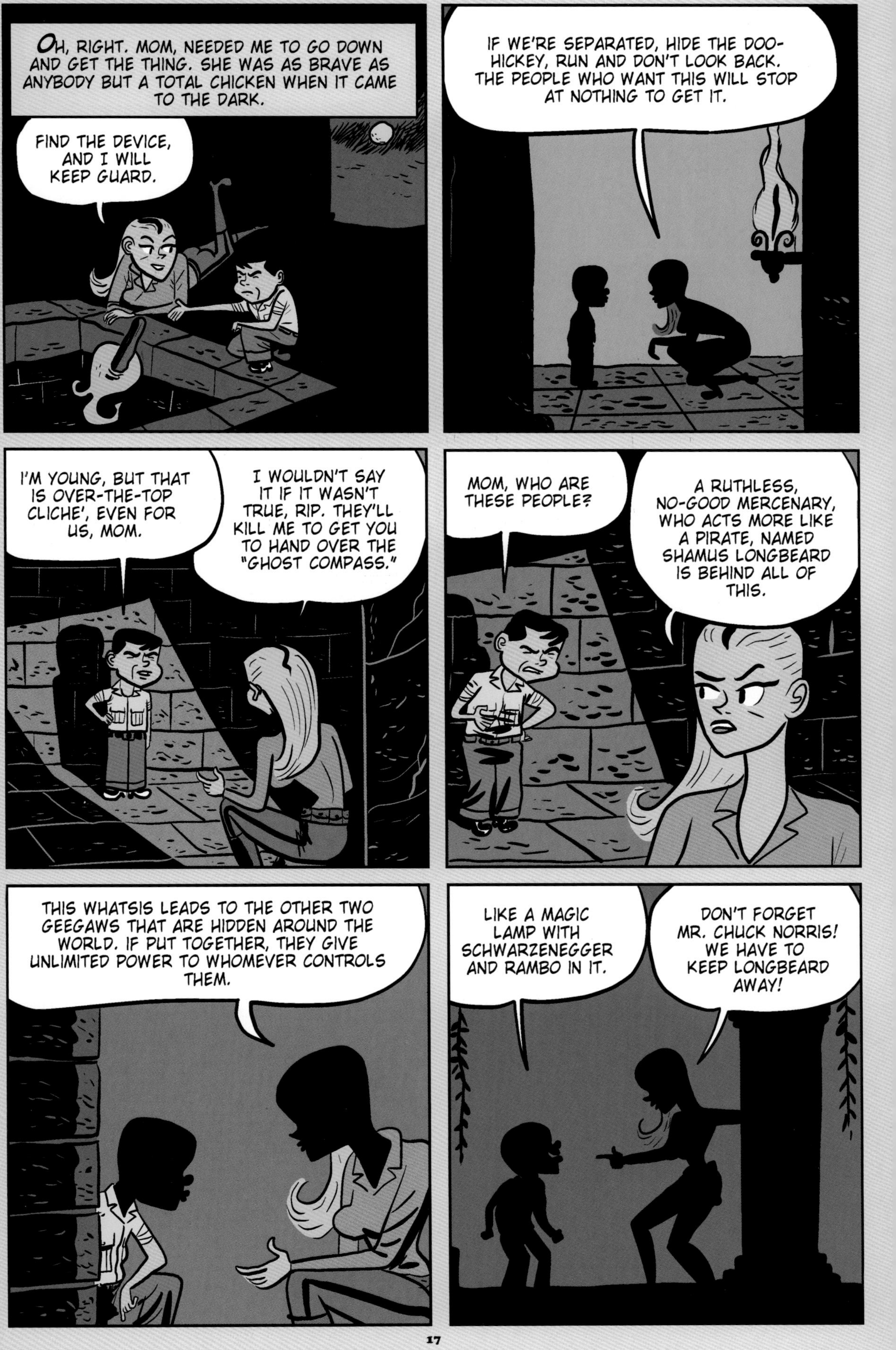
OH, RIGHT. MOM, NEEDED ME TO GO DOWN AND GET THE THING. SHE WAS AS BRAVE AS ANYBODY BUT A TOTAL CHICKEN WHEN IT CAME TO THE DARK.
FIND THE DEVICE, AND I WILL KEEP GUARD.
IF WE'RE SEPARATED, HIDE THE DOO-HICKEY, RUN AND DON'T LOOK BACK. THE PEOPLE WHO WANT THIS WILL STOP AT NOTHING TO GET IT.
I'M YOUNG, BUT THAT IS OVER-THE-TOP CLICHE', EVEN FOR US, MOM.
I WOULDN'T SAY IT IF IT WASN'T TRUE, RIP. THEY'LL KILL ME TO GET YOU TO HAND OVER THE "GHOST COMPASS."
MOM, WHO ARE THESE PEOPLE?
A RUTHLESS, NO-GOOD MERCENARY, WHO ACTS MORE LIKE A PIRATE, NAMED SHAMUS LONGBEARD IS BEHIND ALL OF THIS.
THIS WHATSIS LEADS TO THE OTHER TWO GEEGAWS THAT ARE HIDDEN AROUND THE WORLD. IF PUT TOGETHER, THEY GIVE UNLIMITED POWER TO WHOMEVER CONTROLS THEM.
LIKE A MAGIC LAMP WITH SCHWARZENEGGER AND RAMBO IN IT.
DON'T FORGET MR. CHUCK NORRIS! WE HAVE TO KEEP LONGBEARD AWAY!

WHILE I WAS IN THE TUNNEL TRACKING DOWN THE "GHOST COMPASS." LONGBEARD AND HIS CREW SURPRISED MOM, LIKE A SCALE AT THE DOCTOR'S OFFICE THAT TELLS YOU YOUR REAL WEIGHT.

I'M ALONE, LONGBEARD, THE DEVICE IS GONE, SO DO WHAT YOU WANT WITH ME! I'LL NEVER TALK!

ALONE, REALLY? BECAUSE I SEEM TO REMEMBER SEEING YOUR BRAT WITH YOU WHEN YOU CAME IN HERE.

ULP!

KILL THE BOY.

DUSTIN' A KID WILL COST YOU EXTRA. WE'RE NOT ANIMALS YOU KNOW!

PUT IT ON MY TAB.

WE'LL BE IN THE SUBMARINE. DON'T COME BACK IF YOU DON'T HAVE THE THINGAMABOBBER AND THE BODY OF THAT KID.

THEY NEVER TELL YOU THIS STUFF IN THE JOB DESCRIPTION.

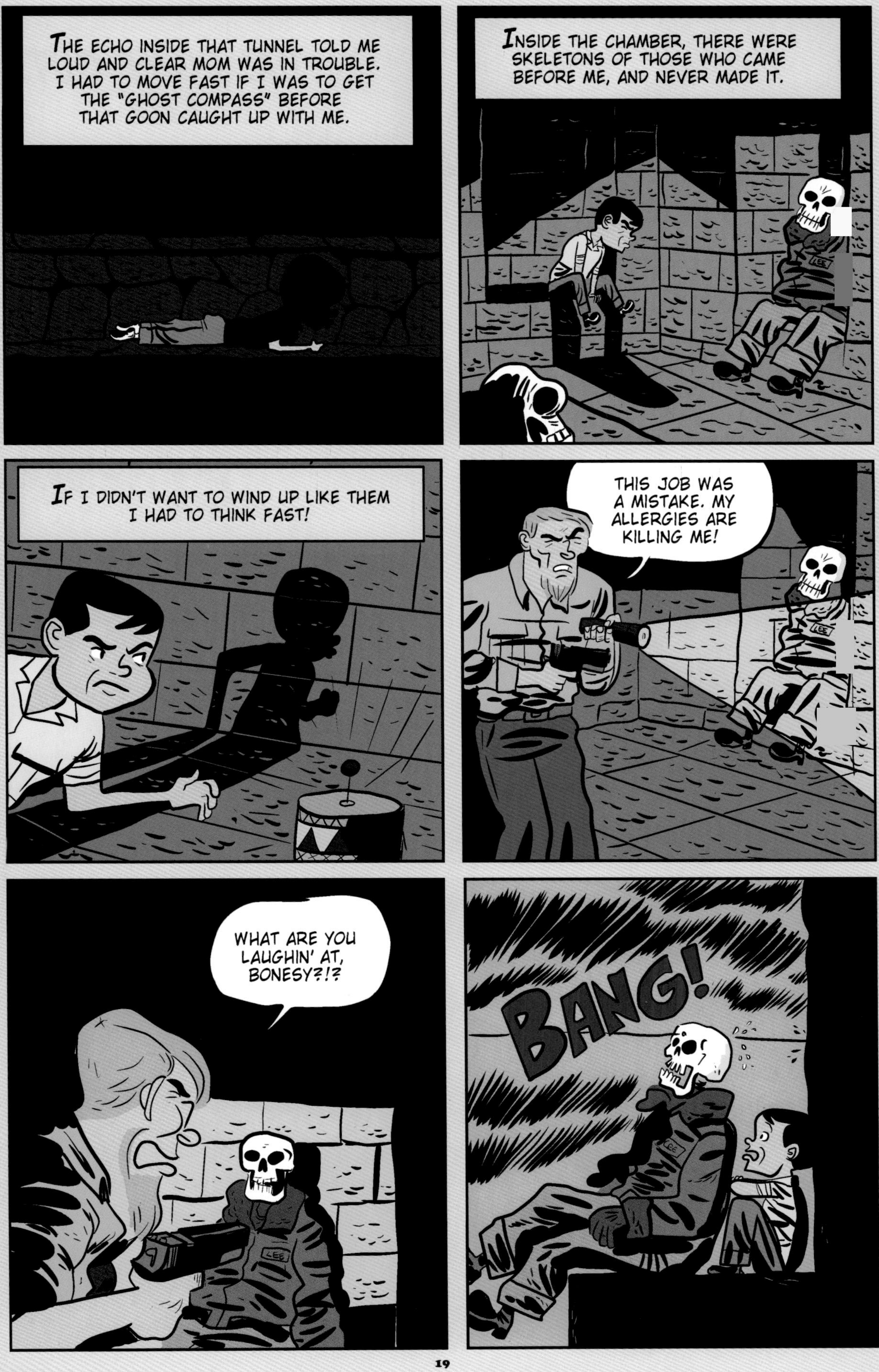
THE ECHO INSIDE THAT TUNNEL TOLD ME LOUD AND CLEAR MOM WAS IN TROUBLE. I HAD TO MOVE FAST IF I WAS TO GET THE "GHOST COMPASS" BEFORE THAT GOON CAUGHT UP WITH ME.
INSIDE THE CHAMBER, THERE WERE SKELETONS OF THOSE WHO CAME BEFORE ME, AND NEVER MADE IT.
LEE
IF I DIDN'T WANT TO WIND UP LIKE THEM I HAD TO THINK FAST!
THIS JOB WAS A MISTAKE. MY ALLERGIES ARE KILLING ME!
LEE
WHAT ARE YOU LAUGHIN' AT, BONESY?!?
LEE
BANG!
LEE

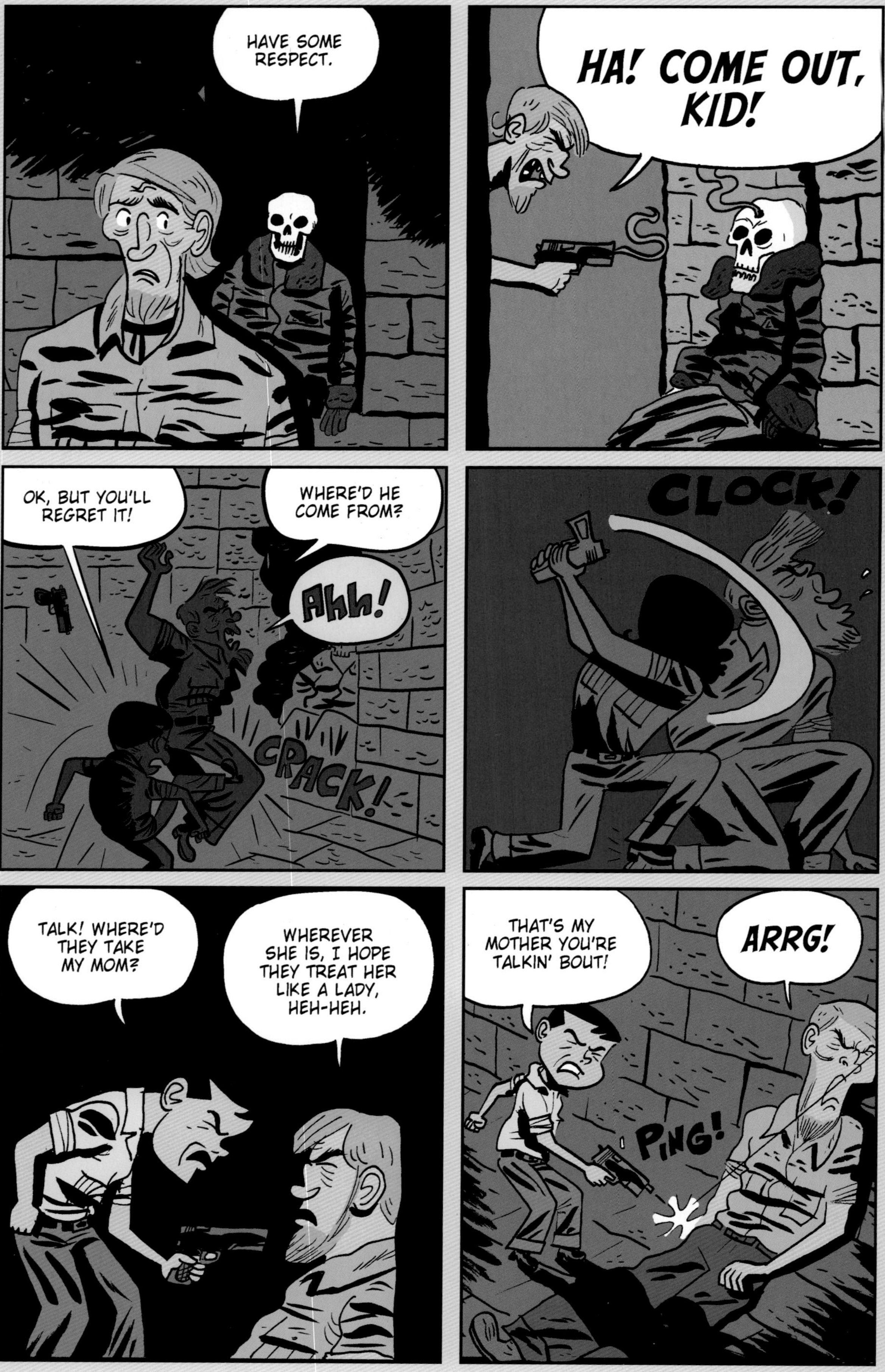
HAVE SOME RESPECT.
HA! COME OUT, KID!
OK, BUT YOU'LL REGRET IT!
WHERE'D HE COME FROM?
Ahh!
CRACK!
CLOCK!
TALK! WHERE'D THEY TAKE MY MOM?
WHEREVER SHE IS, I HOPE THEY TREAT HER LIKE A LADY, HEH-HEH.
THAT'S MY MOTHER YOU'RE TALKIN' BOUT!
ARRG!
PING!

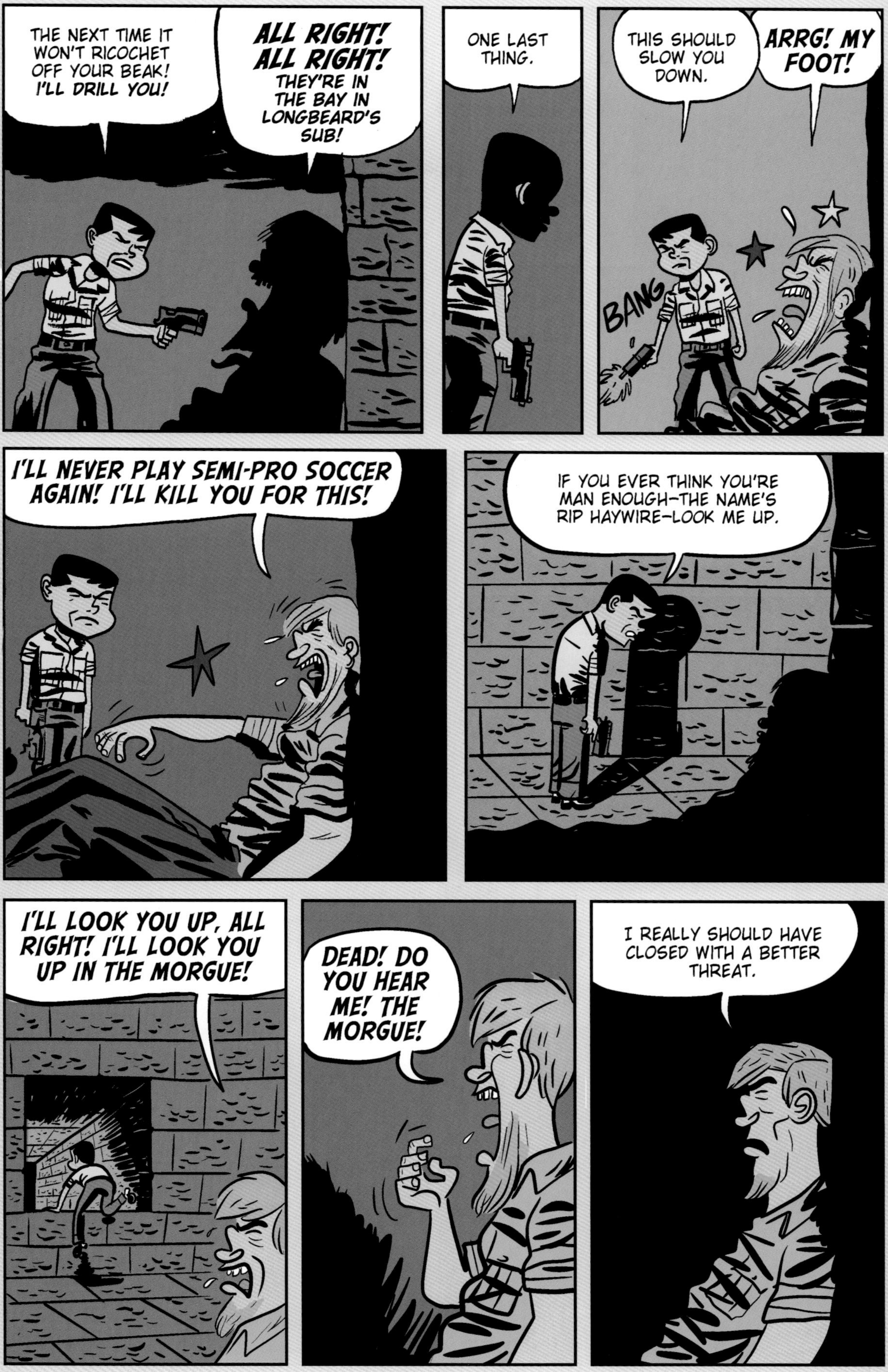
THE NEXT TIME IT WON'T RICOCHET OFF YOUR BEAK! I'LL DRILL YOU!
ALL RIGHT! ALL RIGHT! THEY'RE IN THE BAY IN LONGBEARD'S SUB!
ONE LAST THING.
THIS SHOULD SLOW YOU DOWN.
ARRG! MY FOOT!
BANG
I'LL NEVER PLAY SEMI-PRO SOCCER AGAIN! I'LL KILL YOU FOR THIS!
IF YOU EVER THINK YOU'RE MAN ENOUGH—THE NAME'S RIP HAYWIRE—LOOK ME UP.
I'LL LOOK YOU UP, ALL RIGHT! I'LL LOOK YOU UP IN THE MORGUE!
DEAD! DO YOU HEAR ME! THE MORGUE!
I REALLY SHOULD HAVE CLOSED WITH A BETTER THREAT.

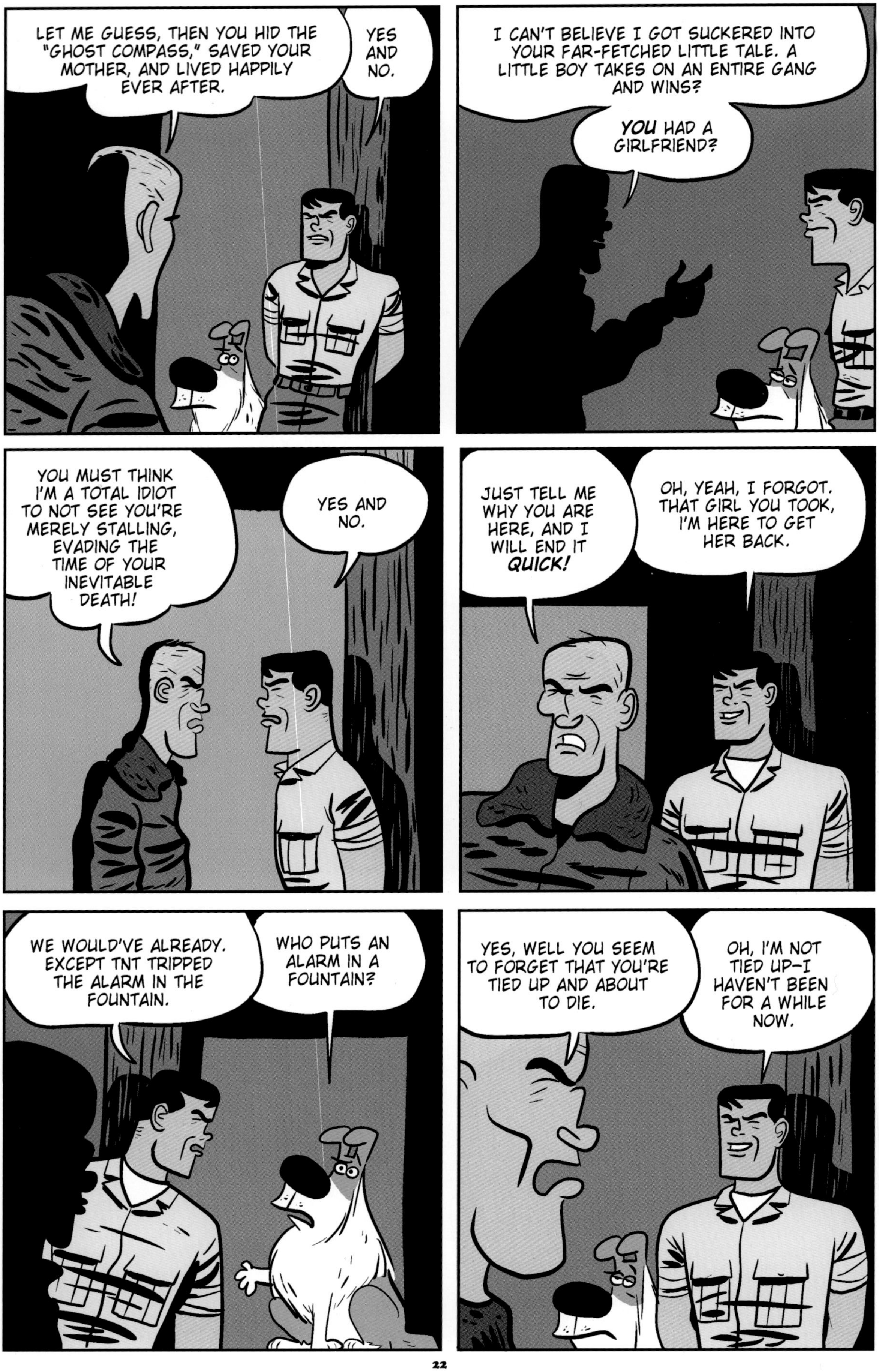
LET ME GUESS, THEN YOU HID THE "GHOST COMPASS," SAVED YOUR MOTHER, AND LIVED HAPPILY EVER AFTER.
YES AND NO.
I CAN'T BELIEVE I GOT SUCKERED INTO YOUR FAR-FETCHED LITTLE TALE. A LITTLE BOY TAKES ON AN ENTIRE GANG AND WINS?
YOU HAD A GIRLFRIEND?
YOU MUST THINK I'M A TOTAL IDIOT TO NOT SEE YOU'RE MERELY STALLING, EVADING THE TIME OF YOUR INEVITABLE DEATH!
YES AND NO.
JUST TELL ME WHY YOU ARE HERE, AND I WILL END IT *QUICK!*
OH, YEAH, I FORGOT. THAT GIRL YOU TOOK, I'M HERE TO GET HER BACK.
WE WOULD'VE ALREADY. EXCEPT TNT TRIPPED THE ALARM IN THE FOUNTAIN.
WHO PUTS AN ALARM IN A FOUNTAIN?
YES, WELL YOU SEEM TO FORGET THAT YOU'RE TIED UP AND ABOUT TO DIE.
OH, I'M NOT TIED UP—I HAVEN'T BEEN FOR A WHILE NOW.

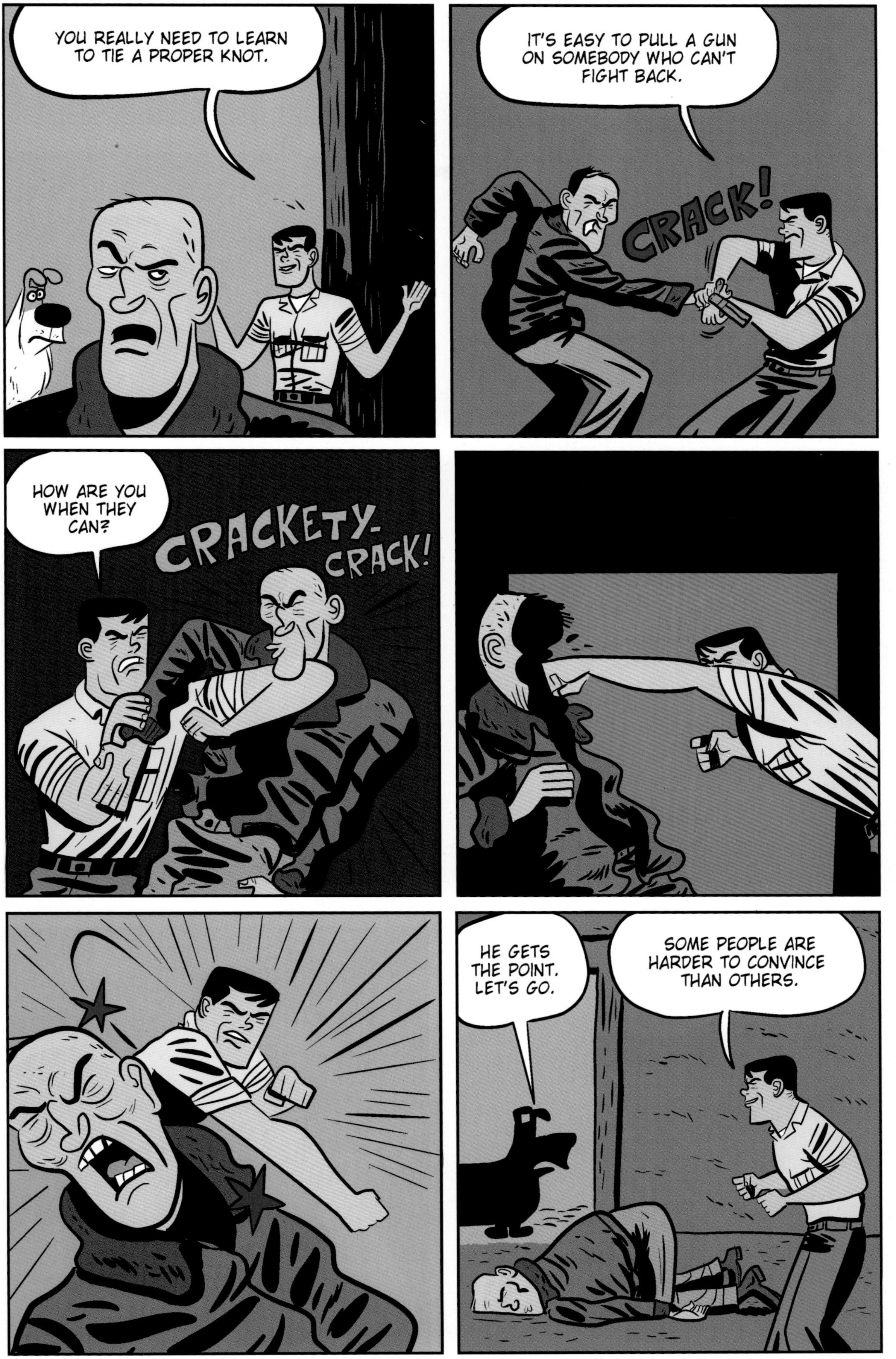
YOU REALLY NEED TO LEARN TO TIE A PROPER KNOT.
IT'S EASY TO PULL A GUN ON SOMEBODY WHO CAN'T FIGHT BACK.
CRACK!
HOW ARE YOU WHEN THEY CAN?
CRACKETY-CRACK!
HE GETS THE POINT. LET'S GO.
SOME PEOPLE ARE HARDER TO CONVINCE THAN OTHERS.

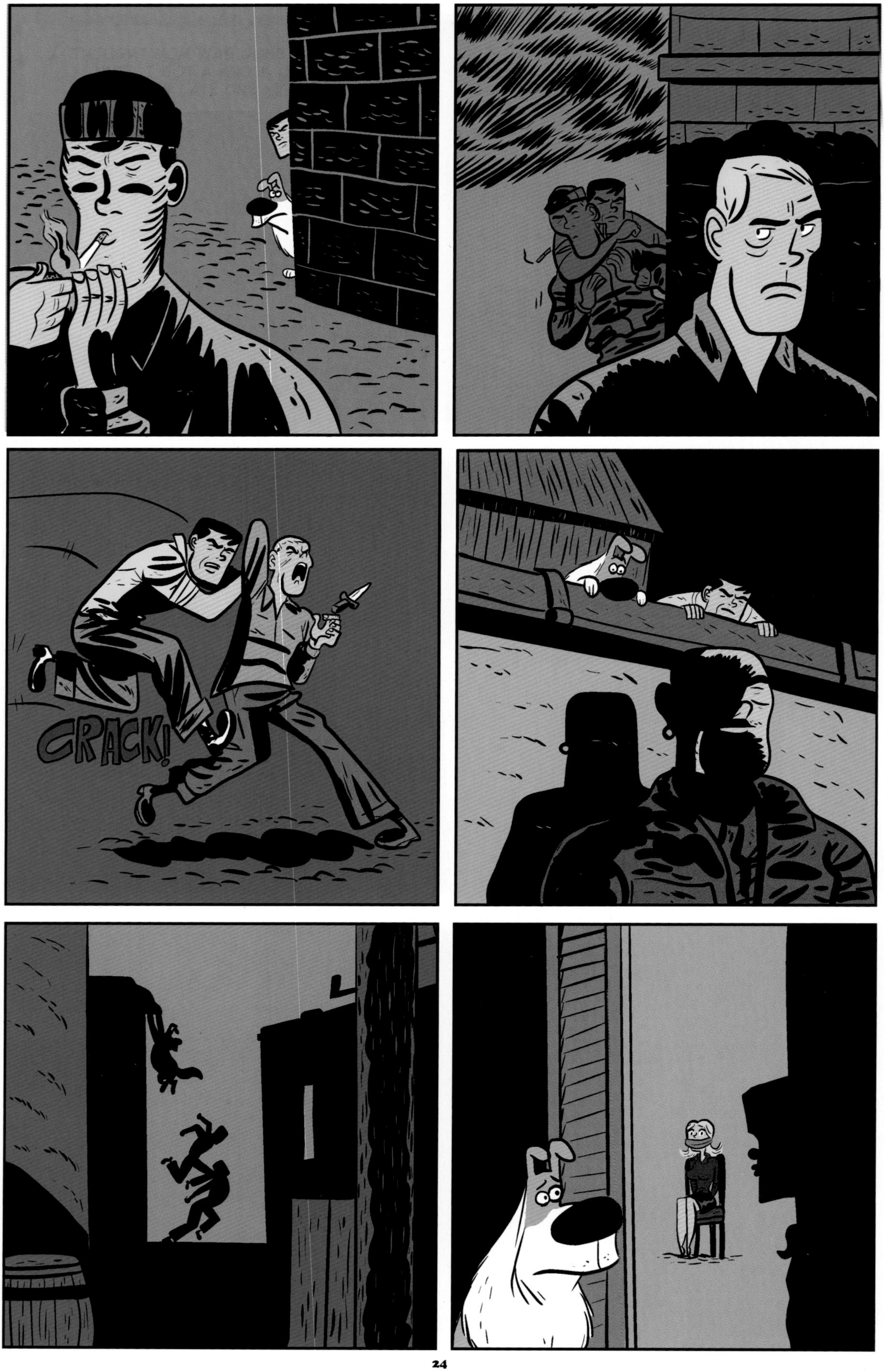
CRACK!

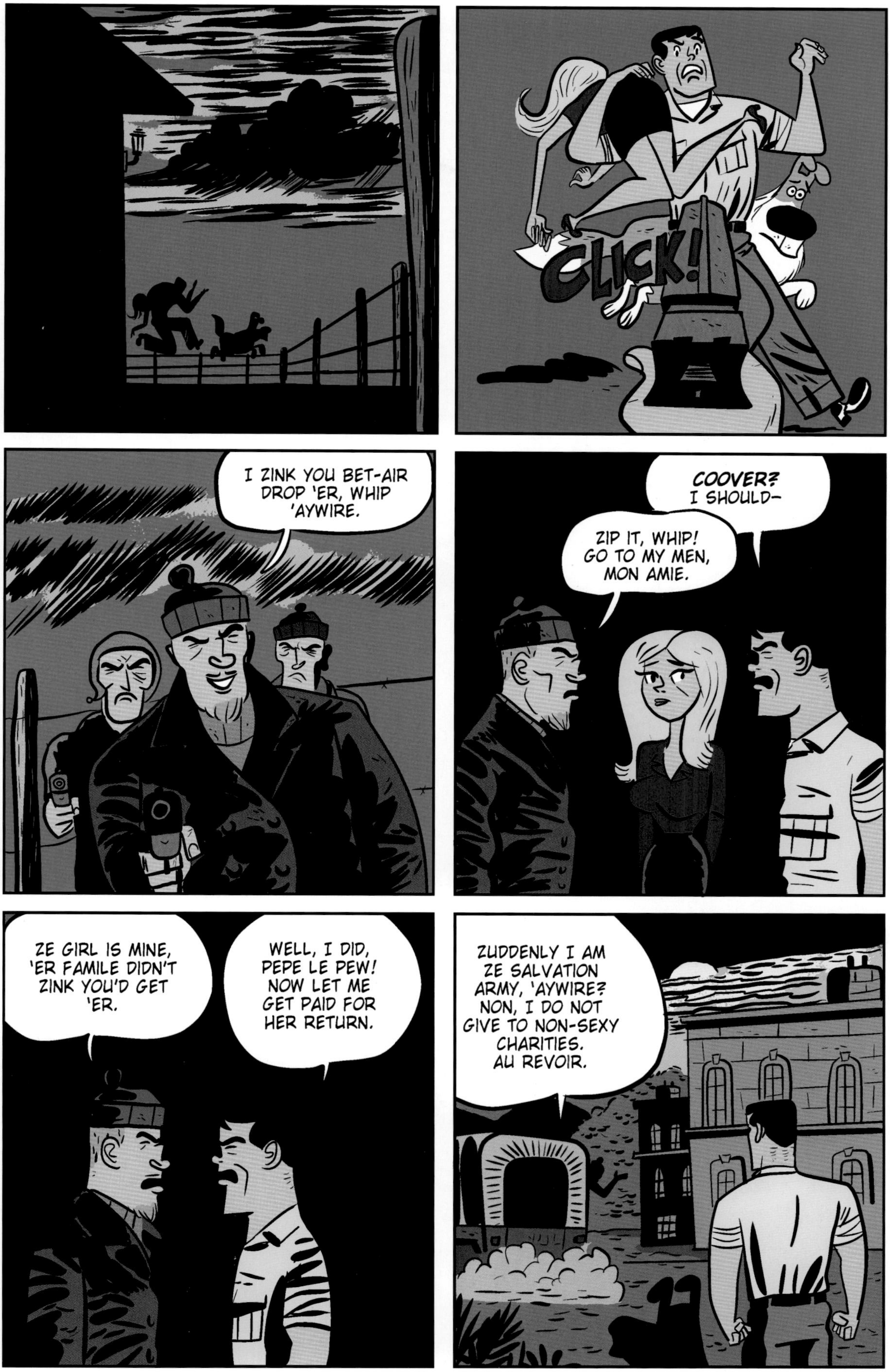
CLICK!
I ZINK YOU BET-AIR DROP 'ER, WHIP 'AYWIRE.
COOVER? I SHOULD—
ZIP IT, WHIP! GO TO MY MEN, MON AMIE.
ZE GIRL IS MINE, 'ER FAMILE DIDN'T ZINK YOU'D GET 'ER.
WELL, I DID, PEPE LE PEW! NOW LET ME GET PAID FOR HER RETURN.
ZUDDENLY I AM ZE SALVATION ARMY, 'AYWIRE? NON, I DO NOT GIVE TO NON-SEXY CHARITIES. AU REVOIR.

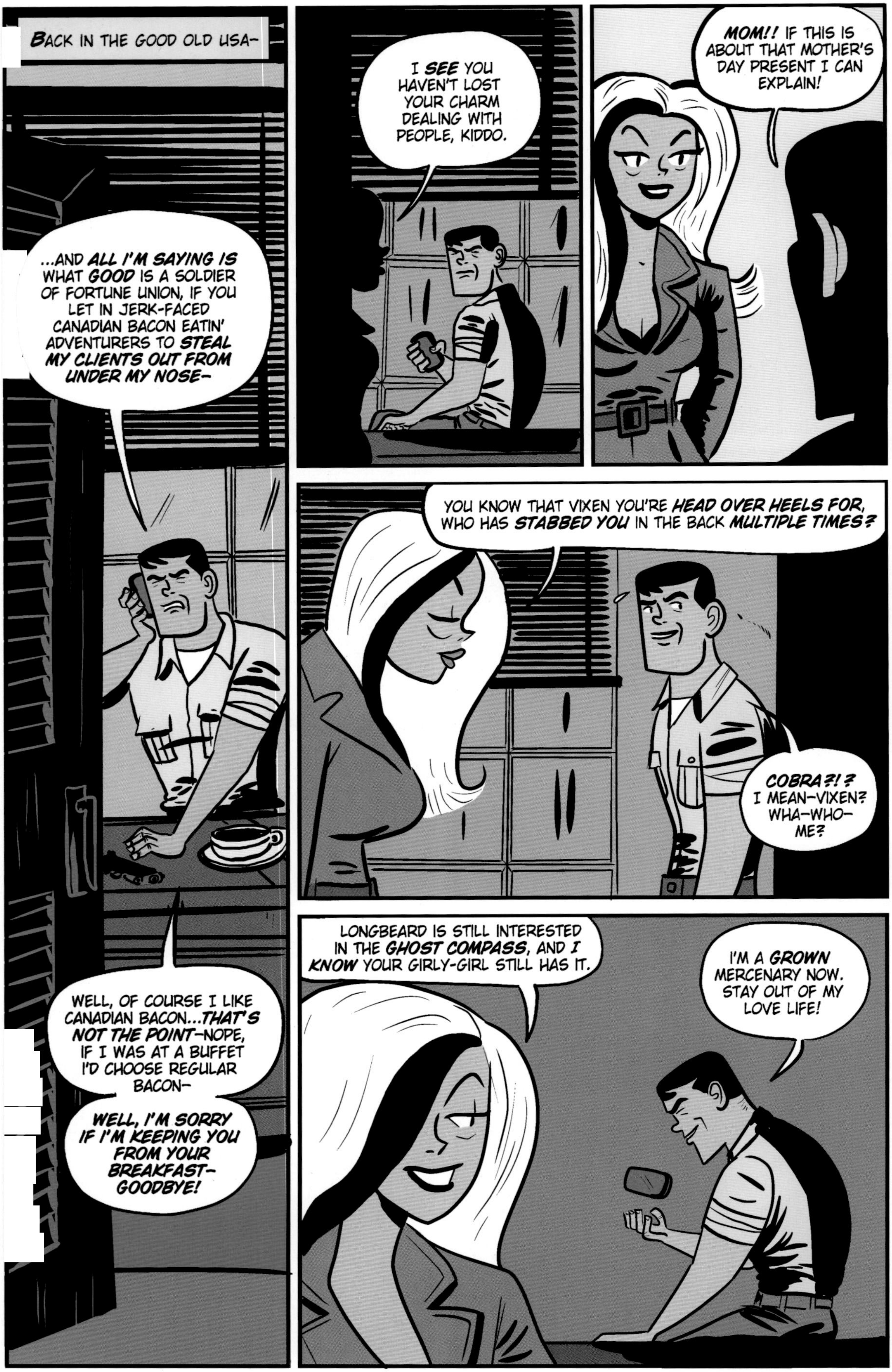

BACK IN THE GOOD OLD USA-
...AND ALL I'M SAYING IS WHAT GOOD IS A SOLDIER OF FORTUNE UNION, IF YOU LET IN JERK-FACED CANADIAN BACON EATIN' ADVENTURERS TO STEAL MY CLIENTS OUT FROM UNDER MY NOSE-
WELL, OF COURSE I LIKE CANADIAN BACON...THAT'S NOT THE POINT-NOPE, IF I WAS AT A BUFFET I'D CHOOSE REGULAR BACON-
WELL, I'M SORRY IF I'M KEEPING YOU FROM YOUR BREAKFAST-GOODBYE!
I SEE YOU HAVEN'T LOST YOUR CHARM DEALING WITH PEOPLE, KIDDO.
MOM!! IF THIS IS ABOUT THAT MOTHER'S DAY PRESENT I CAN EXPLAIN!
YOU KNOW THAT VIXEN YOU'RE HEAD OVER HEELS FOR, WHO HAS STABBED YOU IN THE BACK MULTIPLE TIMES?
COBRA?!? I MEAN-VIXEN? WHA-WHO-ME?
LONGBEARD IS STILL INTERESTED IN THE GHOST COMPASS, AND I KNOW YOUR GIRLY-GIRL STILL HAS IT.
I'M A GROWN MERCENARY NOW. STAY OUT OF MY LOVE LIFE!

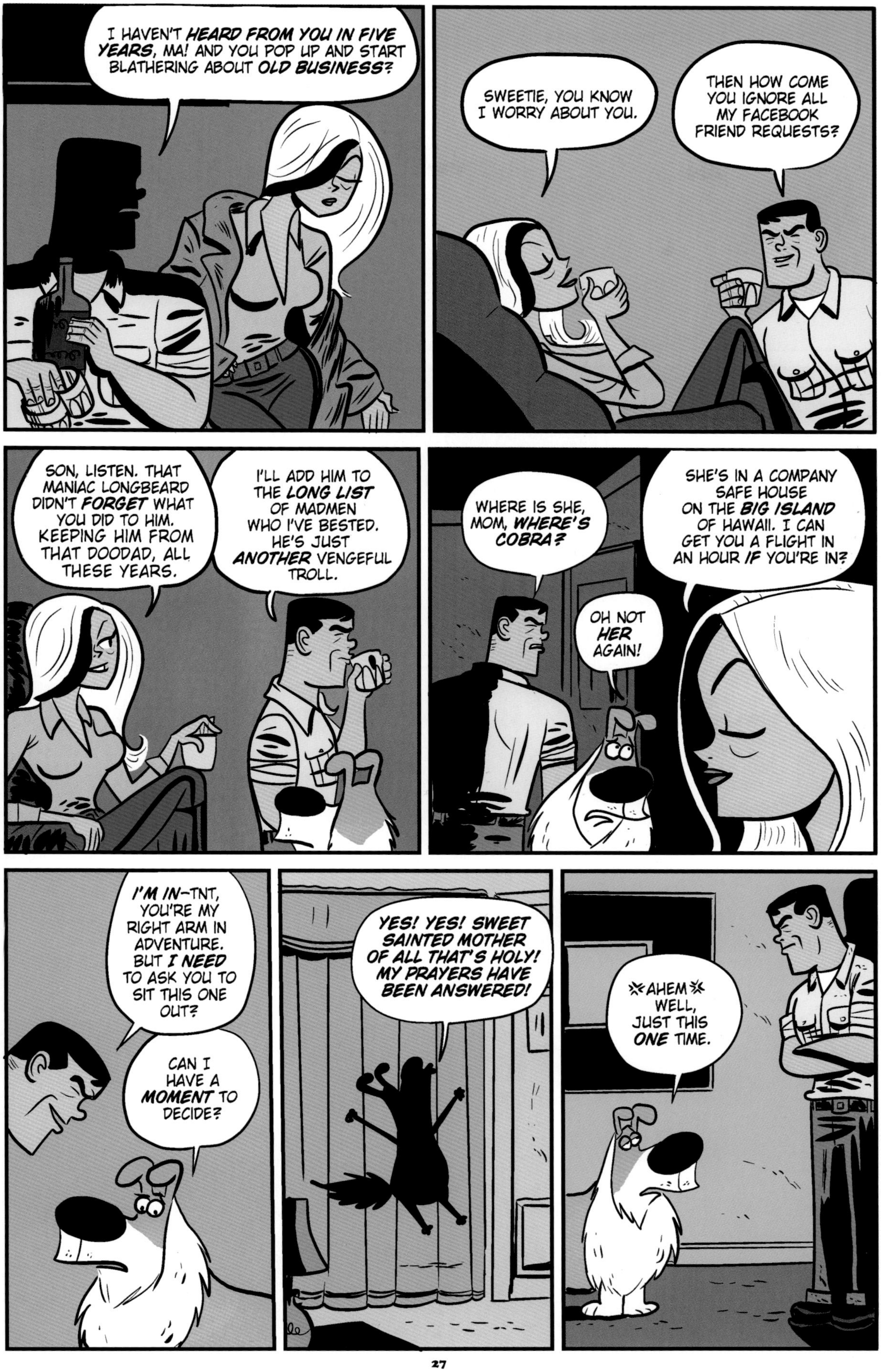
I HAVEN'T **HEARD FROM YOU IN FIVE YEARS**, MA! AND YOU POP UP AND START BLATHERING ABOUT **OLD BUSINESS**?
SWEETIE, YOU KNOW I WORRY ABOUT YOU.
THEN HOW COME YOU IGNORE ALL MY FACEBOOK FRIEND REQUESTS?
SON, LISTEN. THAT MANIAC LONGBEARD DIDN'T **FORGET** WHAT YOU DID TO HIM. KEEPING HIM FROM THAT DOODAD, ALL THESE YEARS.
I'LL ADD HIM TO THE **LONG LIST** OF MADMEN WHO I'VE BESTED. HE'S JUST **ANOTHER** VENGEFUL TROLL.
WHERE IS SHE, MOM, **WHERE'S COBRA**?
SHE'S IN A COMPANY SAFE HOUSE ON THE **BIG ISLAND** OF HAWAII. I CAN GET YOU A FLIGHT IN AN HOUR **IF** YOU'RE IN?
OH NOT **HER** AGAIN!
I'M IN—TNT, YOU'RE MY RIGHT ARM IN ADVENTURE. BUT **I NEED** TO ASK YOU TO SIT THIS ONE OUT?
CAN I HAVE A **MOMENT** TO DECIDE?
YES! YES! SWEET SAINTED MOTHER OF ALL THAT'S HOLY! MY PRAYERS HAVE BEEN ANSWERED!
AHEM WELL, JUST THIS **ONE** TIME.

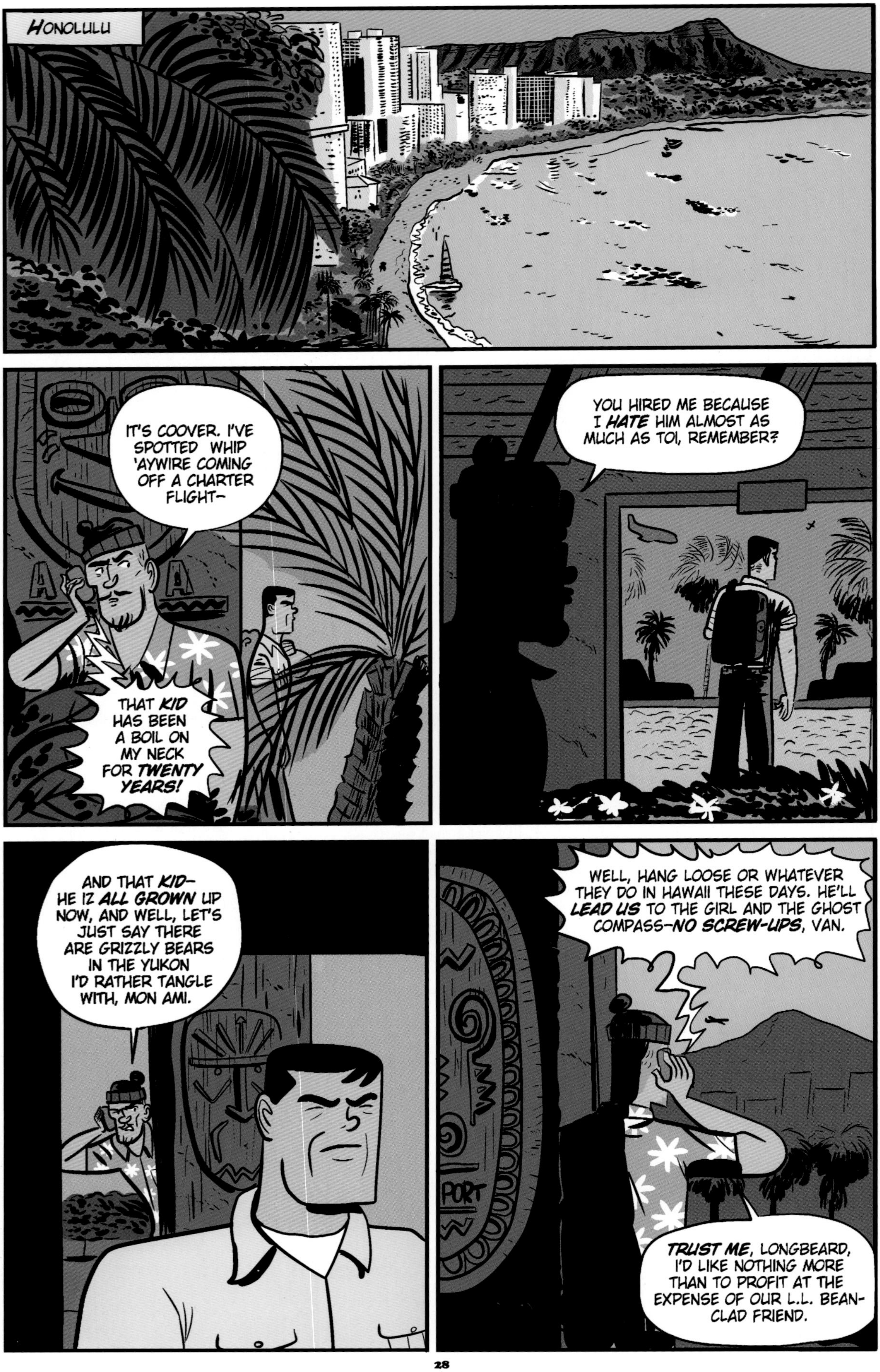
HONOLULU
IT'S COOVER. I'VE SPOTTED WHIP 'AYWIRE COMING OFF A CHARTER FLIGHT-
THAT KID HAS BEEN A BOIL ON MY NECK FOR TWENTY YEARS!
YOU HIRED ME BECAUSE I HATE HIM ALMOST AS MUCH AS TOI, REMEMBER?
AND THAT KID- HE IZ ALL GROWN UP NOW, AND WELL, LET'S JUST SAY THERE ARE GRIZZLY BEARS IN THE YUKON I'D RATHER TANGLE WITH, MON AMI.
WELL, HANG LOOSE OR WHATEVER THEY DO IN HAWAII THESE DAYS. HE'LL LEAD US TO THE GIRL AND THE GHOST COMPASS-NO SCREW-UPS, VAN.
TRUST ME, LONGBEARD, I'D LIKE NOTHING MORE THAN TO PROFIT AT THE EXPENSE OF OUR L.L. BEAN-CLAD FRIEND.

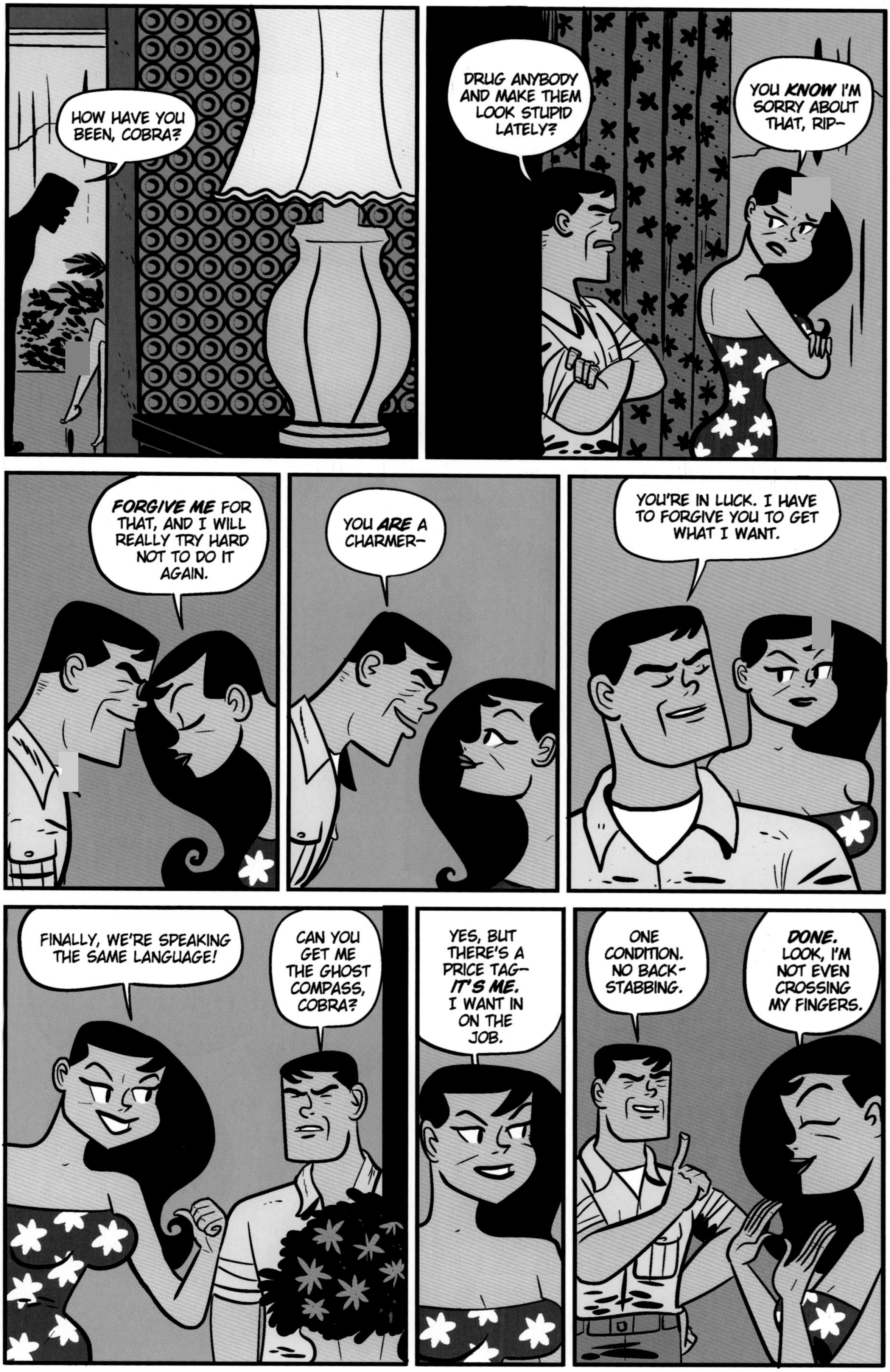
HOW HAVE YOU BEEN, COBRA?
DRUG ANYBODY AND MAKE THEM LOOK STUPID LATELY?
YOU *KNOW* I'M SORRY ABOUT THAT, RIP—
FORGIVE ME FOR THAT, AND I WILL REALLY TRY HARD NOT TO DO IT AGAIN.
YOU *ARE* A CHARMER—
YOU'RE IN LUCK. I HAVE TO FORGIVE YOU TO GET WHAT I WANT.
FINALLY, WE'RE SPEAKING THE SAME LANGUAGE!
CAN YOU GET ME THE GHOST COMPASS, COBRA?
YES, BUT THERE'S A PRICE TAG— *IT'S ME.* I WANT IN ON THE JOB.
ONE CONDITION. NO BACK-STABBING.
DONE. LOOK, I'M NOT EVEN CROSSING MY FINGERS.

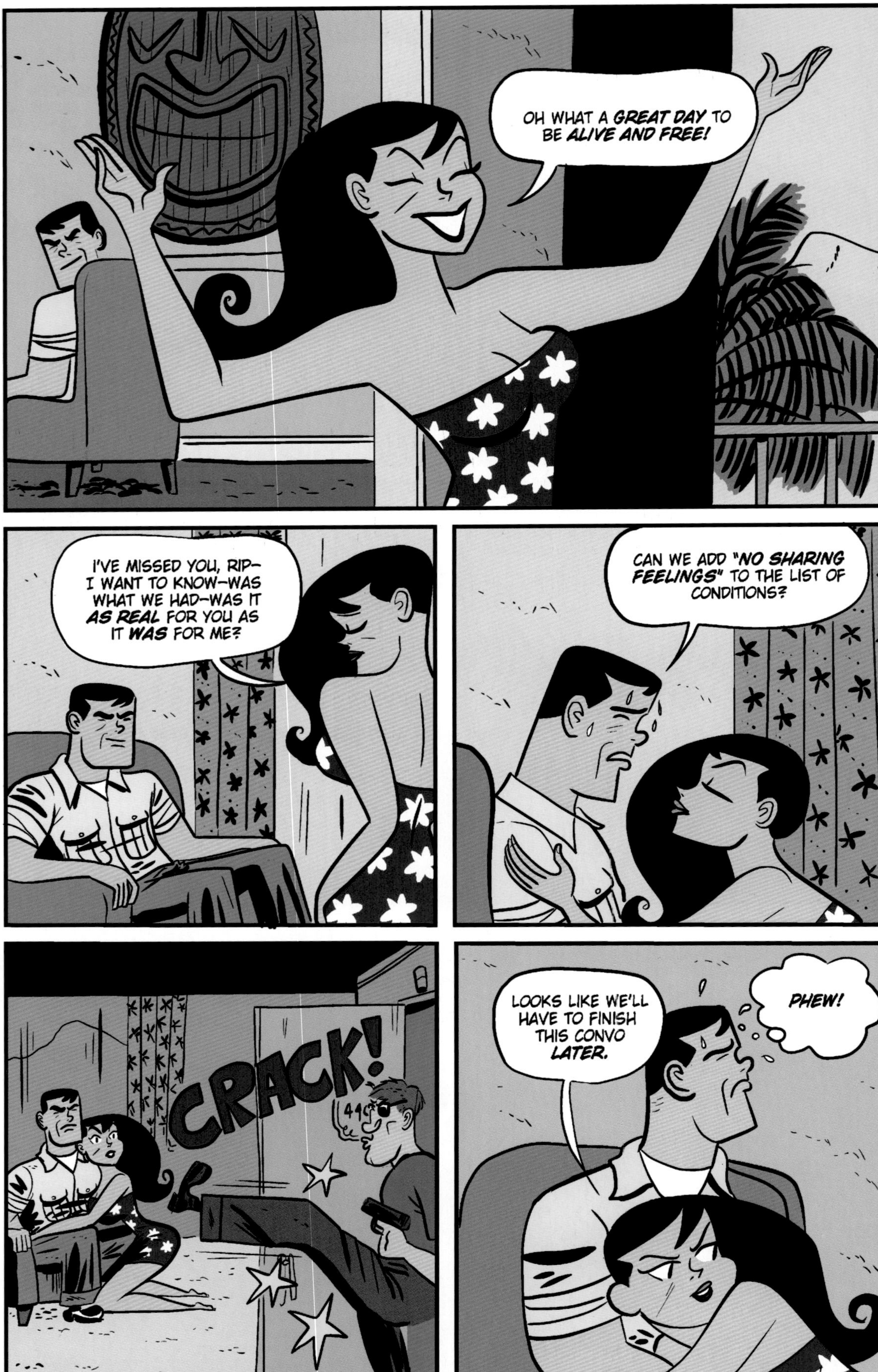
OH WHAT A **GREAT DAY** TO BE **ALIVE AND FREE!**
I'VE MISSED YOU, RIP— I WANT TO KNOW—WAS WHAT WE HAD—WAS IT **AS REAL** FOR YOU AS IT **WAS** FOR ME?
CAN WE ADD "**NO SHARING FEELINGS**" TO THE LIST OF CONDITIONS?
CRACK!
LOOKS LIKE WE'LL HAVE TO FINISH THIS CONVO **LATER.**
PHEW!

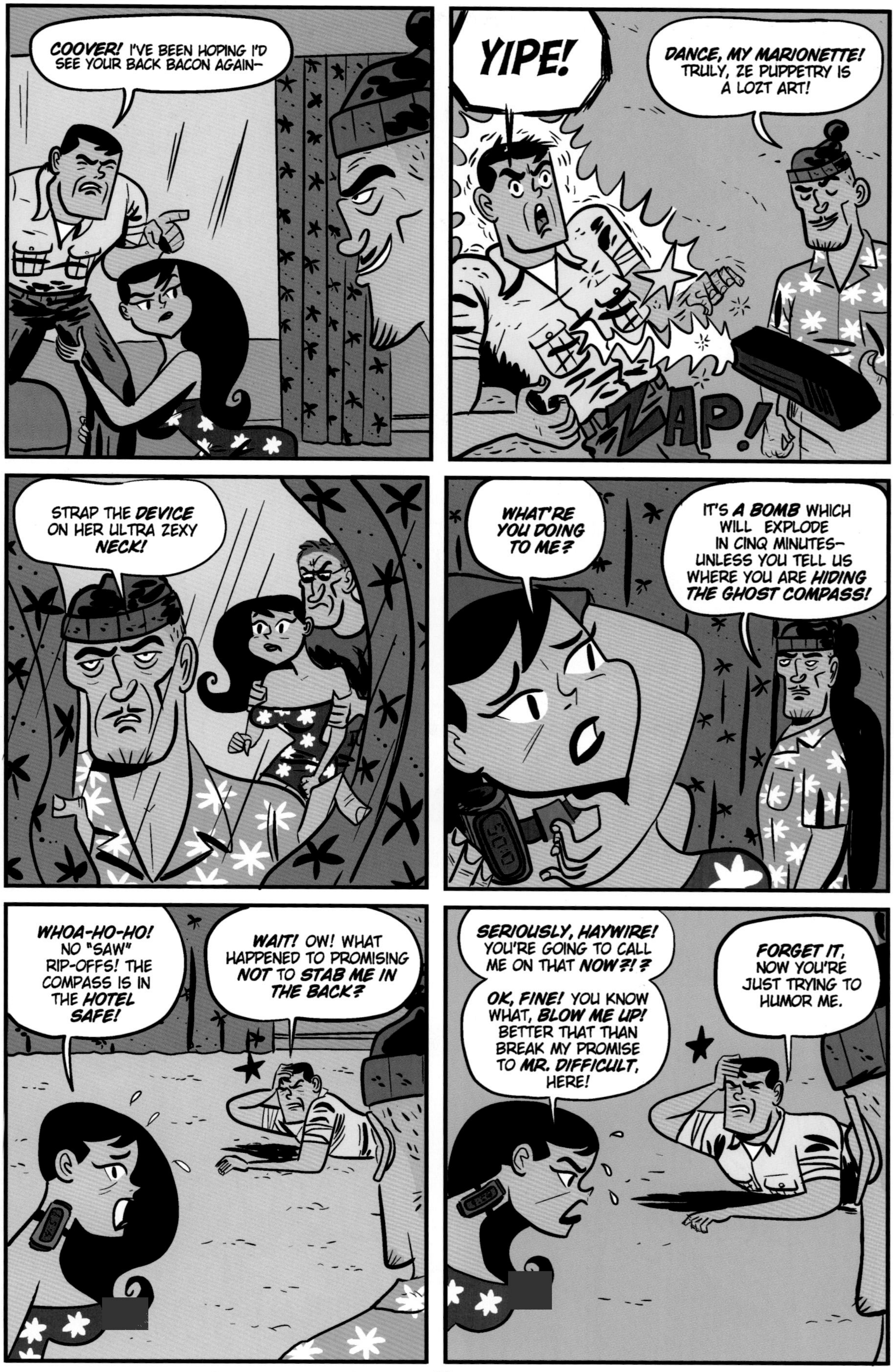
COOVER! I'VE BEEN HOPING I'D SEE YOUR BACK BACON AGAIN–
YIPE!
DANCE, MY MARIONETTE! TRULY, ZE PUPPETRY IS A LOZT ART!
ZAP!
STRAP THE DEVICE ON HER ULTRA ZEXY NECK!
WHAT'RE YOU DOING TO ME?
IT'S A BOMB WHICH WILL EXPLODE IN CINQ MINUTES– UNLESS YOU TELL US WHERE YOU ARE HIDING THE GHOST COMPASS!
WHOA-HO-HO! NO "SAW" RIP-OFFS! THE COMPASS IS IN THE HOTEL SAFE!
WAIT! OW! WHAT HAPPENED TO PROMISING NOT TO STAB ME IN THE BACK?
SERIOUSLY, HAYWIRE! YOU'RE GOING TO CALL ME ON THAT NOW?!?
OK, FINE! YOU KNOW WHAT, BLOW ME UP! BETTER THAT THAN BREAK MY PROMISE TO MR. DIFFICULT, HERE!
FORGET IT, NOW YOU'RE JUST TRYING TO HUMOR ME.

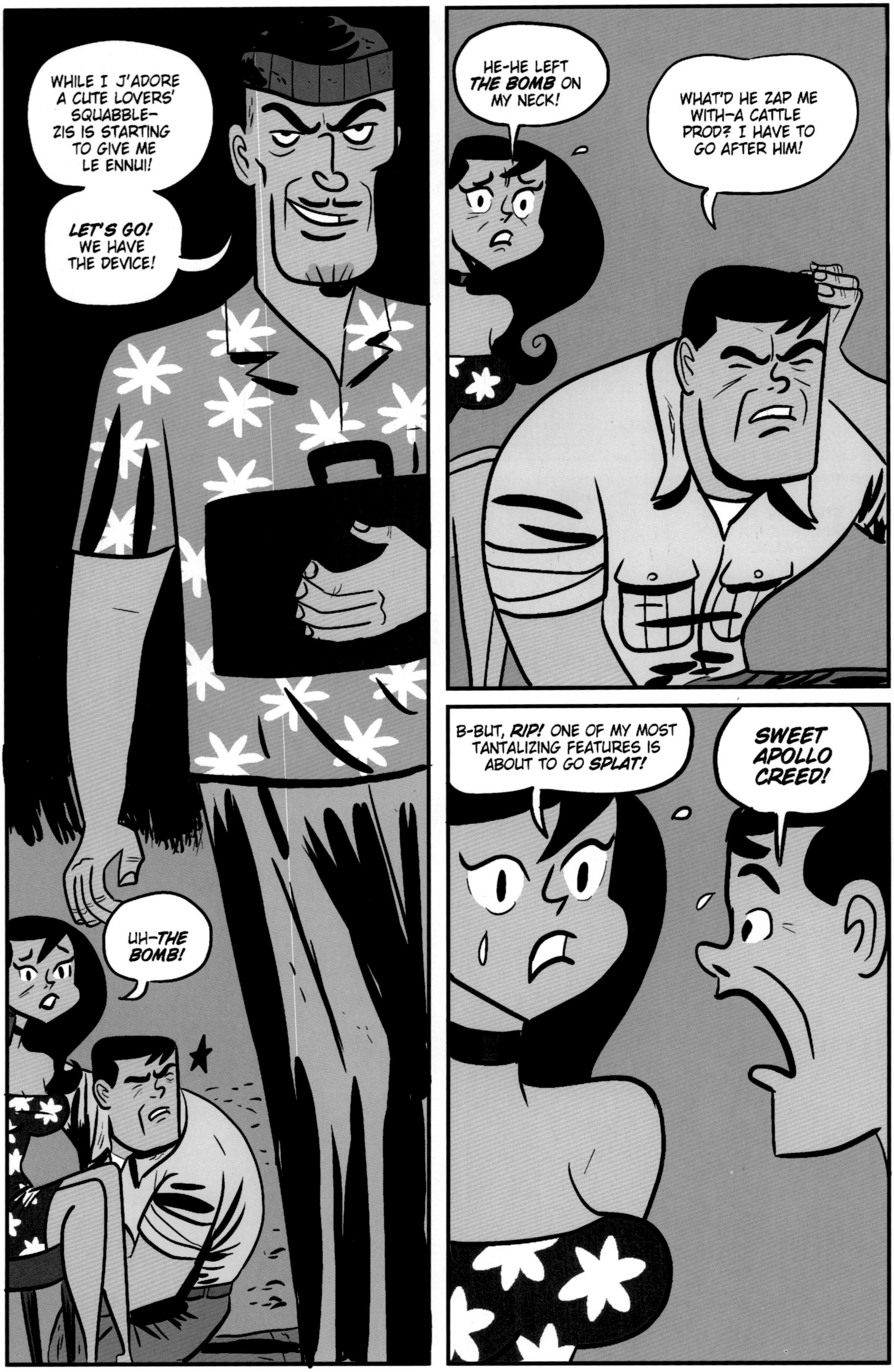

WHILE I J'ADORE A CUTE LOVERS' SQUABBLE- ZIS IS STARTING TO GIVE ME LE ENNUI!
LET'S GO! WE HAVE THE DEVICE!
UH-THE BOMB!
HE-HE LEFT THE BOMB ON MY NECK!
WHAT'D HE ZAP ME WITH-A CATTLE PROD? I HAVE TO GO AFTER HIM!
B-BUT, RIP! ONE OF MY MOST TANTALIZING FEATURES IS ABOUT TO GO SPLAT!
SWEET APOLLO CREED!

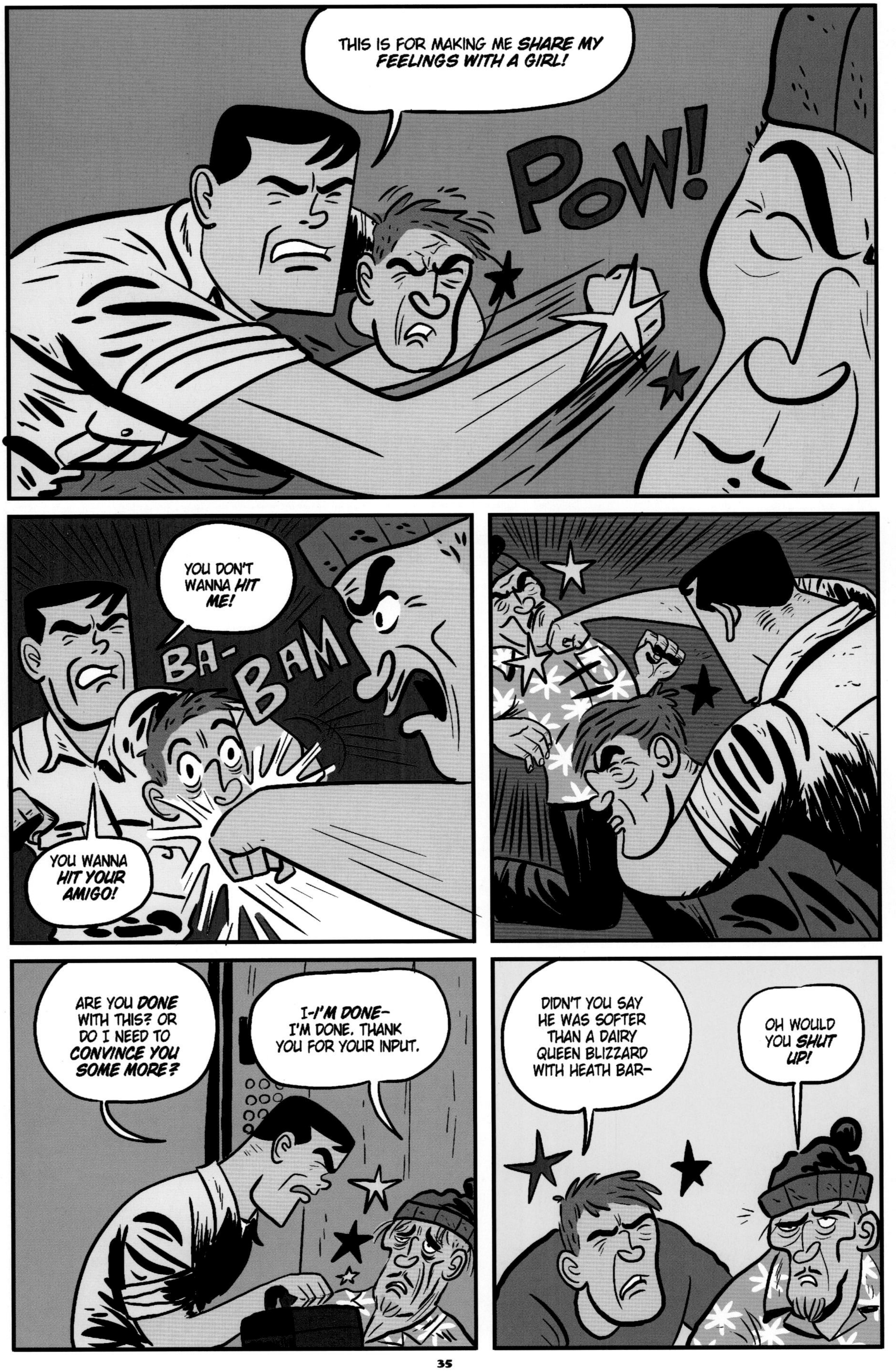
THIS IS FOR MAKING ME SHARE MY FEELINGS WITH A GIRL!
POW!
YOU DON'T WANNA HIT ME!
BA-BAM
YOU WANNA HIT YOUR AMIGO!
ARE YOU DONE WITH THIS? OR DO I NEED TO CONVINCE YOU SOME MORE?
I-I'M DONE- I'M DONE. THANK YOU FOR YOUR INPUT.
DIDN'T YOU SAY HE WAS SOFTER THAN A DAIRY QUEEN BLIZZARD WITH HEATH BAR-
OH WOULD YOU SHUT UP!

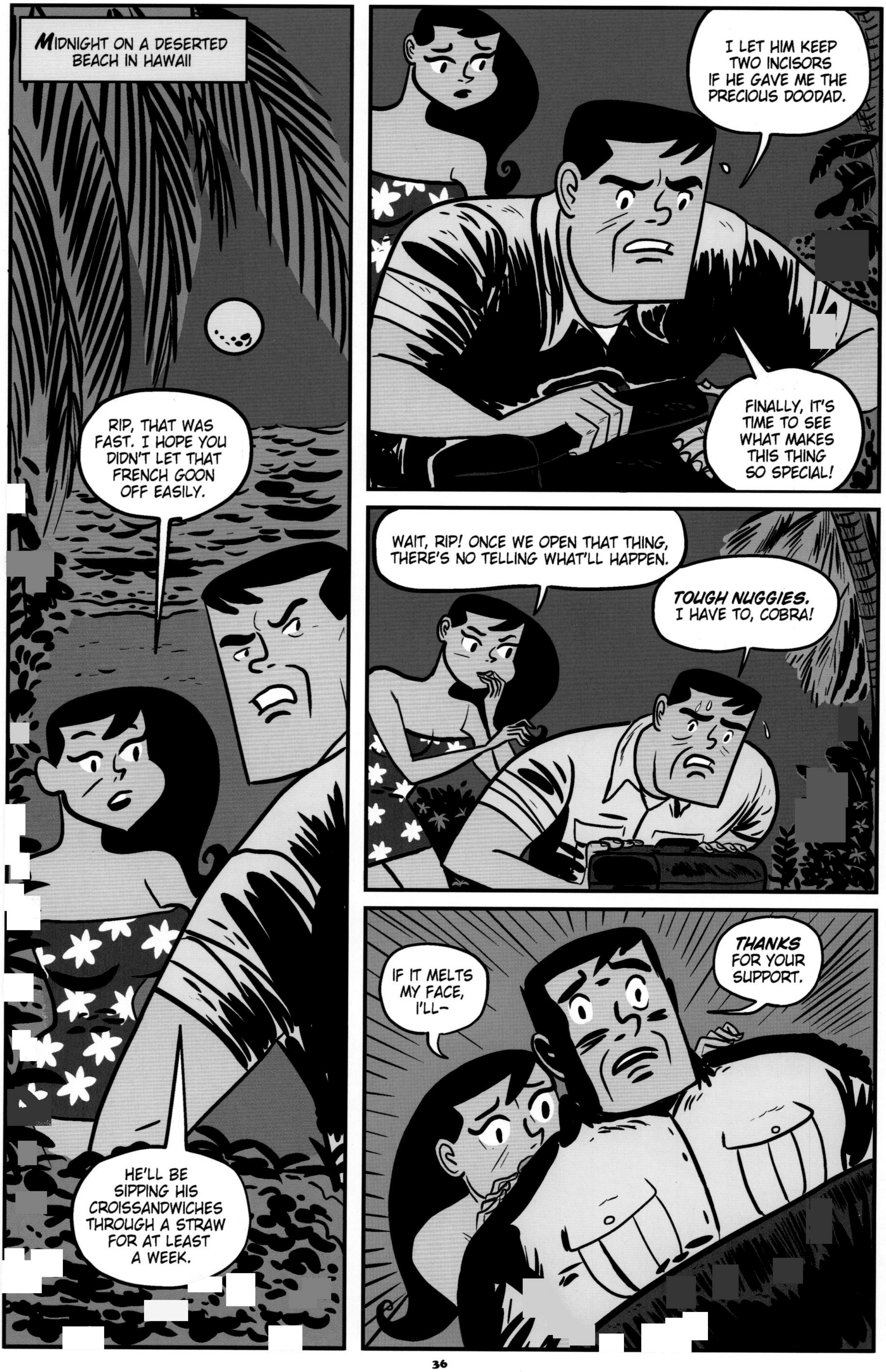
MIDNIGHT ON A DESERTED BEACH IN HAWAII
RIP, THAT WAS FAST. I HOPE YOU DIDN'T LET THAT FRENCH GOON OFF EASILY.
HE'LL BE SIPPING HIS CROISSANDWICHES THROUGH A STRAW FOR AT LEAST A WEEK.
I LET HIM KEEP TWO INCISORS IF HE GAVE ME THE PRECIOUS DOODAD.
FINALLY, IT'S TIME TO SEE WHAT MAKES THIS THING SO SPECIAL!
WAIT, RIP! ONCE WE OPEN THAT THING, THERE'S NO TELLING WHAT'LL HAPPEN.
TOUGH NUGGIES. I HAVE TO, COBRA!
IF IT MELTS MY FACE, I'LL–
THANKS FOR YOUR SUPPORT.

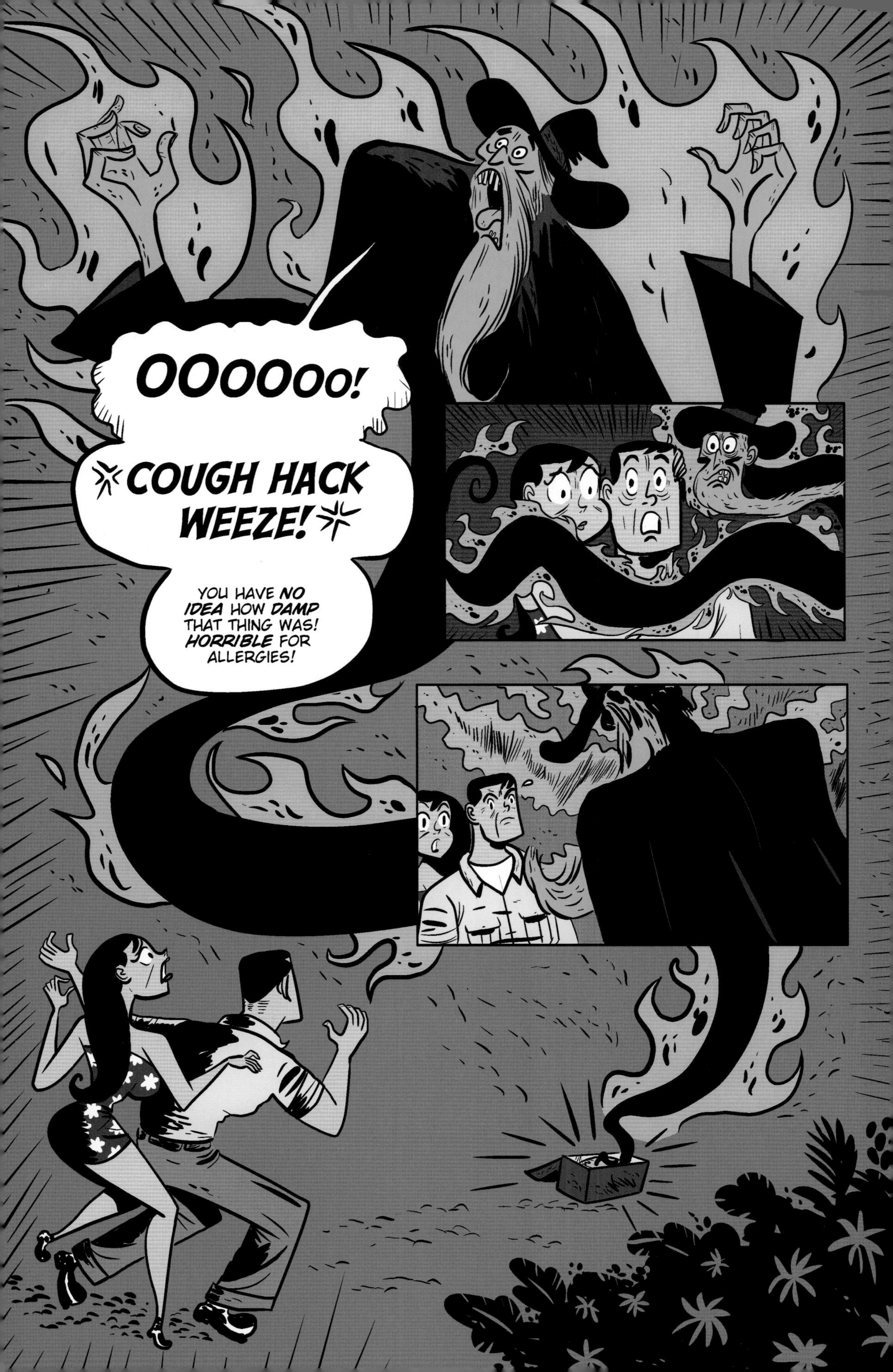
OOOOOo!
COUGH HACK WEEZE!
YOU HAVE NO IDEA HOW DAMP THAT THING WAS! HORRIBLE FOR ALLERGIES!

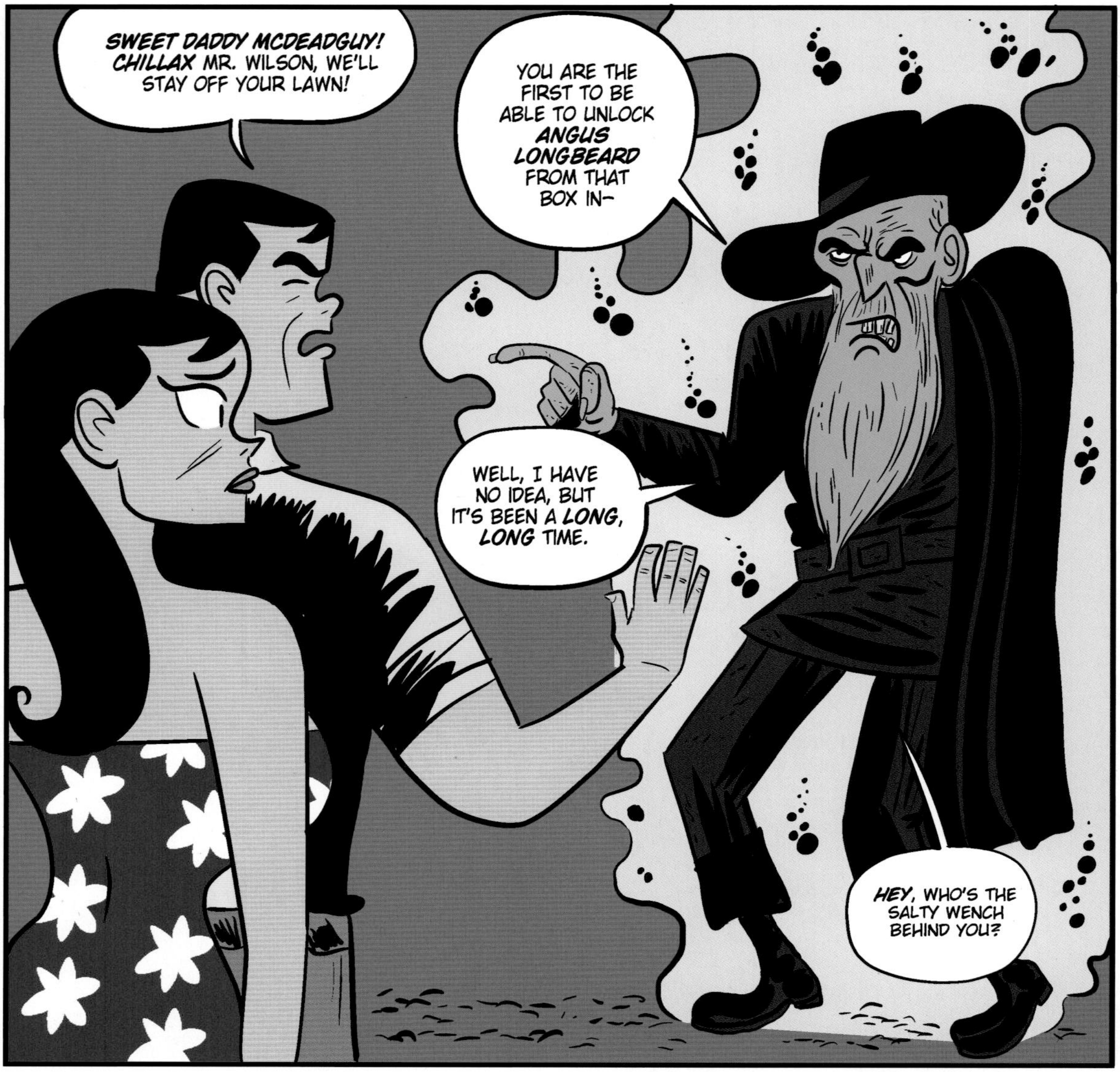
SWEET DADDY MCDEADGUY! CHILLAX MR. WILSON, WE'LL STAY OFF YOUR LAWN!
YOU ARE THE FIRST TO BE ABLE TO UNLOCK ANGUS LONGBEARD FROM THAT BOX IN-
WELL, I HAVE NO IDEA, BUT IT'S BEEN A LONG, LONG TIME.
HEY, WHO'S THE SALTY WENCH BEHIND YOU?

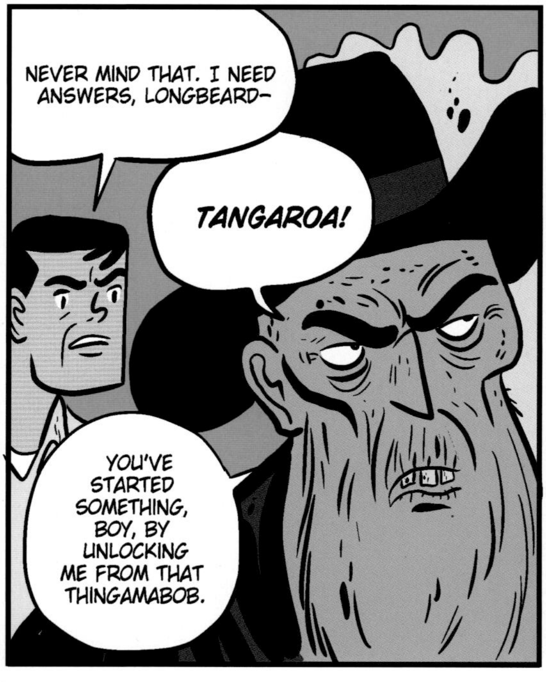
NEVER MIND THAT. I NEED ANSWERS, LONGBEARD-
TANGAROA!
YOU'VE STARTED SOMETHING, BOY, BY UNLOCKING ME FROM THAT THINGAMABOB.

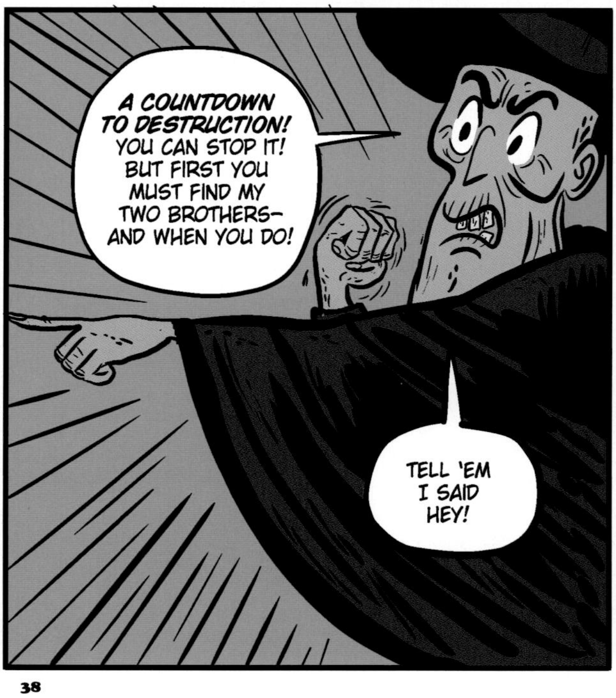
A COUNTDOWN TO DESTRUCTION! YOU CAN STOP IT! BUT FIRST YOU MUST FIND MY TWO BROTHERS- AND WHEN YOU DO!
TELL 'EM I SAID HEY!

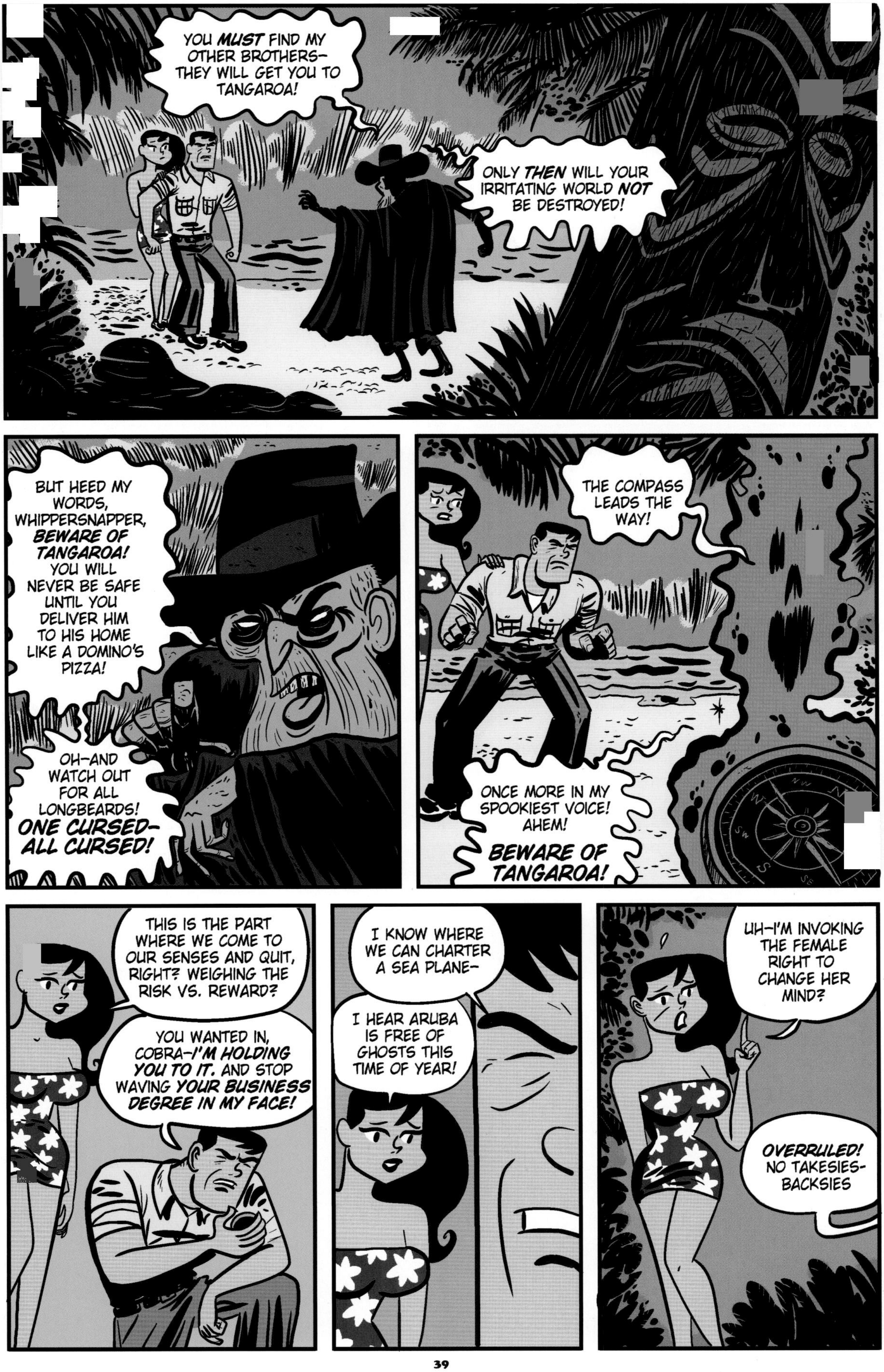
YOU MUST FIND MY OTHER BROTHERS–THEY WILL GET YOU TO TANGAROA!
ONLY THEN WILL YOUR IRRITATING WORLD NOT BE DESTROYED!
BUT HEED MY WORDS, WHIPPERSNAPPER, BEWARE OF TANGAROA! YOU WILL NEVER BE SAFE UNTIL YOU DELIVER HIM TO HIS HOME LIKE A DOMINO'S PIZZA!
OH–AND WATCH OUT FOR ALL LONGBEARDS! ONE CURSED–ALL CURSED!
THE COMPASS LEADS THE WAY!
ONCE MORE IN MY SPOOKIEST VOICE! AHEM!
BEWARE OF TANGAROA!
THIS IS THE PART WHERE WE COME TO OUR SENSES AND QUIT, RIGHT? WEIGHING THE RISK VS. REWARD?
YOU WANTED IN, COBRA–I'M HOLDING YOU TO IT. AND STOP WAVING YOUR BUSINESS DEGREE IN MY FACE!
I KNOW WHERE WE CAN CHARTER A SEA PLANE–
I HEAR ARUBA IS FREE OF GHOSTS THIS TIME OF YEAR!
UH–I'M INVOKING THE FEMALE RIGHT TO CHANGE HER MIND?
OVERRULED! NO TAKESIES-BACKSIES

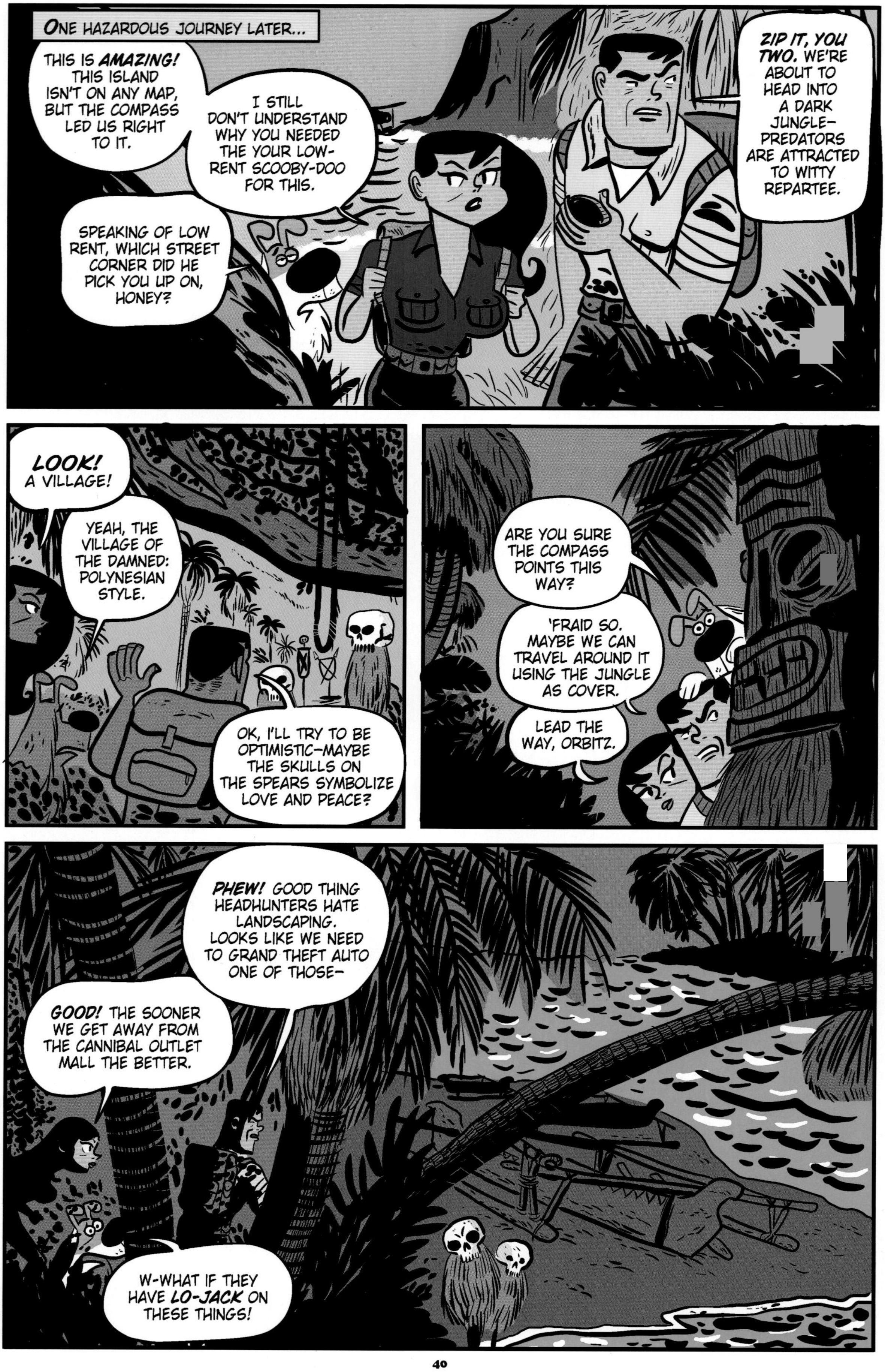

ONE HAZARDOUS JOURNEY LATER...
THIS IS AMAZING! THIS ISLAND ISN'T ON ANY MAP, BUT THE COMPASS LED US RIGHT TO IT.
I STILL DON'T UNDERSTAND WHY YOU NEEDED THE YOUR LOW-RENT SCOOBY-DOO FOR THIS.
SPEAKING OF LOW RENT, WHICH STREET CORNER DID HE PICK YOU UP ON, HONEY?
ZIP IT, YOU TWO. WE'RE ABOUT TO HEAD INTO A DARK JUNGLE– PREDATORS ARE ATTRACTED TO WITTY REPARTEE.
LOOK! A VILLAGE!
YEAH, THE VILLAGE OF THE DAMNED: POLYNESIAN STYLE.
OK, I'LL TRY TO BE OPTIMISTIC–MAYBE THE SKULLS ON THE SPEARS SYMBOLIZE LOVE AND PEACE?
ARE YOU SURE THE COMPASS POINTS THIS WAY?
'FRAID SO. MAYBE WE CAN TRAVEL AROUND IT USING THE JUNGLE AS COVER.
LEAD THE WAY, ORBITZ.
PHEW! GOOD THING HEADHUNTERS HATE LANDSCAPING. LOOKS LIKE WE NEED TO GRAND THEFT AUTO ONE OF THOSE–
GOOD! THE SOONER WE GET AWAY FROM THE CANNIBAL OUTLET MALL THE BETTER.
W-WHAT IF THEY HAVE LO-JACK ON THESE THINGS!

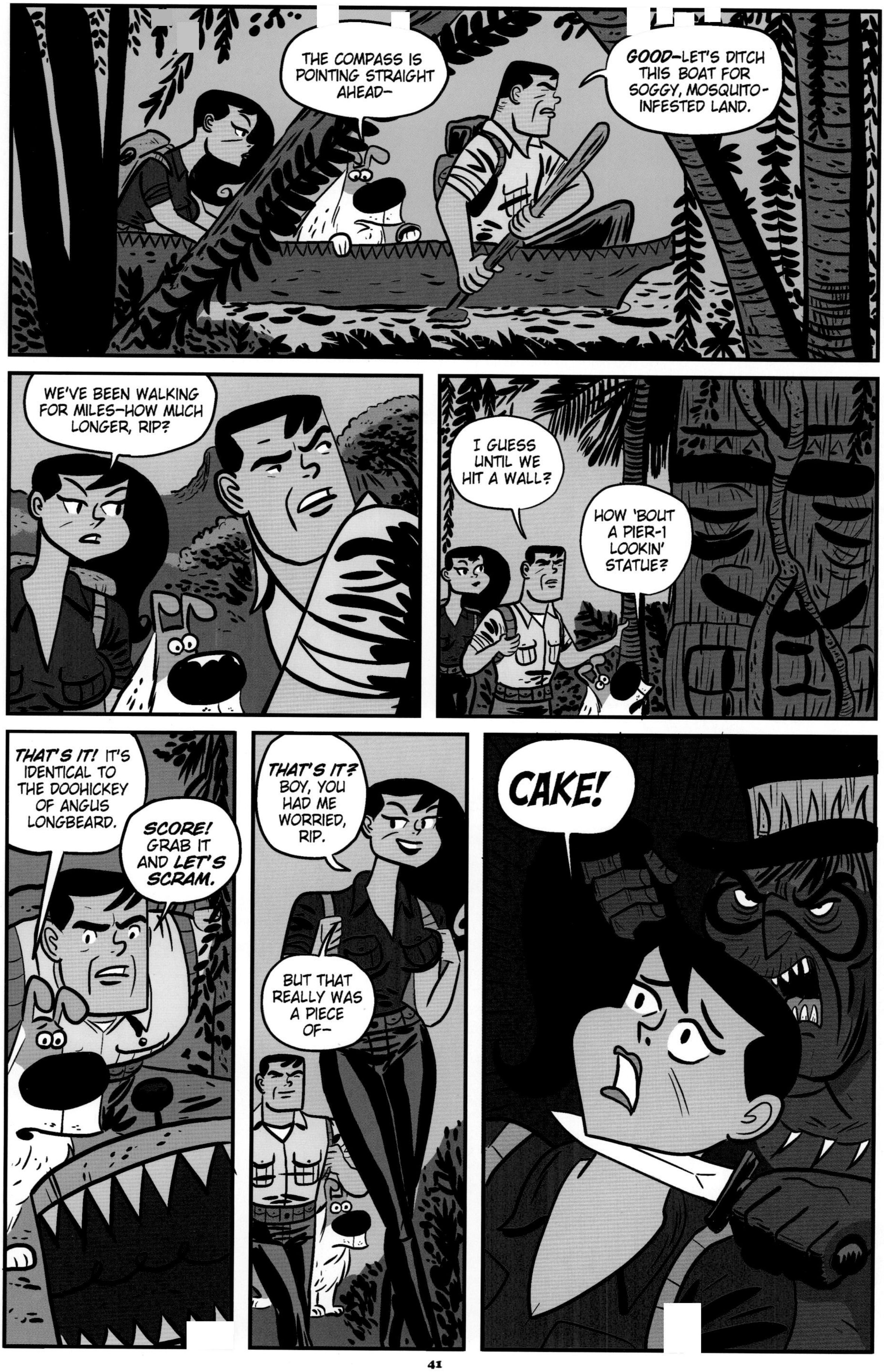
THE COMPASS IS POINTING STRAIGHT AHEAD–
GOOD–LET'S DITCH THIS BOAT FOR SOGGY, MOSQUITO-INFESTED LAND.
WE'VE BEEN WALKING FOR MILES–HOW MUCH LONGER, RIP?
I GUESS UNTIL WE HIT A WALL?
HOW 'BOUT A PIER-1 LOOKIN' STATUE?
THAT'S IT! IT'S IDENTICAL TO THE DOOHICKEY OF ANGUS LONGBEARD.
SCORE! GRAB IT AND LET'S SCRAM.
THAT'S IT? BOY, YOU HAD ME WORRIED, RIP.
BUT THAT REALLY WAS A PIECE OF–
CAKE!

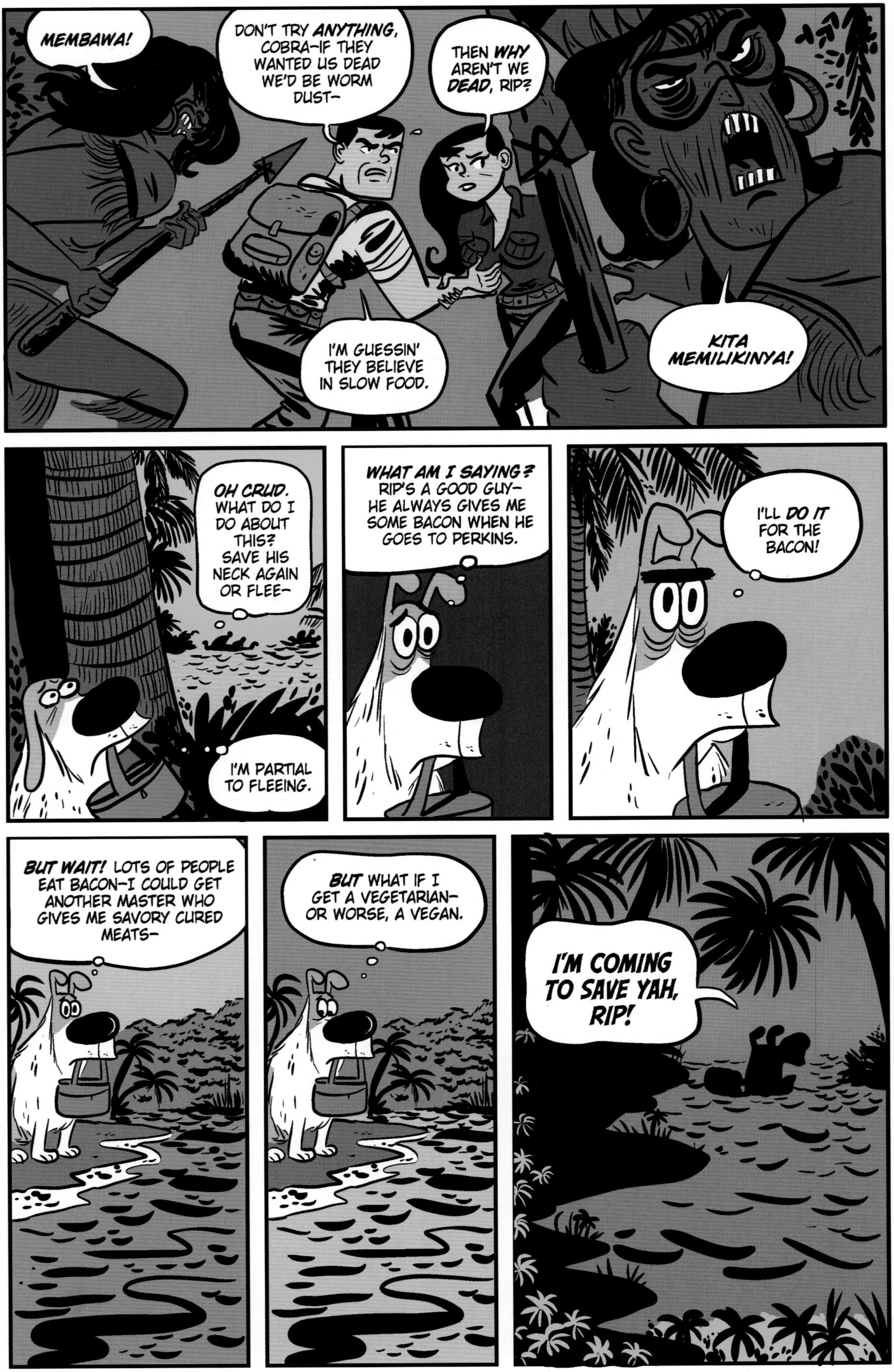
MEMBAWA!
DON'T TRY ANYTHING, COBRA—IF THEY WANTED US DEAD WE'D BE WORM DUST—
THEN WHY AREN'T WE DEAD, RIP?
I'M GUESSIN' THEY BELIEVE IN SLOW FOOD.
KITA MEMILIKINYA!
OH CRUD. WHAT DO I DO ABOUT THIS? SAVE HIS NECK AGAIN OR FLEE—
I'M PARTIAL TO FLEEING.
WHAT AM I SAYING? RIP'S A GOOD GUY—HE ALWAYS GIVES ME SOME BACON WHEN HE GOES TO PERKINS.
I'LL DO IT FOR THE BACON!
BUT WAIT! LOTS OF PEOPLE EAT BACON—I COULD GET ANOTHER MASTER WHO GIVES ME SAVORY CURED MEATS—
BUT WHAT IF I GET A VEGETARIAN—OR WORSE, A VEGAN.
I'M COMING TO SAVE YAH, RIP!

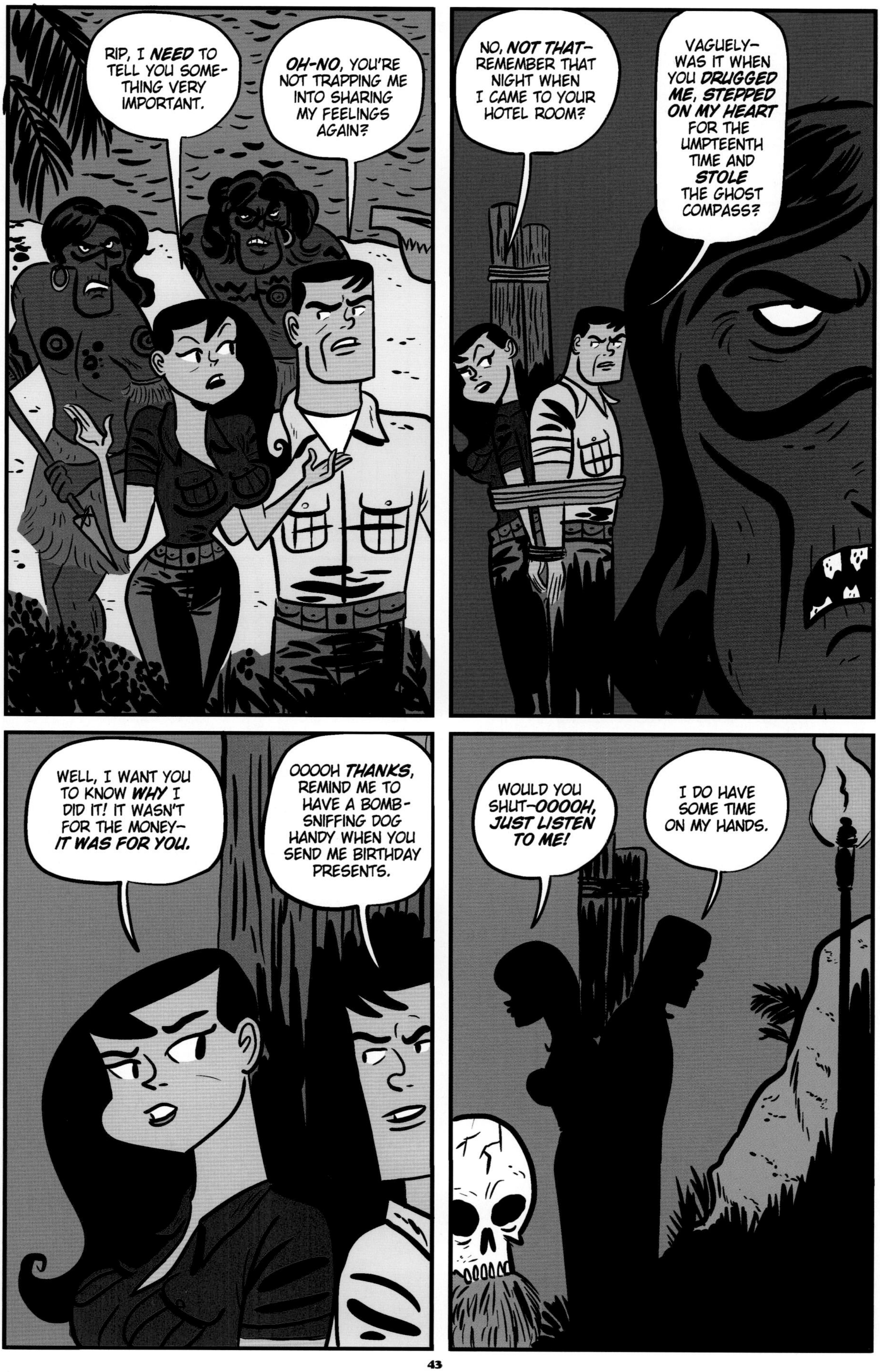
RIP, I **NEED** TO TELL YOU SOMETHING VERY IMPORTANT.
OH-NO, YOU'RE NOT TRAPPING ME INTO SHARING MY FEELINGS AGAIN?
NO, **NOT THAT**- REMEMBER THAT NIGHT WHEN I CAME TO YOUR HOTEL ROOM?
VAGUELY- WAS IT WHEN YOU **DRUGGED ME, STEPPED ON MY HEART** FOR THE UMPTEENTH TIME AND **STOLE** THE GHOST COMPASS?
WELL, I WANT YOU TO KNOW **WHY** I DID IT! IT WASN'T FOR THE MONEY- **IT WAS FOR YOU.**
OOOOH **THANKS**, REMIND ME TO HAVE A BOMB-SNIFFING DOG HANDY WHEN YOU SEND ME BIRTHDAY PRESENTS.
WOULD YOU SHUT-**OOOOH, JUST LISTEN TO ME!**
I DO HAVE SOME TIME ON MY HANDS.

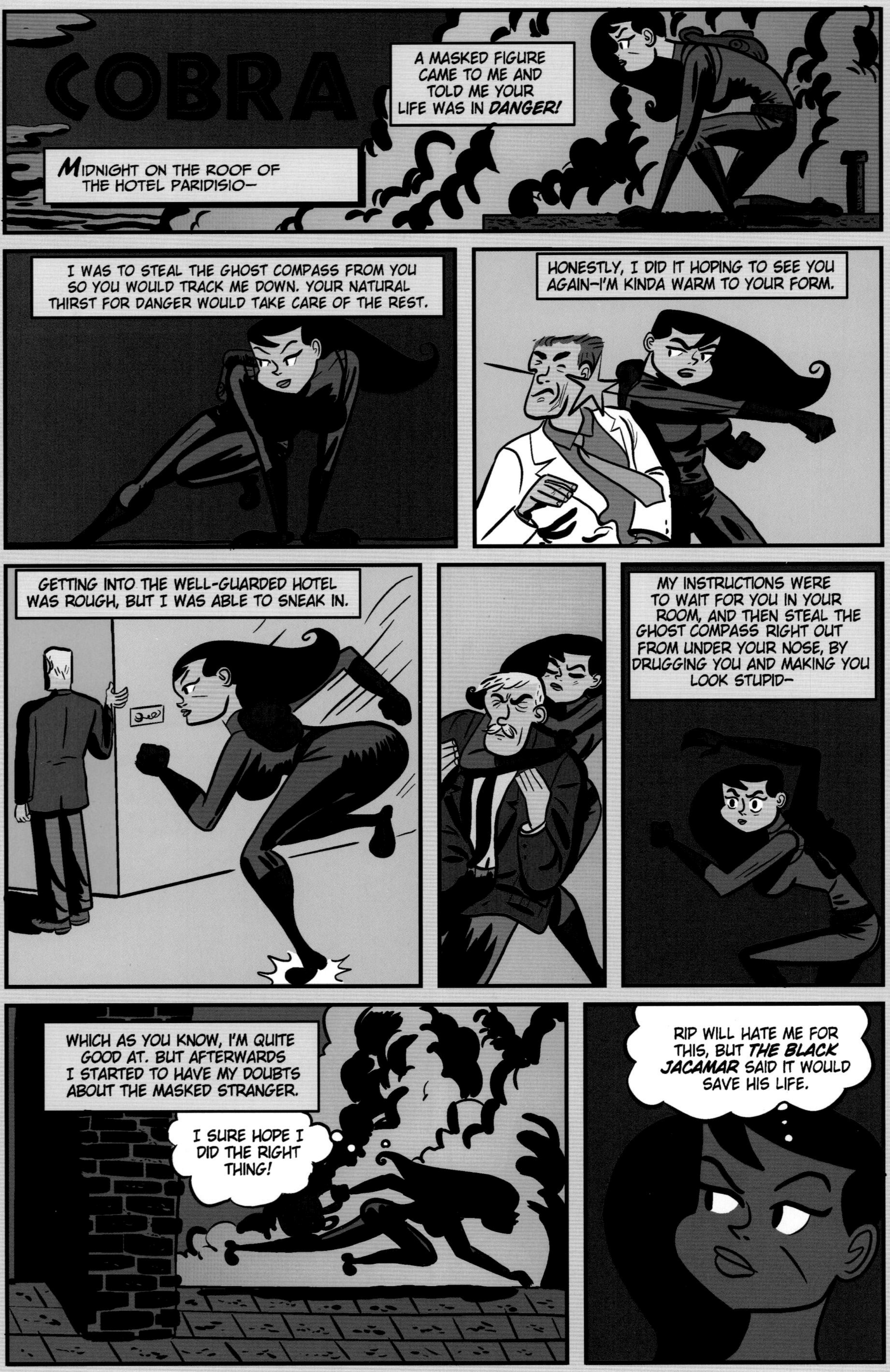
COBRA
MIDNIGHT ON THE ROOF OF THE HOTEL PARIDISIO—
A MASKED FIGURE CAME TO ME AND TOLD ME YOUR LIFE WAS IN DANGER!
I WAS TO STEAL THE GHOST COMPASS FROM YOU SO YOU WOULD TRACK ME DOWN. YOUR NATURAL THIRST FOR DANGER WOULD TAKE CARE OF THE REST.
HONESTLY, I DID IT HOPING TO SEE YOU AGAIN—I'M KINDA WARM TO YOUR FORM.
GETTING INTO THE WELL-GUARDED HOTEL WAS ROUGH, BUT I WAS ABLE TO SNEAK IN.
MY INSTRUCTIONS WERE TO WAIT FOR YOU IN YOUR ROOM, AND THEN STEAL THE GHOST COMPASS RIGHT OUT FROM UNDER YOUR NOSE, BY DRUGGING YOU AND MAKING YOU LOOK STUPID—
WHICH AS YOU KNOW, I'M QUITE GOOD AT. BUT AFTERWARDS I STARTED TO HAVE MY DOUBTS ABOUT THE MASKED STRANGER.
I SURE HOPE I DID THE RIGHT THING!
RIP WILL HATE ME FOR THIS, BUT THE BLACK JACAMAR SAID IT WOULD SAVE HIS LIFE.

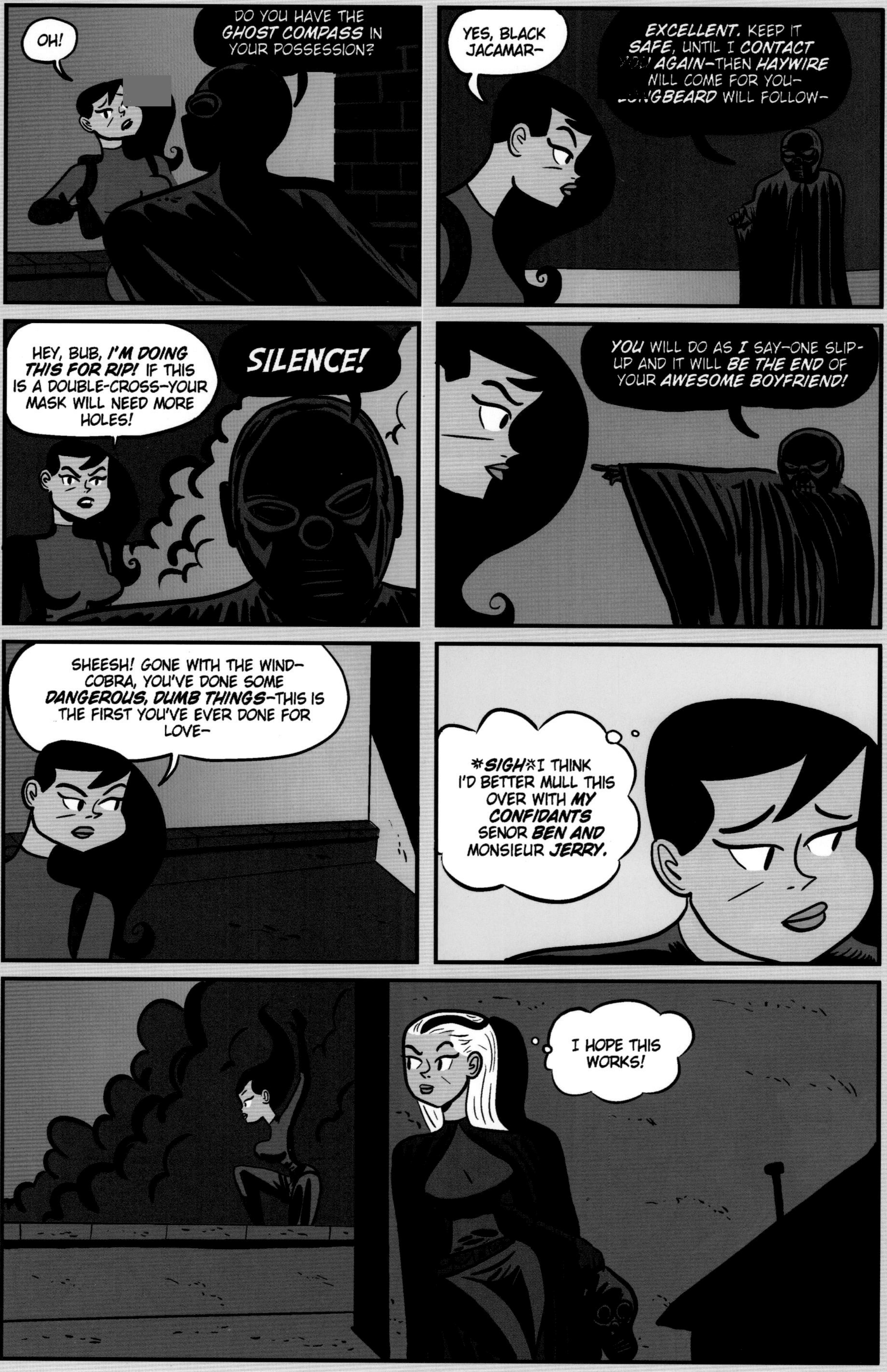
OH!
DO YOU HAVE THE GHOST COMPASS IN YOUR POSSESSION?
YES, BLACK JACAMAR-
EXCELLENT. KEEP IT SAFE, UNTIL I CONTACT
AGAIN-THEN HAYWIRE
NILL COME FOR YOU-
GBEARD WILL FOLLOW-
HEY, BUB, I'M DOING THIS FOR RIP! IF THIS IS A DOUBLE-CROSS-YOUR MASK WILL NEED MORE HOLES!
SILENCE!
YOU WILL DO AS I SAY-ONE SLIP-UP AND IT WILL BE THE END OF YOUR AWESOME BOYFRIEND!
SHEESH! GONE WITH THE WIND-COBRA, YOU'VE DONE SOME DANGEROUS, DUMB THINGS-THIS IS THE FIRST YOU'VE EVER DONE FOR LOVE-
SIGH I THINK I'D BETTER MULL THIS OVER WITH MY CONFIDANTS SENOR BEN AND MONSIEUR JERRY.
I HOPE THIS WORKS!

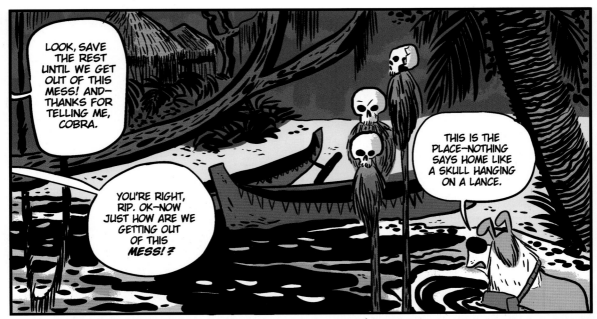

LOOK, SAVE THE REST UNTIL WE GET OUT OF THIS MESS! AND—THANKS FOR TELLING ME, COBRA.

YOU'RE RIGHT, RIP. OK—NOW JUST HOW ARE WE GETTING OUT OF THIS *MESS!?*

THIS IS THE PLACE—NOTHING SAYS HOME LIKE A SKULL HANGING ON A LANCE.

WHAT IF TNT CAN'T SAVE US?

MY DOG IS LOYAL. HE'LL FIGHT TO SAVE MY LIFE.

I'M SORRY, DO YOU HAVE ANOTHER DOG I'M NOT AWARE OF?

TRUST ME— HE'S RAMBO WITH FURRY PAWS— I TRAINED HIM MYSELF.

SORRY I'M LATE, I STEPPED ON A *SLUG*, AND IT WAS GROSS. I WOULDN'T TAKE ANOTHER STEP UNTIL I GOT THE *SLIMY SMOOSH* OUT OF MY *SILKY FUR.*

THERE'S RAMBO NOW!

TNT, THERE'S A GUARD WITH A SPEAR—*TAKE HIM OUT*, AND THEN USE THE SPEAR TO CUT US LOOSE!

NO CAN DO, BIG GUY, I HATE HAND-TO-HAND COMBAT—

IS THERE A SLEEPING PILL I COULD SLIP INTO HIS JAMBA JUICE, OR SOMETHING?

QUIT GIVING ME GUFF—WHEN I THINK OF ALL THE MONEY I SPENT ON A POSH ATTACK DOG SCHOOL—

ALL RIGHT, ALL RIGHT! I GET IT, GUILTY TRIPPENSTEIN.

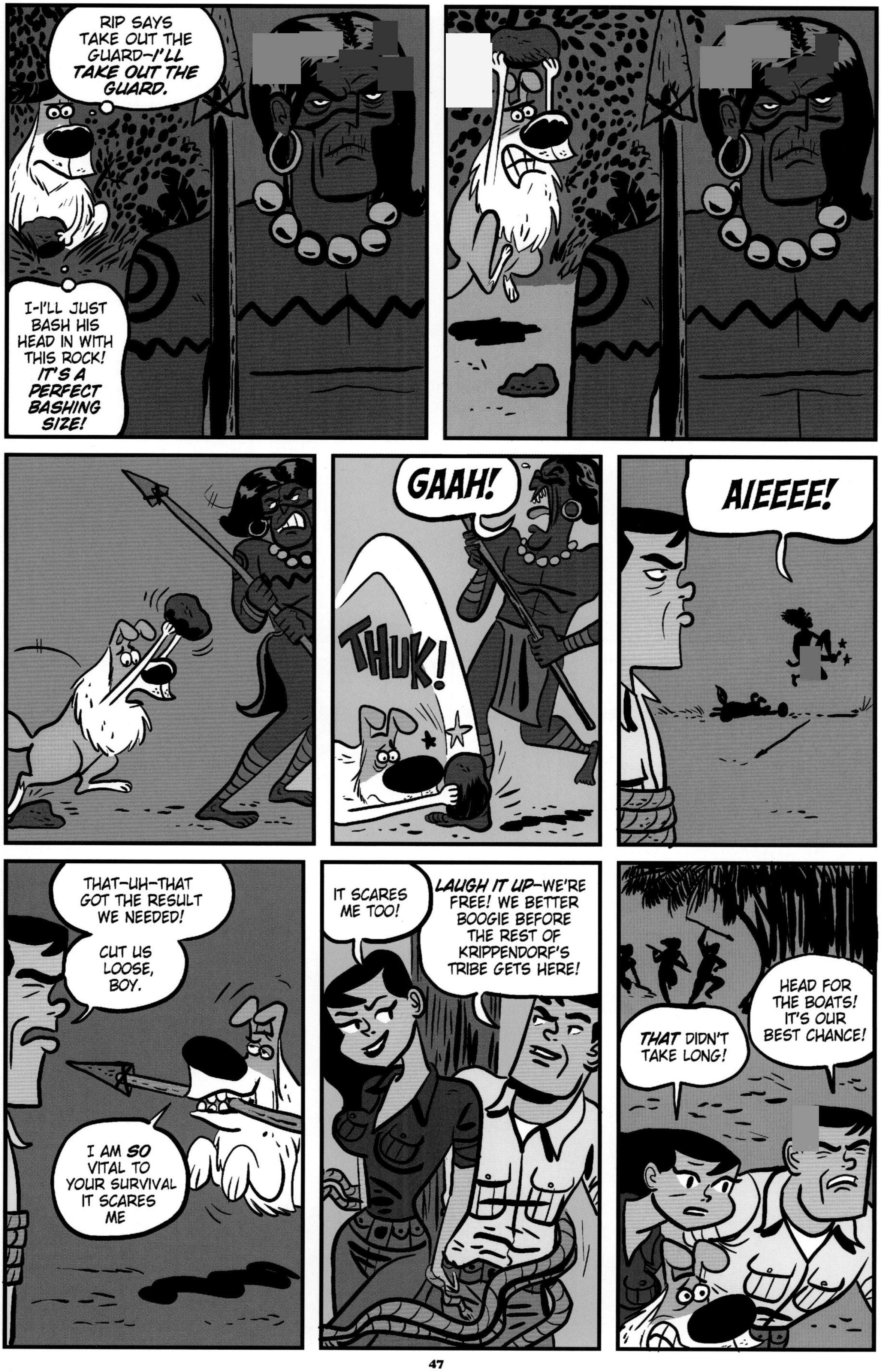
RIP SAYS TAKE OUT THE GUARD—*I'LL TAKE OUT THE GUARD.*
I-I'LL JUST BASH HIS HEAD IN WITH THIS ROCK! *IT'S A PERFECT BASHING SIZE!*
GAAH!
THUK!
AIEEEE!
THAT—UH—THAT GOT THE RESULT WE NEEDED!
CUT US LOOSE, BOY.
I AM *SO* VITAL TO YOUR SURVIVAL IT SCARES ME
IT SCARES ME TOO!
LAUGH IT UP—WE'RE FREE! WE BETTER BOOGIE BEFORE THE REST OF KRIPPENDORF'S TRIBE GETS HERE!
THAT DIDN'T TAKE LONG!
HEAD FOR THE BOATS! IT'S OUR BEST CHANCE!

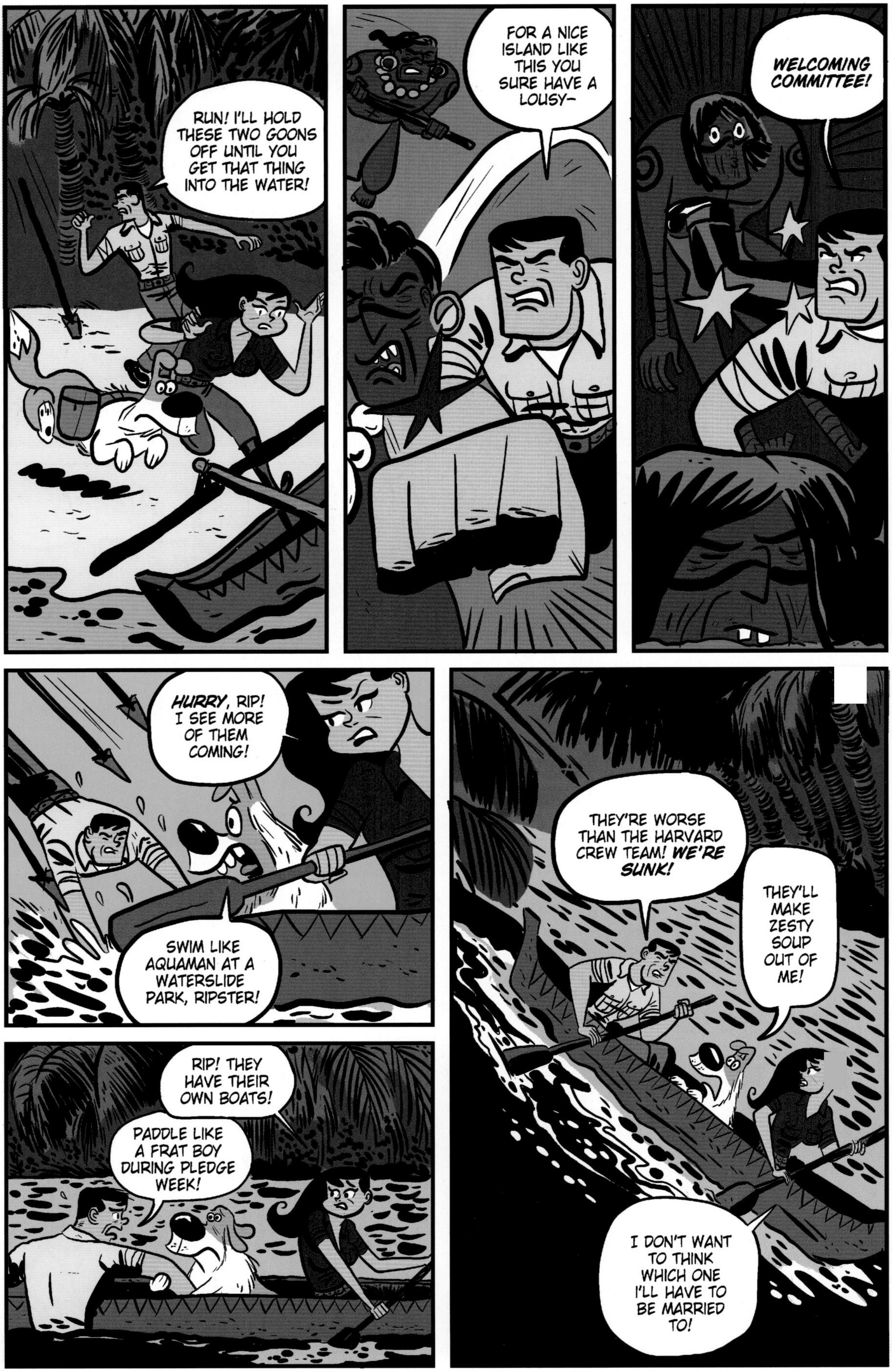
RUN! I'LL HOLD THESE TWO GOONS OFF UNTIL YOU GET THAT THING INTO THE WATER!
FOR A NICE ISLAND LIKE THIS YOU SURE HAVE A LOUSY–
WELCOMING COMMITTEE!
HURRY, RIP! I SEE MORE OF THEM COMING!
SWIM LIKE AQUAMAN AT A WATERSLIDE PARK, RIPSTER!
RIP! THEY HAVE THEIR OWN BOATS!
PADDLE LIKE A FRAT BOY DURING PLEDGE WEEK!
THEY'RE WORSE THAN THE HARVARD CREW TEAM! WE'RE SUNK!
THEY'LL MAKE ZESTY SOUP OUT OF ME!
I DON'T WANT TO THINK WHICH ONE I'LL HAVE TO BE MARRIED TO!

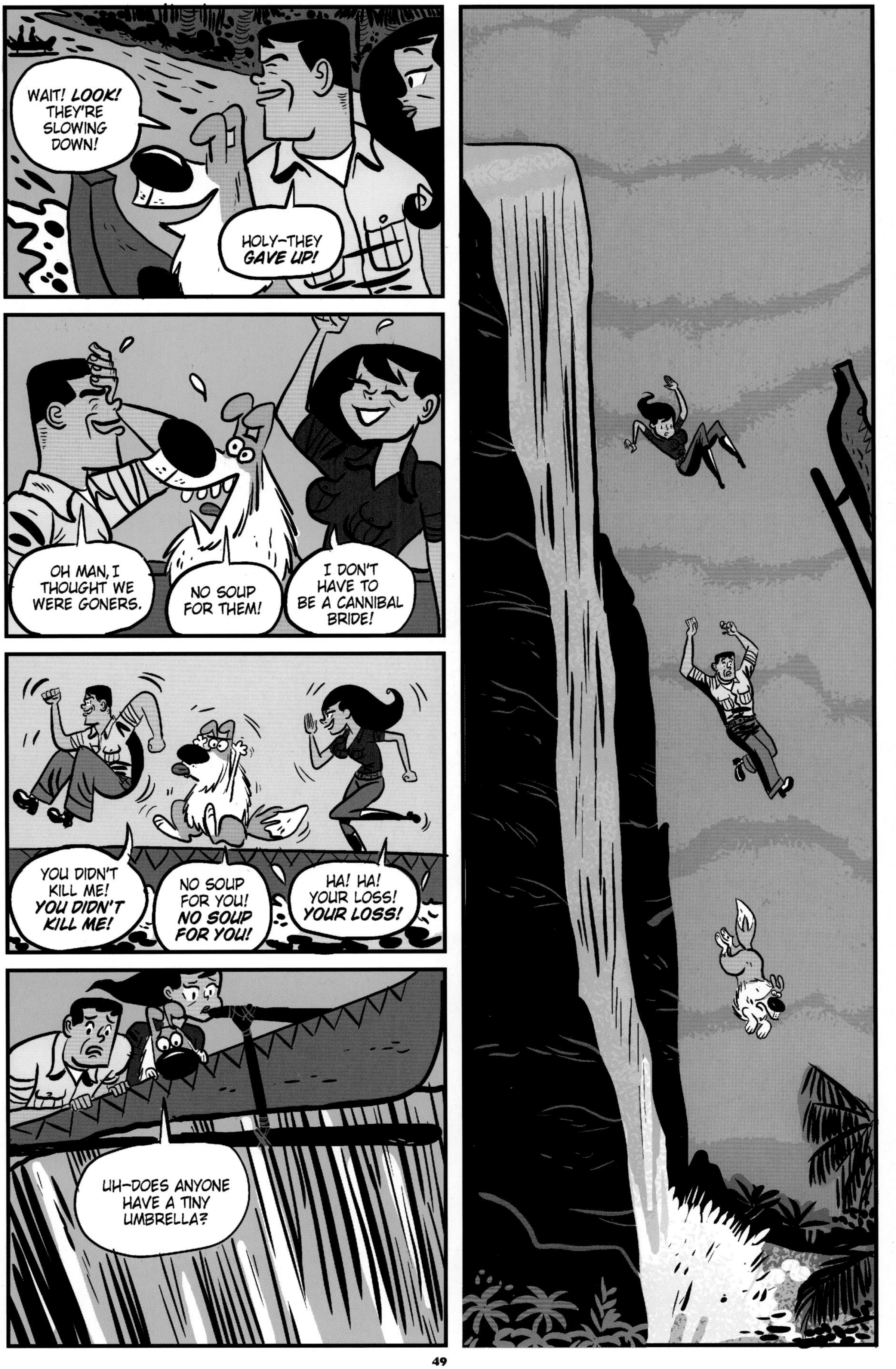
WAIT! LOOK! THEY'RE SLOWING DOWN!
HOLY–THEY GAVE UP!
OH MAN, I THOUGHT WE WERE GONERS.
NO SOUP FOR THEM!
I DON'T HAVE TO BE A CANNIBAL BRIDE!
YOU DIDN'T KILL ME! YOU DIDN'T KILL ME!
NO SOUP FOR YOU! NO SOUP FOR YOU!
HA! HA! YOUR LOSS! YOUR LOSS!
UH–DOES ANYONE HAVE A TINY UMBRELLA?

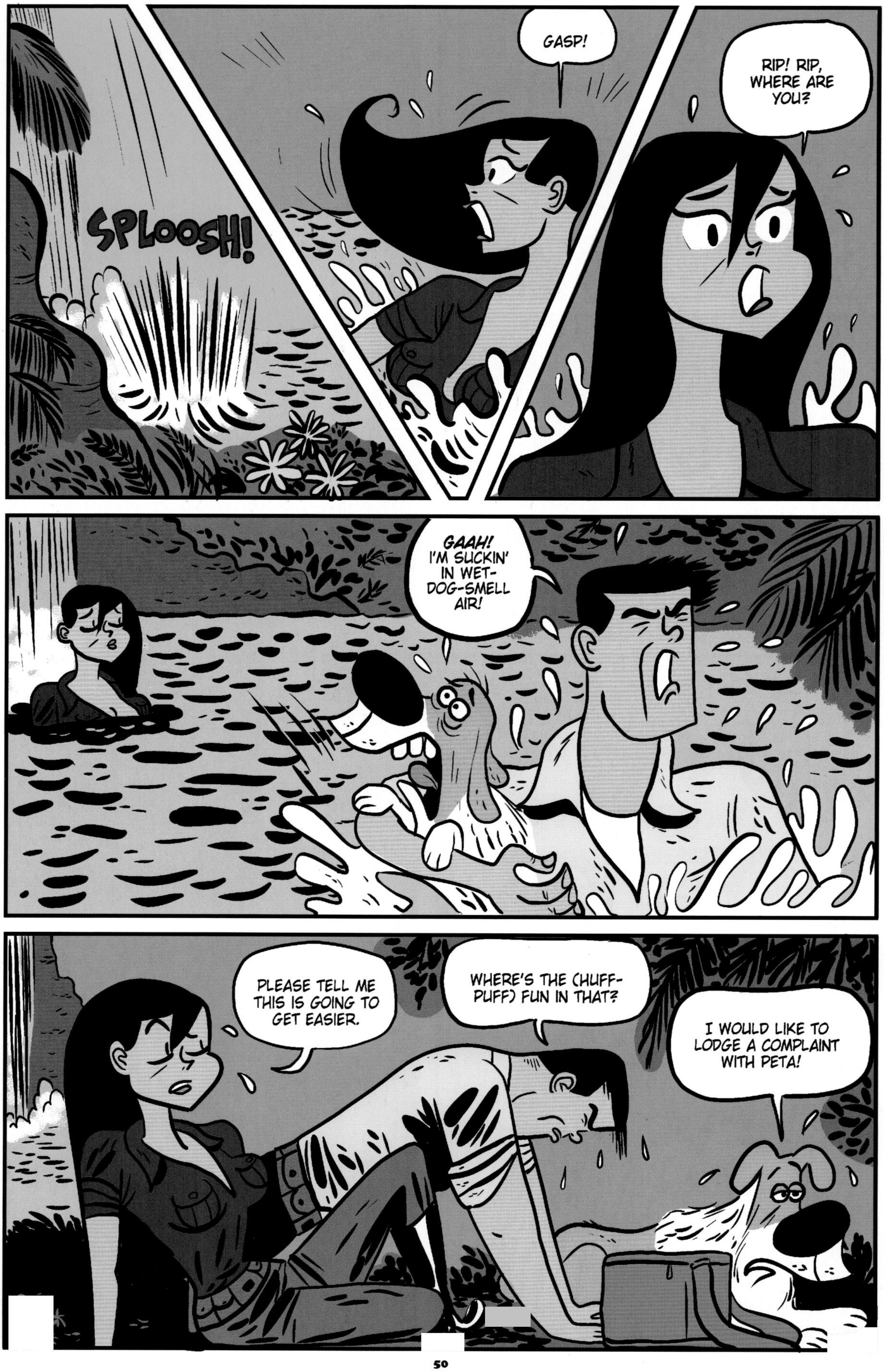
SPLOOSH!
GASP!
RIP! RIP, WHERE ARE YOU?
GAAH! I'M SUCKIN' IN WET-DOG-SMELL AIR!
PLEASE TELL ME THIS IS GOING TO GET EASIER.
WHERE'S THE (HUFF-PUFF) FUN IN THAT?
I WOULD LIKE TO LODGE A COMPLAINT WITH PETA!

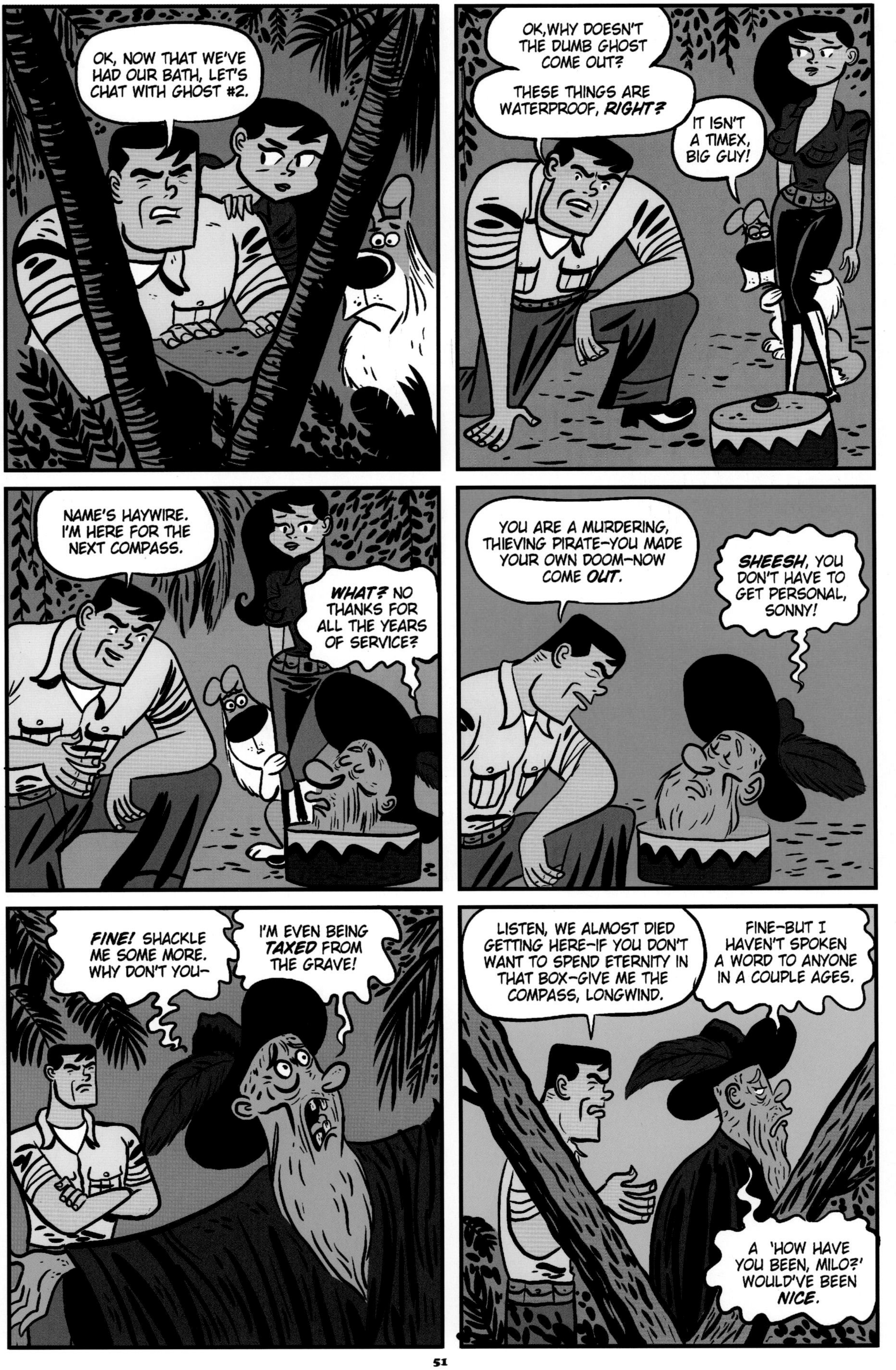
OK, NOW THAT WE'VE HAD OUR BATH, LET'S CHAT WITH GHOST #2.
OK, WHY DOESN'T THE DUMB GHOST COME OUT?
THESE THINGS ARE WATERPROOF, RIGHT?
IT ISN'T A TIMEX, BIG GUY!
NAME'S HAYWIRE. I'M HERE FOR THE NEXT COMPASS.
WHAT? NO THANKS FOR ALL THE YEARS OF SERVICE?
YOU ARE A MURDERING, THIEVING PIRATE–YOU MADE YOUR OWN DOOM–NOW COME OUT.
SHEESH, YOU DON'T HAVE TO GET PERSONAL, SONNY!
FINE! SHACKLE ME SOME MORE. WHY DON'T YOU–
I'M EVEN BEING TAXED FROM THE GRAVE!
LISTEN, WE ALMOST DIED GETTING HERE–IF YOU DON'T WANT TO SPEND ETERNITY IN THAT BOX–GIVE ME THE COMPASS, LONGWIND.
FINE–BUT I HAVEN'T SPOKEN A WORD TO ANYONE IN A COUPLE AGES.
A 'HOW HAVE YOU BEEN, MILO?' WOULD'VE BEEN NICE.

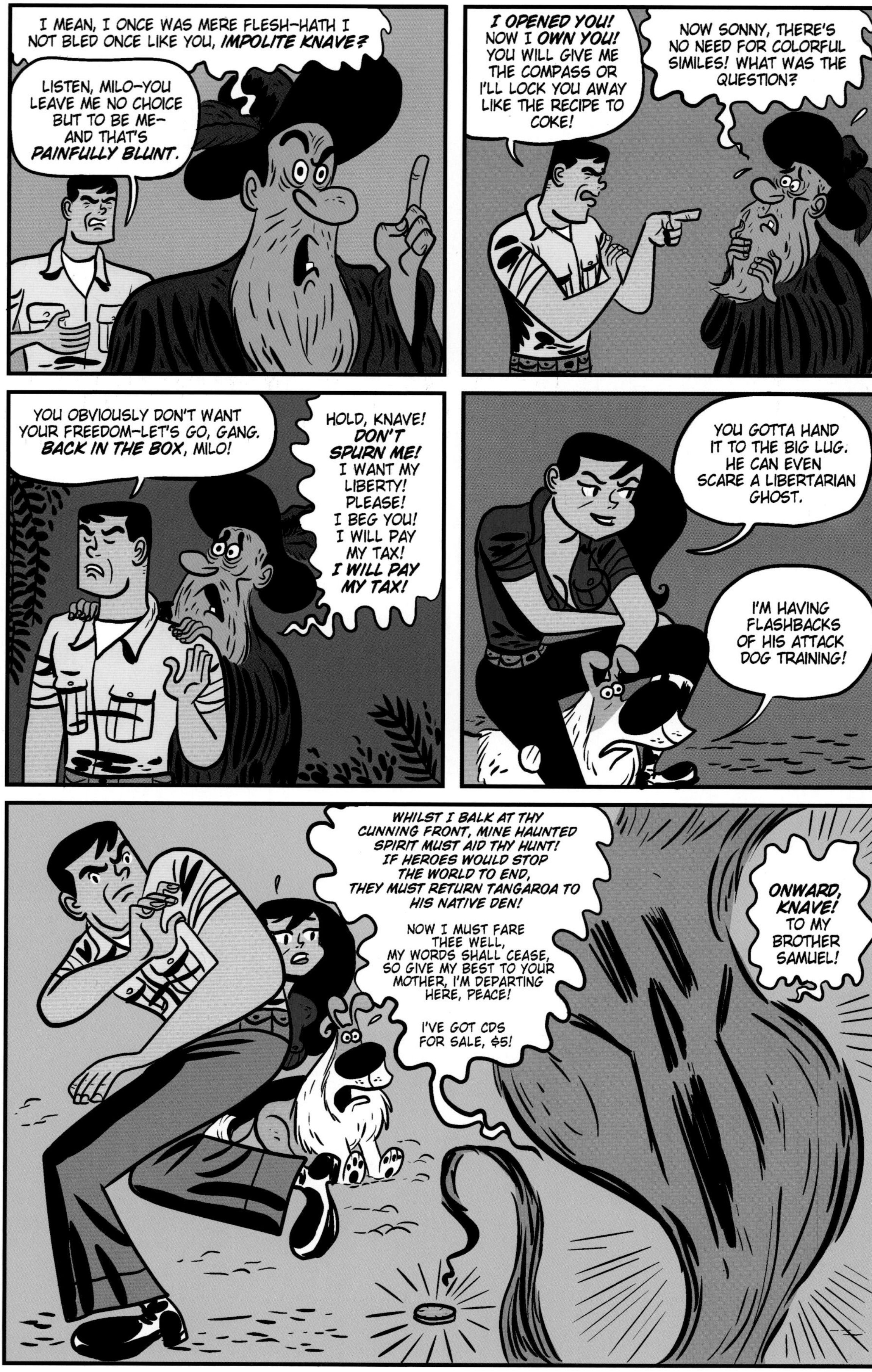
I MEAN, I ONCE WAS MERE FLESH—HATH I NOT BLED ONCE LIKE YOU, *IMPOLITE KNAVE?*
LISTEN, MILO—YOU LEAVE ME NO CHOICE BUT TO BE ME—AND THAT'S *PAINFULLY BLUNT*.
I OPENED YOU! NOW I *OWN YOU!* YOU WILL GIVE ME THE COMPASS OR I'LL LOCK YOU AWAY LIKE THE RECIPE TO COKE!
NOW SONNY, THERE'S NO NEED FOR COLORFUL SIMILES! WHAT WAS THE QUESTION?
YOU OBVIOUSLY DON'T WANT YOUR FREEDOM—LET'S GO, GANG. *BACK IN THE BOX*, MILO!
HOLD, KNAVE! *DON'T SPURN ME!* I WANT MY LIBERTY! PLEASE! I BEG YOU! I WILL PAY MY TAX! *I WILL PAY MY TAX!*
YOU GOTTA HAND IT TO THE BIG LUG. HE CAN EVEN SCARE A LIBERTARIAN GHOST.
I'M HAVING FLASHBACKS OF HIS ATTACK DOG TRAINING!
WHILST I BALK AT THY CUNNING FRONT, MINE HAUNTED SPIRIT MUST AID THY HUNT! IF HEROES WOULD STOP THE WORLD TO END, THEY MUST RETURN TANGAROA TO HIS NATIVE DEN!
NOW I MUST FARE THEE WELL, MY WORDS SHALL CEASE, SO GIVE MY BEST TO YOUR MOTHER, I'M DEPARTING HERE, PEACE!
I'VE GOT CDS FOR SALE, $5!
ONWARD, KNAVE! TO MY BROTHER SAMUEL!

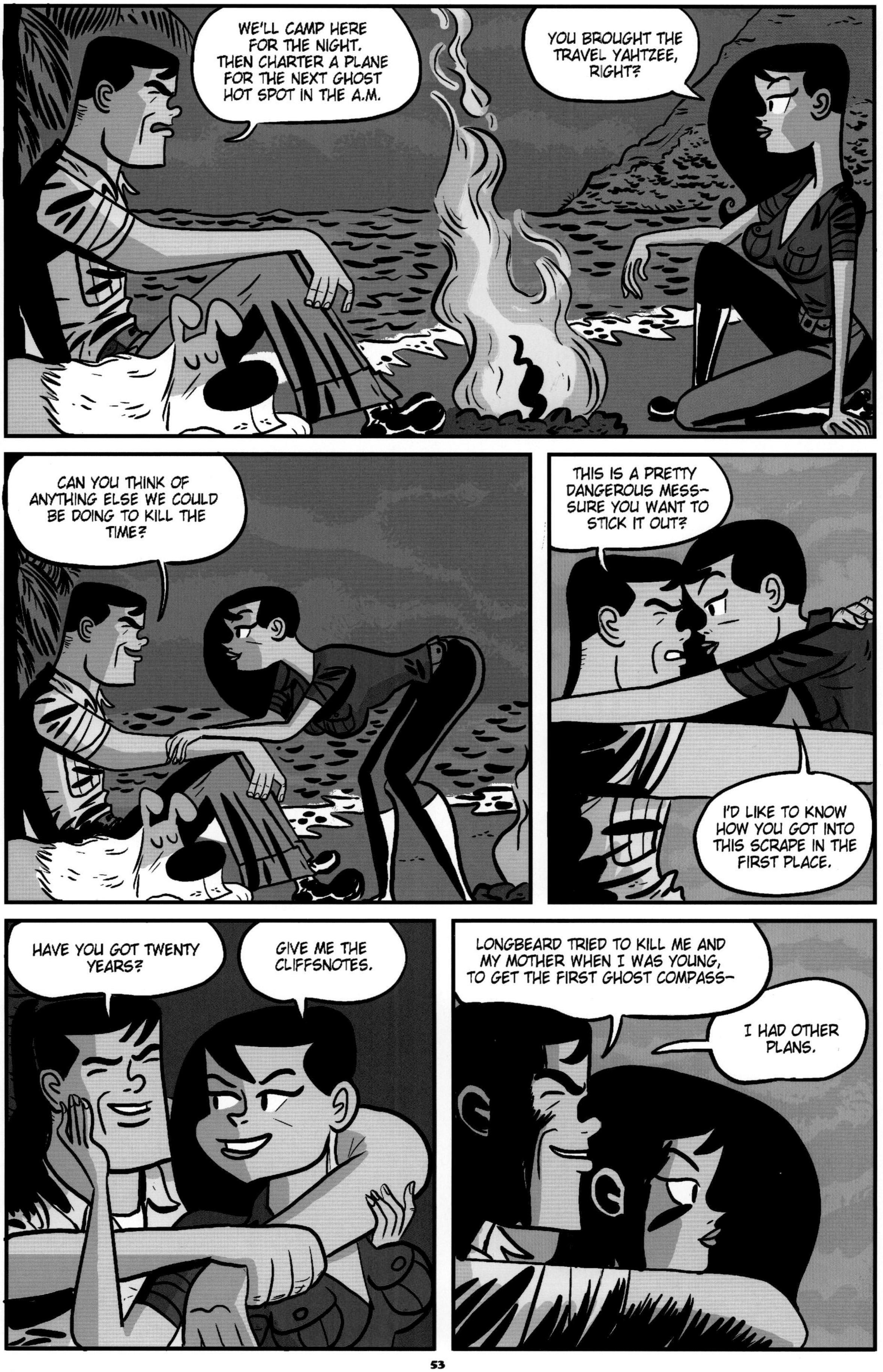
WE'LL CAMP HERE FOR THE NIGHT. THEN CHARTER A PLANE FOR THE NEXT GHOST HOT SPOT IN THE A.M.
YOU BROUGHT THE TRAVEL YAHTZEE, RIGHT?
CAN YOU THINK OF ANYTHING ELSE WE COULD BE DOING TO KILL THE TIME?
THIS IS A PRETTY DANGEROUS MESS-SURE YOU WANT TO STICK IT OUT?
I'D LIKE TO KNOW HOW YOU GOT INTO THIS SCRAPE IN THE FIRST PLACE.
HAVE YOU GOT TWENTY YEARS?
GIVE ME THE CLIFFSNOTES.
LONGBEARD TRIED TO KILL ME AND MY MOTHER WHEN I WAS YOUNG, TO GET THE FIRST GHOST COMPASS-
I HAD OTHER PLANS.

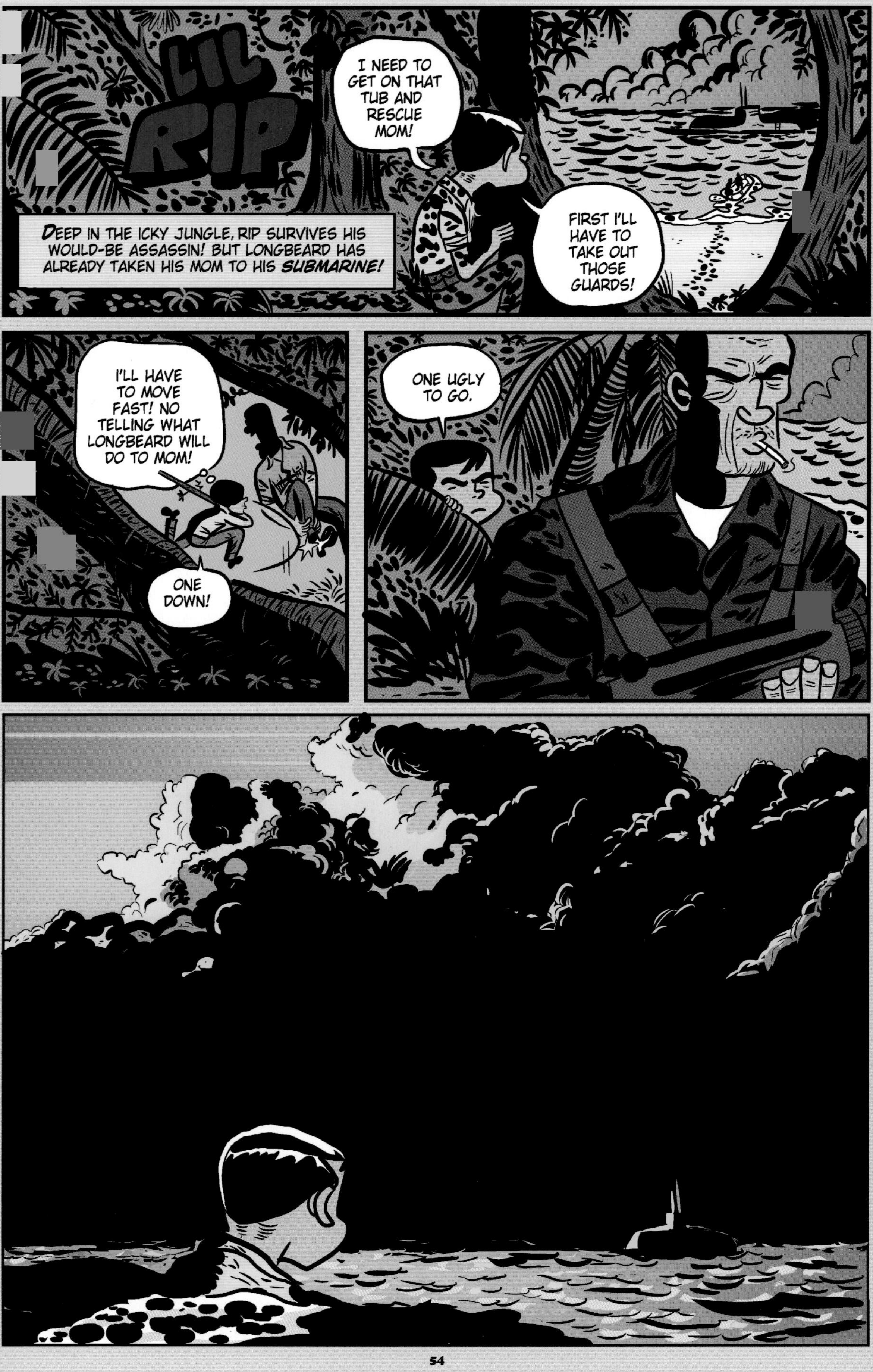
LIL RIP
DEEP IN THE ICKY JUNGLE, RIP SURVIVES HIS WOULD-BE ASSASSIN! BUT LONGBEARD HAS ALREADY TAKEN HIS MOM TO HIS SUBMARINE!
I NEED TO GET ON THAT TUB AND RESCUE MOM!
FIRST I'LL HAVE TO TAKE OUT THOSE GUARDS!
I'LL HAVE TO MOVE FAST! NO TELLING WHAT LONGBEARD WILL DO TO MOM!
ONE DOWN!
ONE UGLY TO GO.

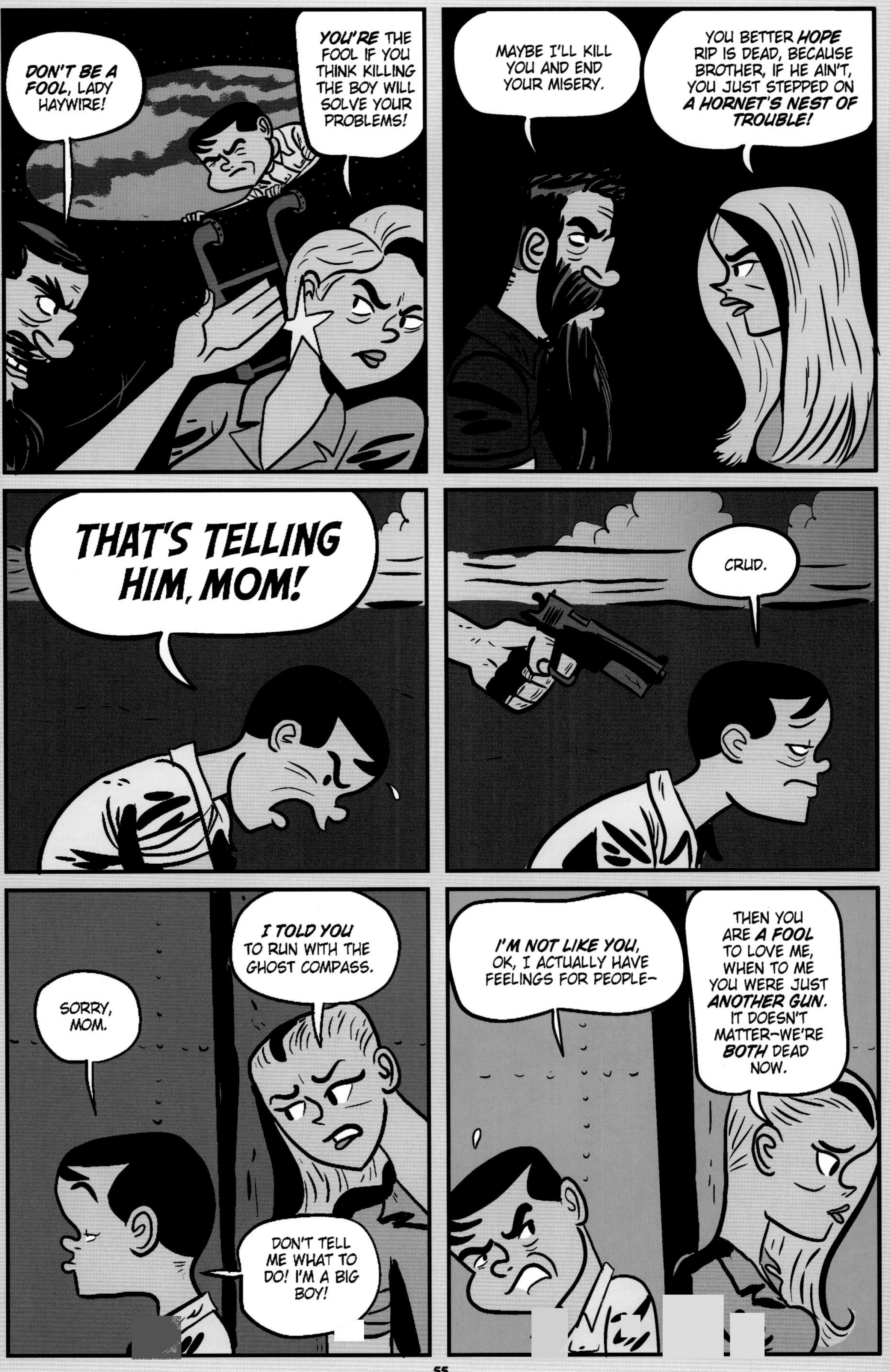
DON'T BE A FOOL, LADY HAYWIRE!
YOU'RE THE FOOL IF YOU THINK KILLING THE BOY WILL SOLVE YOUR PROBLEMS!
MAYBE I'LL KILL YOU AND END YOUR MISERY.
YOU BETTER HOPE RIP IS DEAD, BECAUSE BROTHER, IF HE AIN'T, YOU JUST STEPPED ON A HORNET'S NEST OF TROUBLE!
THAT'S TELLING HIM, MOM!
CRUD.
I TOLD YOU TO RUN WITH THE GHOST COMPASS.
SORRY, MOM.
DON'T TELL ME WHAT TO DO! I'M A BIG BOY!
I'M NOT LIKE YOU, OK, I ACTUALLY HAVE FEELINGS FOR PEOPLE–
THEN YOU ARE A FOOL TO LOVE ME, WHEN TO ME YOU WERE JUST ANOTHER GUN. IT DOESN'T MATTER–WE'RE BOTH DEAD NOW.

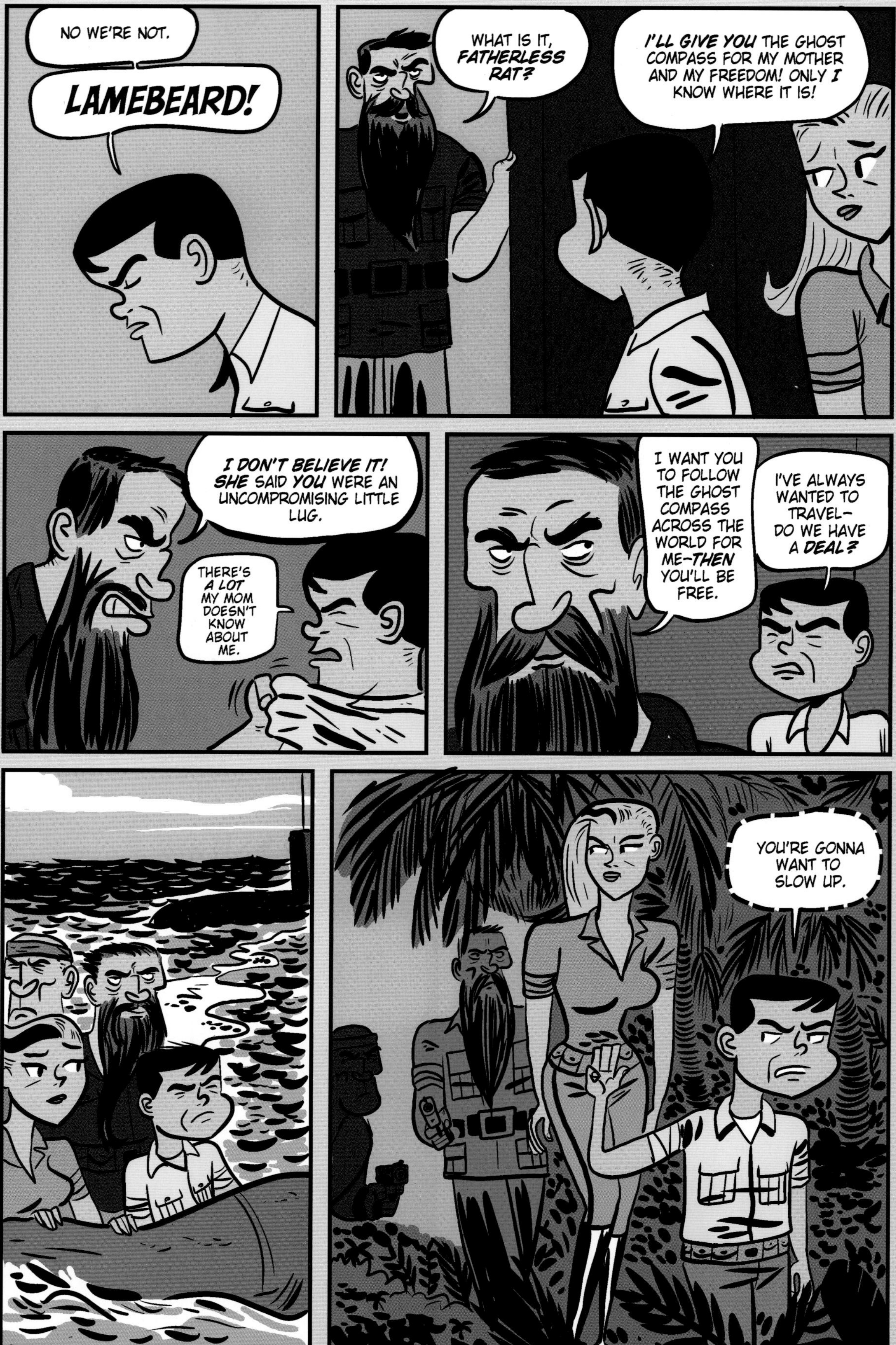
NO WE'RE NOT.
LAMEBEARD!
WHAT IS IT, FATHERLESS RAT?
I'LL GIVE YOU THE GHOST COMPASS FOR MY MOTHER AND MY FREEDOM! ONLY I KNOW WHERE IT IS!
I DON'T BELIEVE IT! SHE SAID YOU WERE AN UNCOMPROMISING LITTLE LUG.
THERE'S A LOT MY MOM DOESN'T KNOW ABOUT ME.
I WANT YOU TO FOLLOW THE GHOST COMPASS ACROSS THE WORLD FOR ME—THEN YOU'LL BE FREE.
I'VE ALWAYS WANTED TO TRAVEL— DO WE HAVE A DEAL?
YOU'RE GONNA WANT TO SLOW UP.

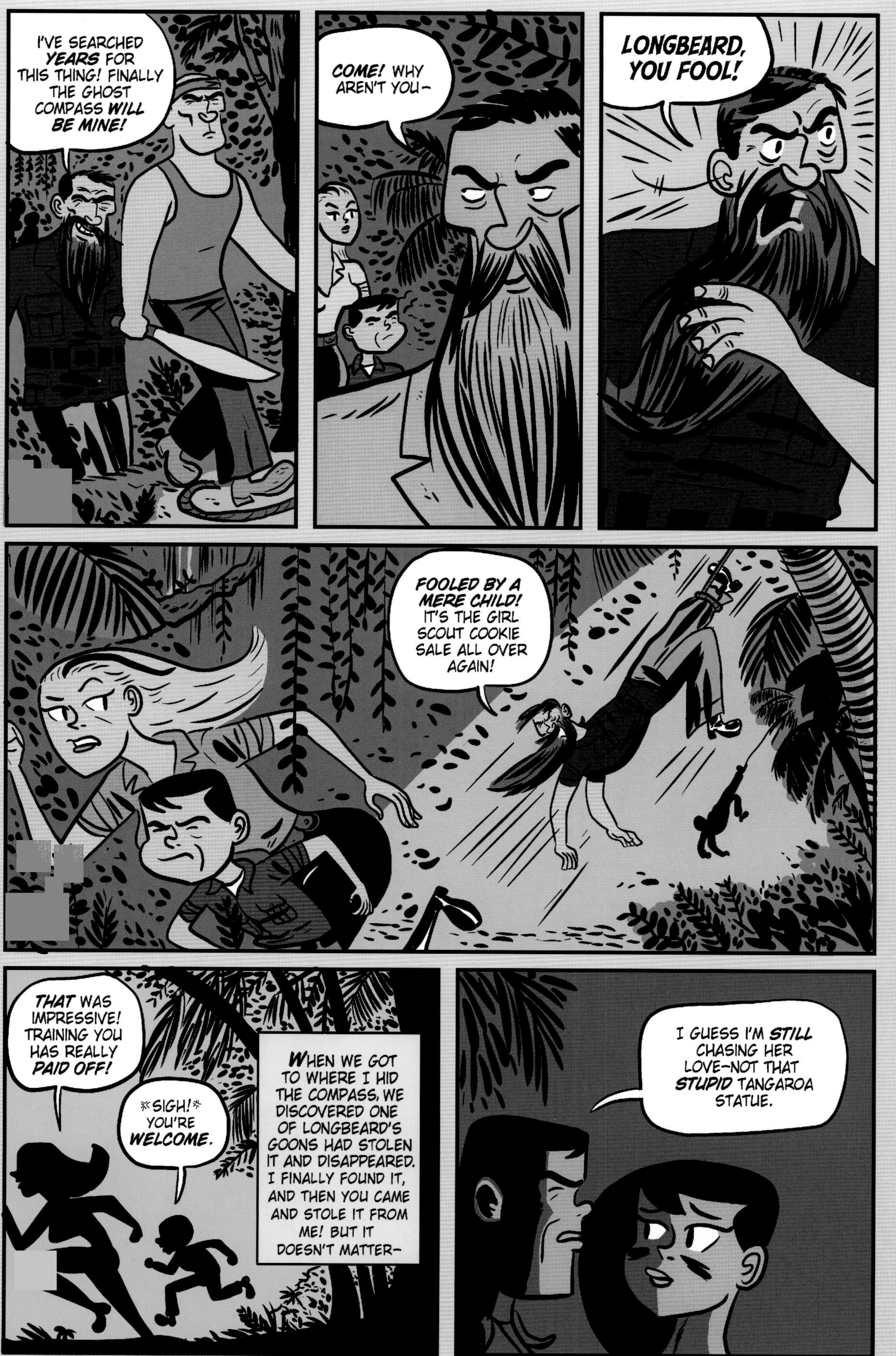
I'VE SEARCHED YEARS FOR THIS THING! FINALLY THE GHOST COMPASS WILL BE MINE!
COME! WHY AREN'T YOU–
LONGBEARD, YOU FOOL!
FOOLED BY A MERE CHILD! IT'S THE GIRL SCOUT COOKIE SALE ALL OVER AGAIN!
THAT WAS IMPRESSIVE! TRAINING YOU HAS REALLY PAID OFF!
SIGH! YOU'RE WELCOME.
WHEN WE GOT TO WHERE I HID THE COMPASS, WE DISCOVERED ONE OF LONGBEARD'S GOONS HAD STOLEN IT AND DISAPPEARED. I FINALLY FOUND IT, AND THEN YOU CAME AND STOLE IT FROM ME! BUT IT DOESN'T MATTER–
I GUESS I'M STILL CHASING HER LOVE–NOT THAT STUPID TANGAROA STATUE.

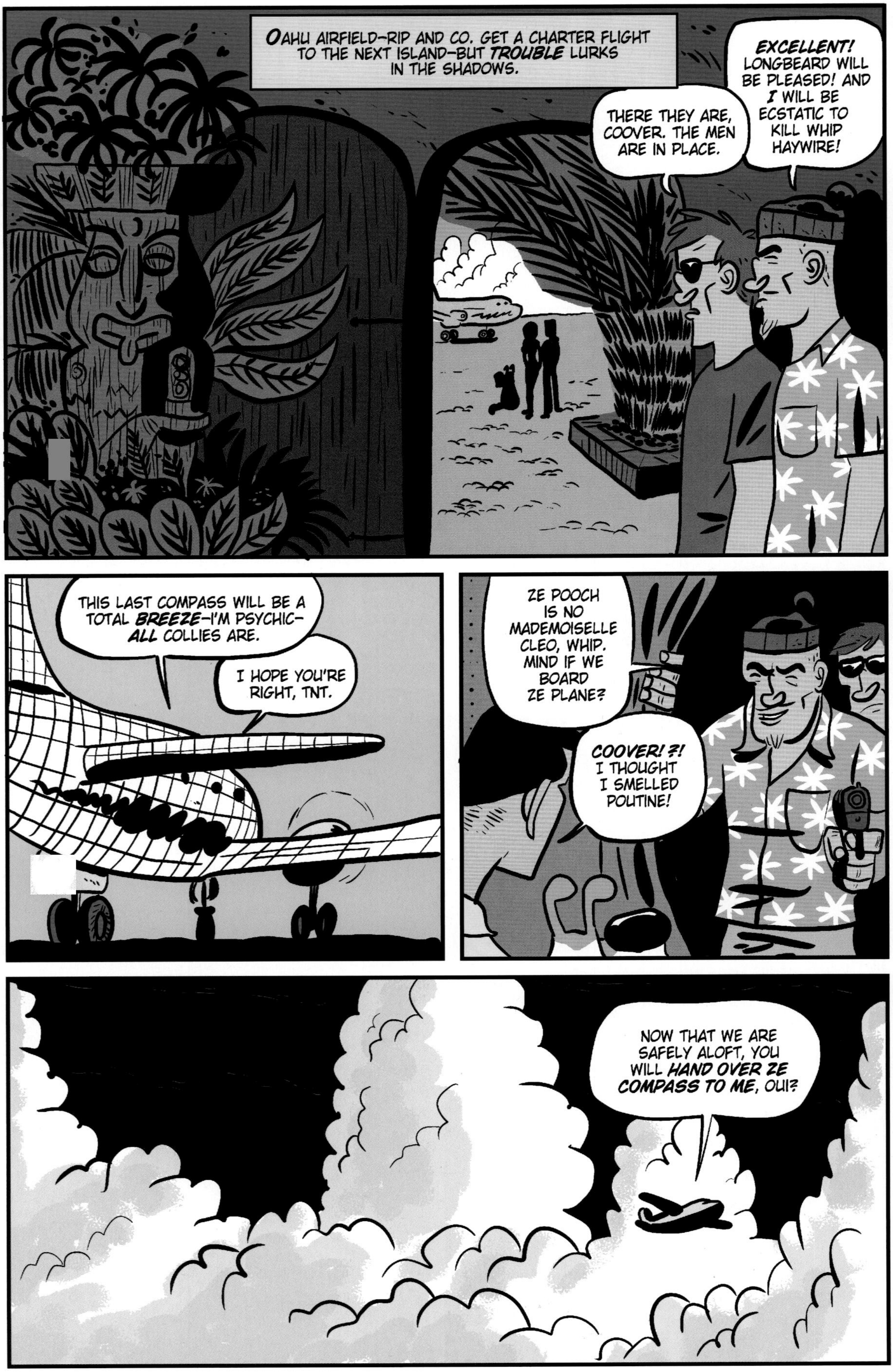
OAHU AIRFIELD—RIP AND CO. GET A CHARTER FLIGHT TO THE NEXT ISLAND—BUT TROUBLE LURKS IN THE SHADOWS.
THERE THEY ARE, COOVER. THE MEN ARE IN PLACE.
EXCELLENT! LONGBEARD WILL BE PLEASED! AND I WILL BE ECSTATIC TO KILL WHIP HAYWIRE!
THIS LAST COMPASS WILL BE A TOTAL BREEZE—I'M PSYCHIC—ALL COLLIES ARE.
I HOPE YOU'RE RIGHT, TNT.
ZE POOCH IS NO MADEMOISELLE CLEO, WHIP. MIND IF WE BOARD ZE PLANE?
COOVER!?! I THOUGHT I SMELLED POUTINE!
NOW THAT WE ARE SAFELY ALOFT, YOU WILL HAND OVER ZE COMPASS TO ME, OUI?

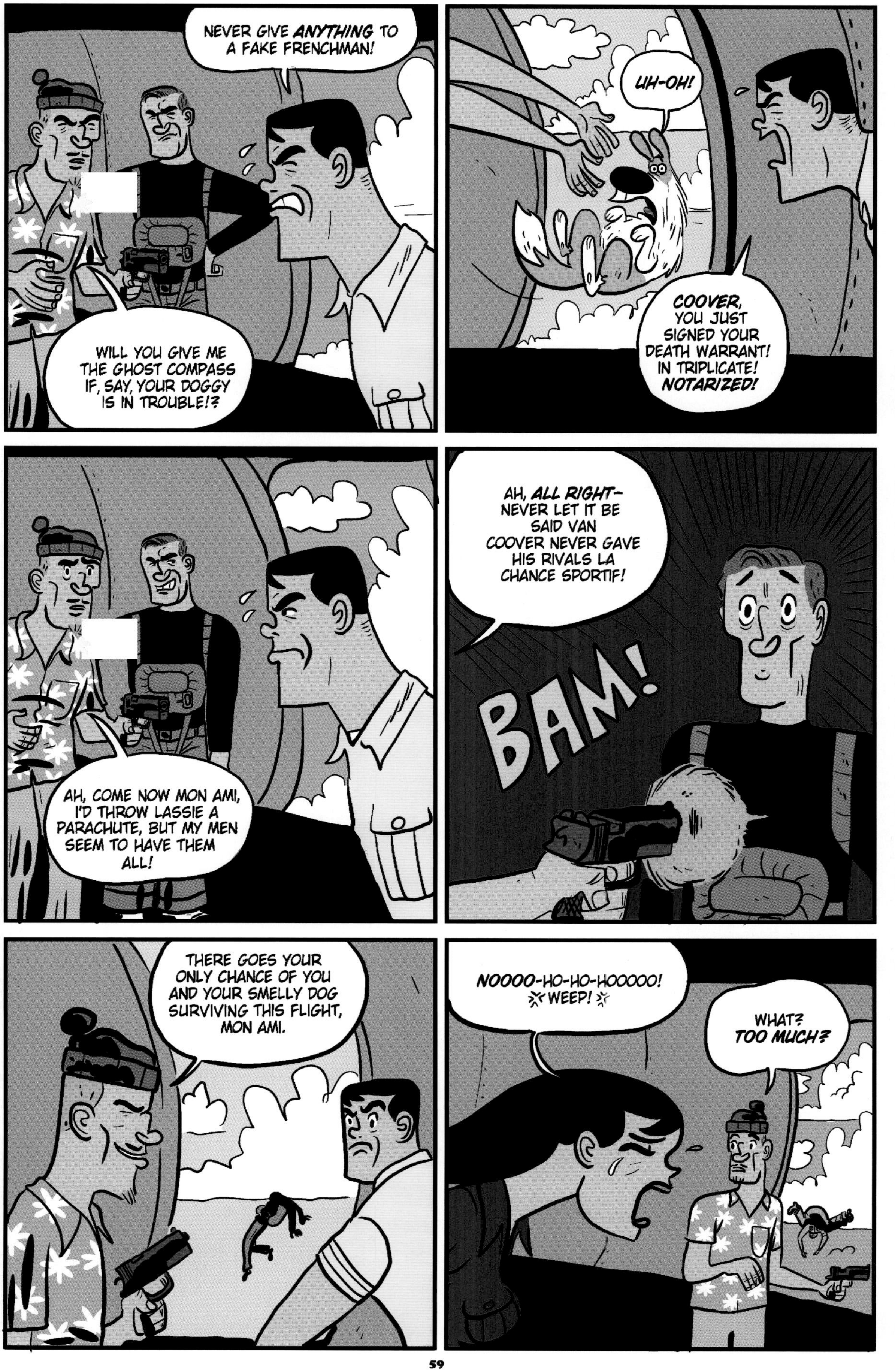
NEVER GIVE ANYTHING TO A FAKE FRENCHMAN!
WILL YOU GIVE ME THE GHOST COMPASS IF, SAY, YOUR DOGGY IS IN TROUBLE!?
UH-OH!
COOVER, YOU JUST SIGNED YOUR DEATH WARRANT! IN TRIPLICATE! NOTARIZED!
AH, COME NOW MON AMI, I'D THROW LASSIE A PARACHUTE, BUT MY MEN SEEM TO HAVE THEM ALL!
AH, ALL RIGHT- NEVER LET IT BE SAID VAN COOVER NEVER GAVE HIS RIVALS LA CHANCE SPORTIF!
BAM!
THERE GOES YOUR ONLY CHANCE OF YOU AND YOUR SMELLY DOG SURVIVING THIS FLIGHT, MON AMI.
NOOOO-HO-HO-HOOOOO! WEEP!
WHAT? TOO MUCH?

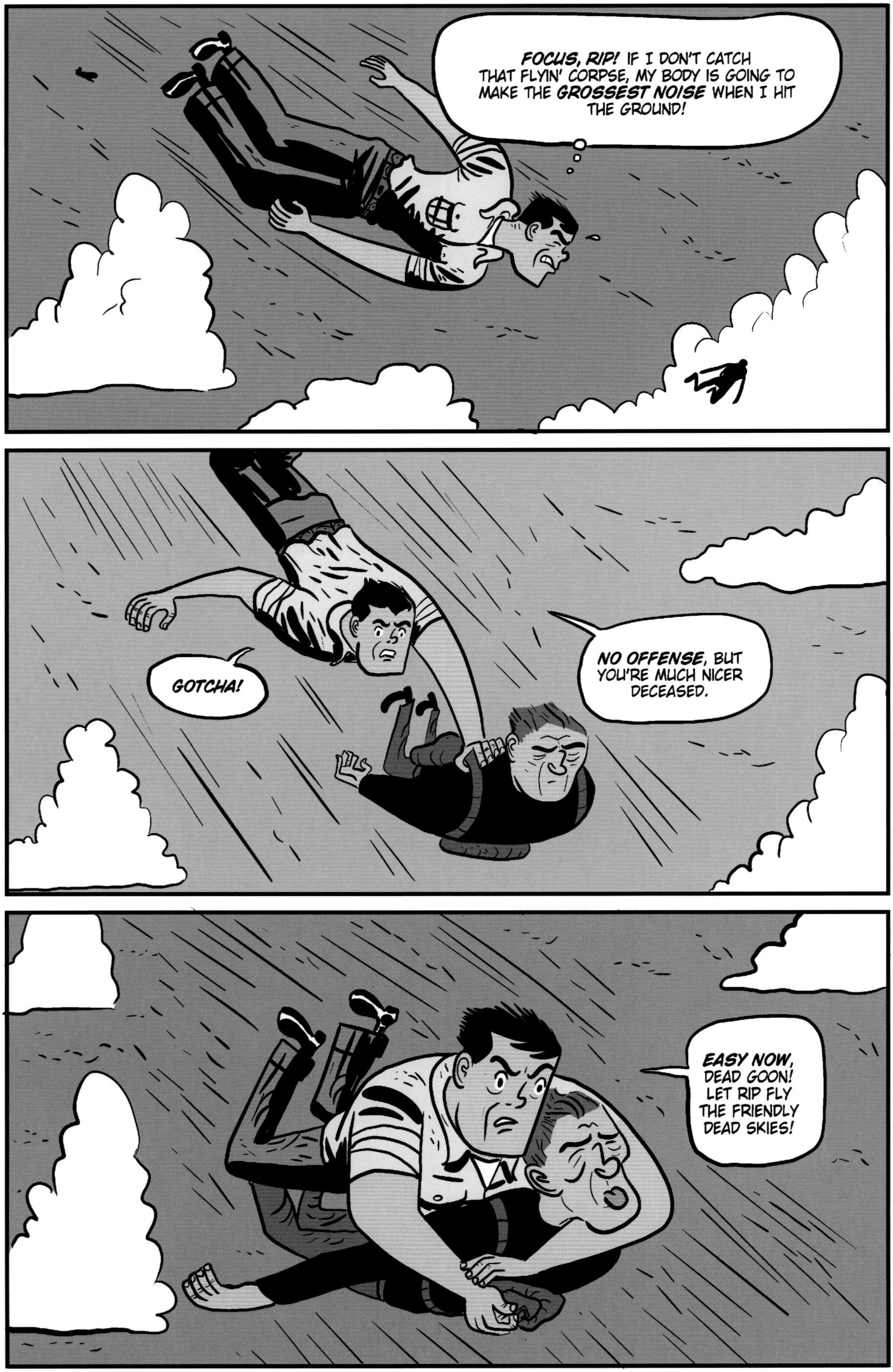
FOCUS, RIP! IF I DON'T CATCH THAT FLYIN' CORPSE, MY BODY IS GOING TO MAKE THE GROSSEST NOISE WHEN I HIT THE GROUND!
GOTCHA!
NO OFFENSE, BUT YOU'RE MUCH NICER DECEASED.
EASY NOW, DEAD GOON! LET RIP FLY THE FRIENDLY DEAD SKIES!

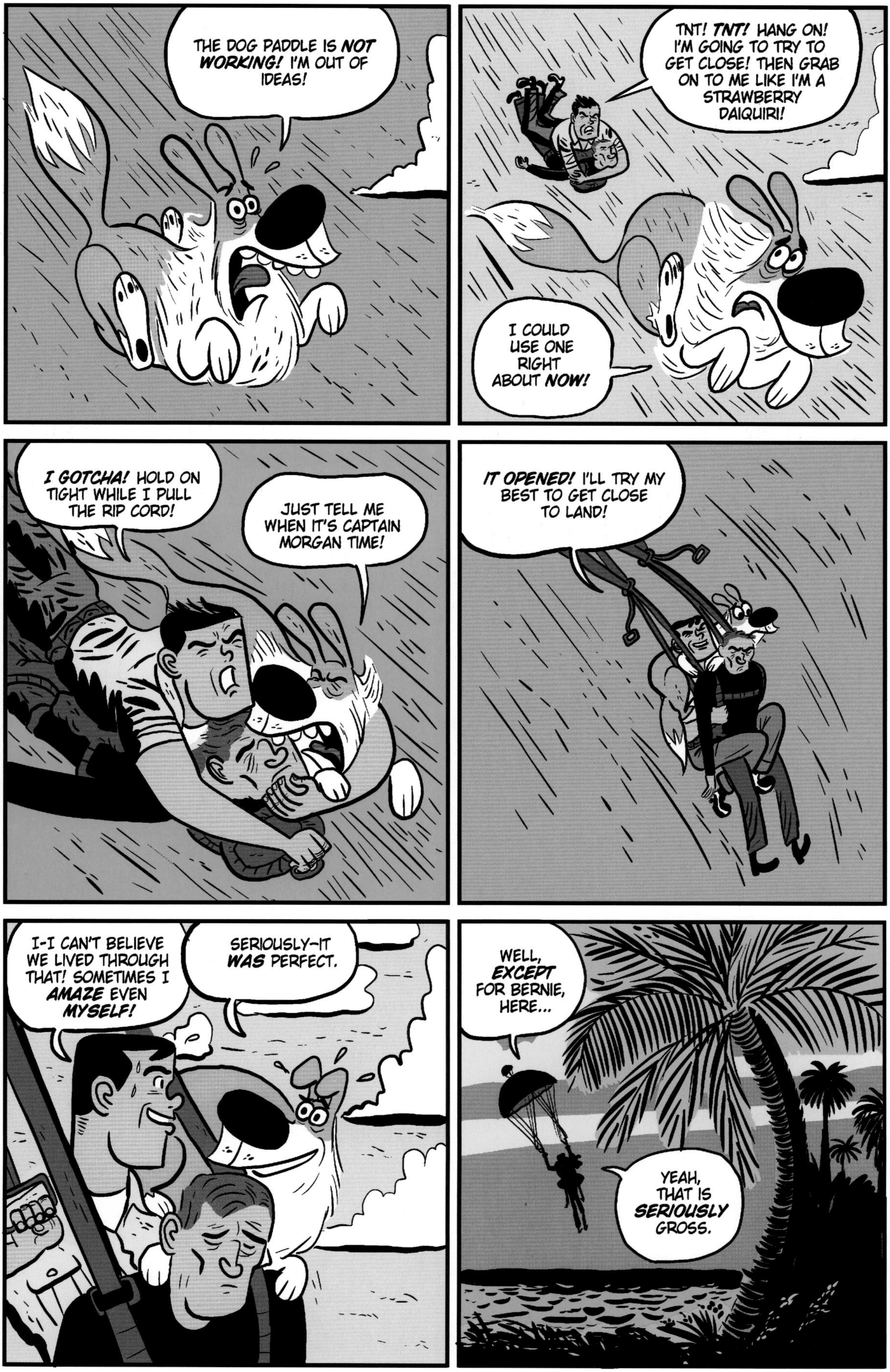
THE DOG PADDLE IS *NOT WORKING!* I'M OUT OF IDEAS!
TNT! *TNT!* HANG ON! I'M GOING TO TRY TO GET CLOSE! THEN GRAB ON TO ME LIKE I'M A STRAWBERRY DAIQUIRI!
I COULD USE ONE RIGHT ABOUT *NOW!*
I GOTCHA! HOLD ON TIGHT WHILE I PULL THE RIP CORD!
JUST TELL ME WHEN IT'S CAPTAIN MORGAN TIME!
IT OPENED! I'LL TRY MY BEST TO GET CLOSE TO LAND!
I-I CAN'T BELIEVE WE LIVED THROUGH THAT! SOMETIMES I *AMAZE* EVEN *MYSELF!*
SERIOUSLY–IT *WAS* PERFECT.
WELL, *EXCEPT* FOR BERNIE, HERE...
YEAH, THAT IS *SERIOUSLY* GROSS.

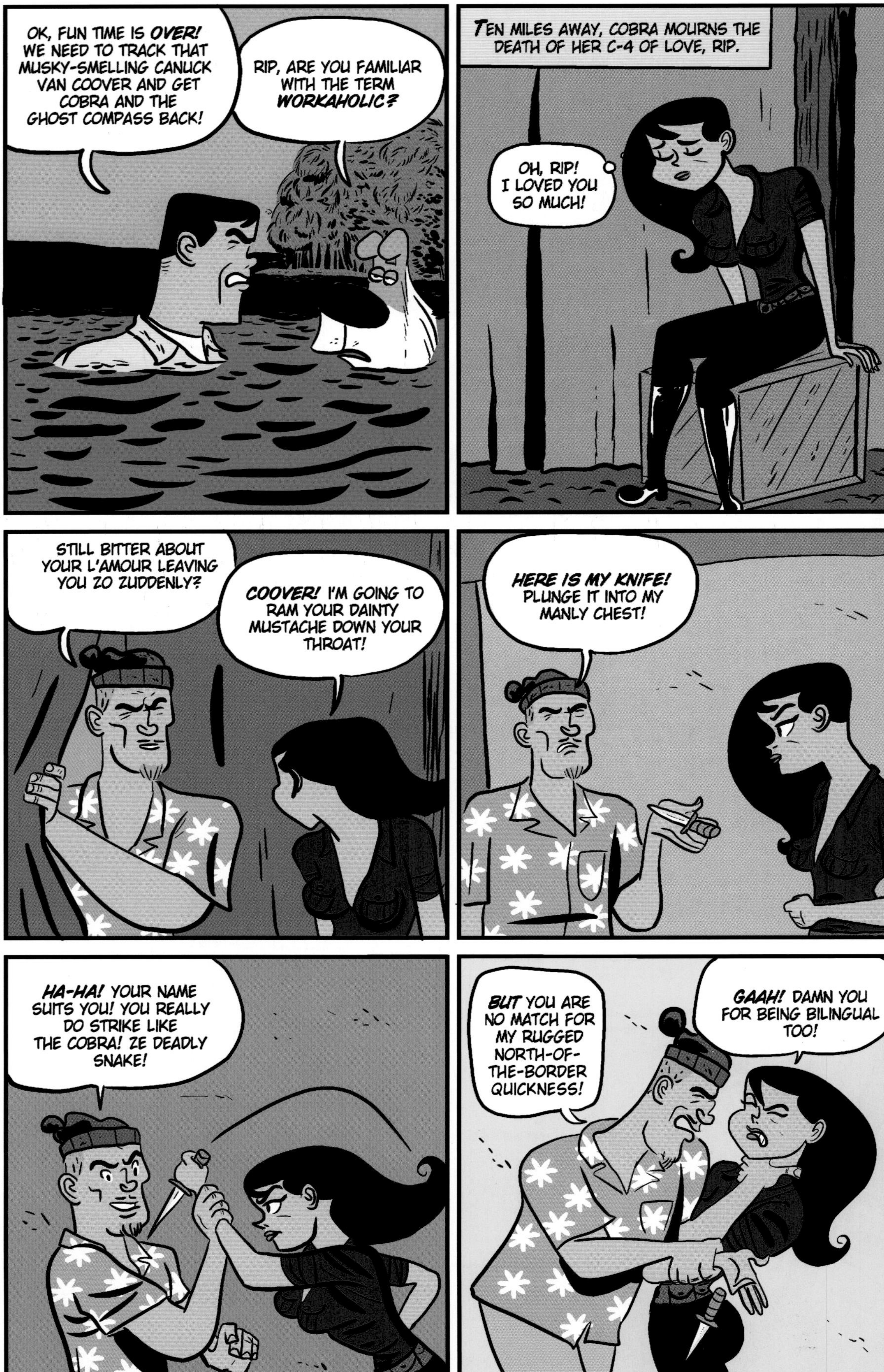

OK, FUN TIME IS OVER! WE NEED TO TRACK THAT MUSKY-SMELLING CANUCK VAN COOVER AND GET COBRA AND THE GHOST COMPASS BACK!
RIP, ARE YOU FAMILIAR WITH THE TERM WORKAHOLIC?
TEN MILES AWAY, COBRA MOURNS THE DEATH OF HER C-4 OF LOVE, RIP.
OH, RIP! I LOVED YOU SO MUCH!
STILL BITTER ABOUT YOUR L'AMOUR LEAVING YOU ZO ZUDDENLY?
COOVER! I'M GOING TO RAM YOUR DAINTY MUSTACHE DOWN YOUR THROAT!
HERE IS MY KNIFE! PLUNGE IT INTO MY MANLY CHEST!
HA-HA! YOUR NAME SUITS YOU! YOU REALLY DO STRIKE LIKE THE COBRA! ZE DEADLY SNAKE!
BUT YOU ARE NO MATCH FOR MY RUGGED NORTH-OF-THE-BORDER QUICKNESS!
GAAH! DAMN YOU FOR BEING BILINGUAL TOO!

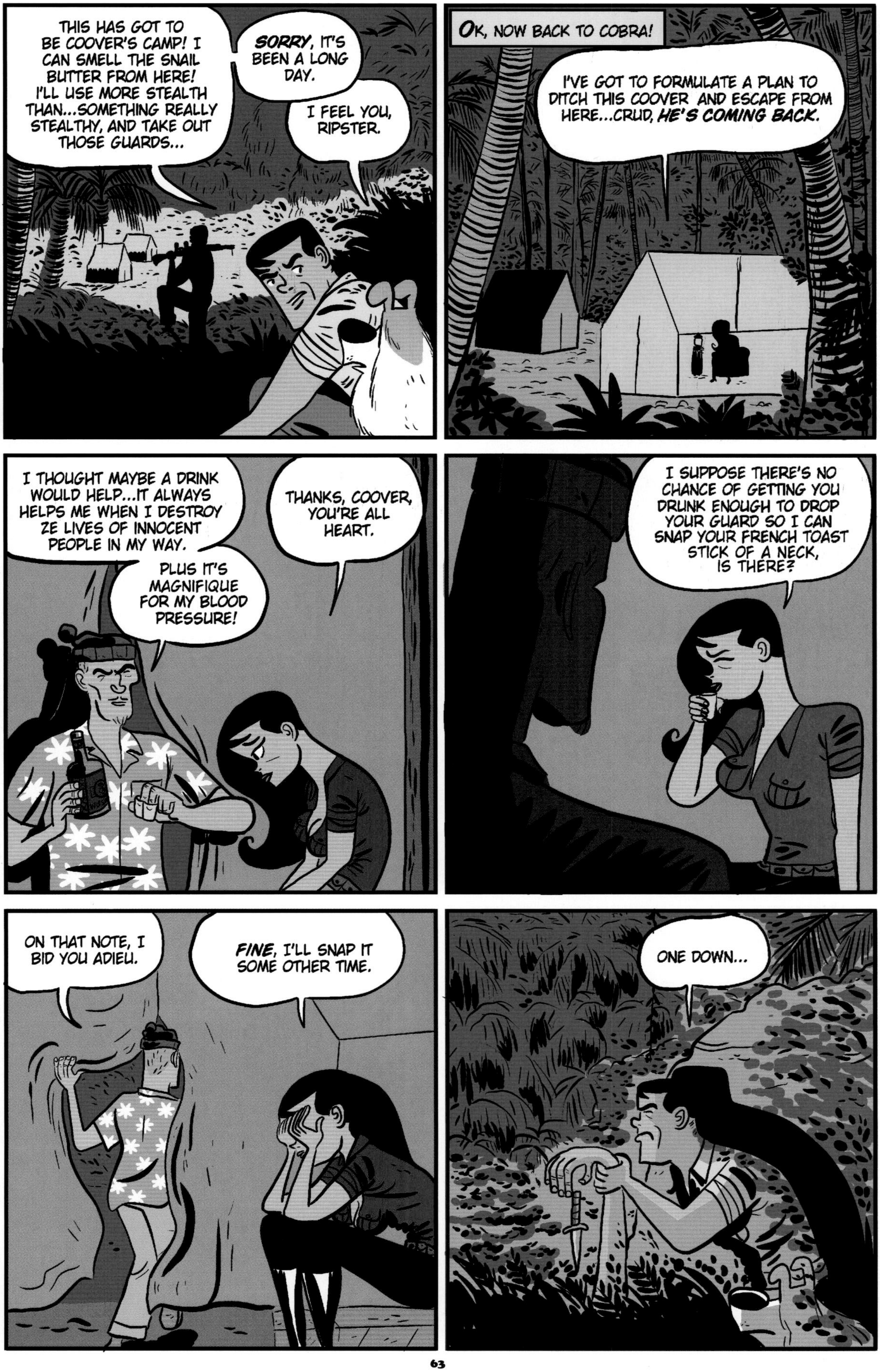
THIS HAS GOT TO BE COOVER'S CAMP! I CAN SMELL THE SNAIL BUTTER FROM HERE! I'LL USE MORE STEALTH THAN...SOMETHING REALLY STEALTHY, AND TAKE OUT THOSE GUARDS...
SORRY, IT'S BEEN A LONG DAY.
I FEEL YOU, RIPSTER.
OK, NOW BACK TO COBRA!
I'VE GOT TO FORMULATE A PLAN TO DITCH THIS COOVER AND ESCAPE FROM HERE...CRUD, HE'S COMING BACK.
I THOUGHT MAYBE A DRINK WOULD HELP...IT ALWAYS HELPS ME WHEN I DESTROY ZE LIVES OF INNOCENT PEOPLE IN MY WAY.
PLUS IT'S MAGNIFIQUE FOR MY BLOOD PRESSURE!
THANKS, COOVER, YOU'RE ALL HEART.
I SUPPOSE THERE'S NO CHANCE OF GETTING YOU DRUNK ENOUGH TO DROP YOUR GUARD SO I CAN SNAP YOUR FRENCH TOAST STICK OF A NECK, IS THERE?
ON THAT NOTE, I BID YOU ADIEU.
FINE, I'LL SNAP IT SOME OTHER TIME.
ONE DOWN...

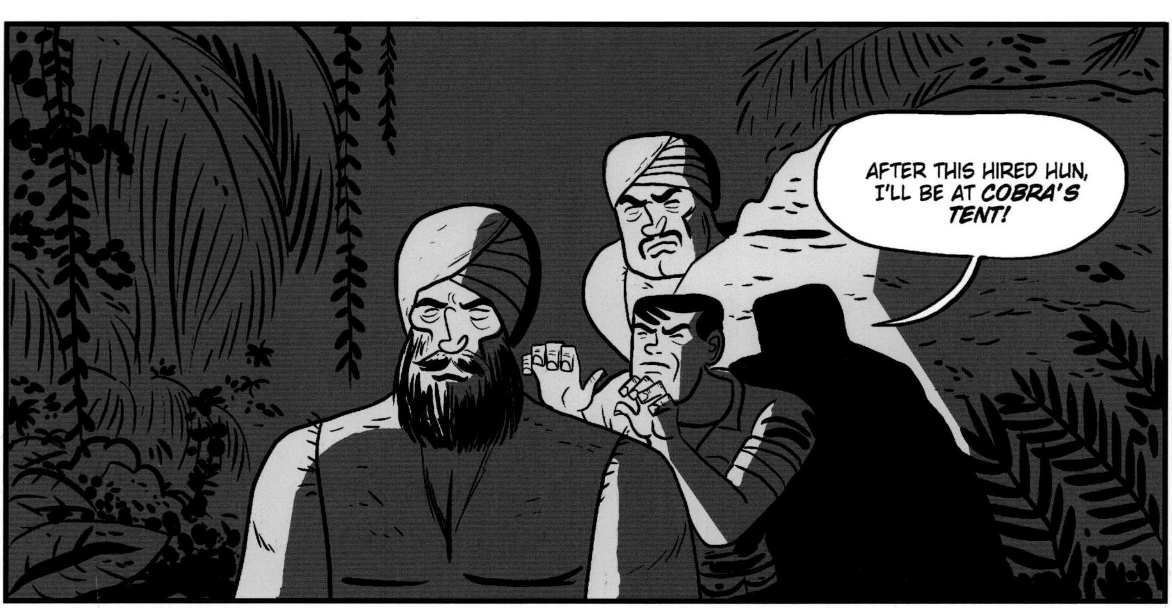
AFTER THIS HIRED HUN, I'LL BE AT COBRA'S TENT!

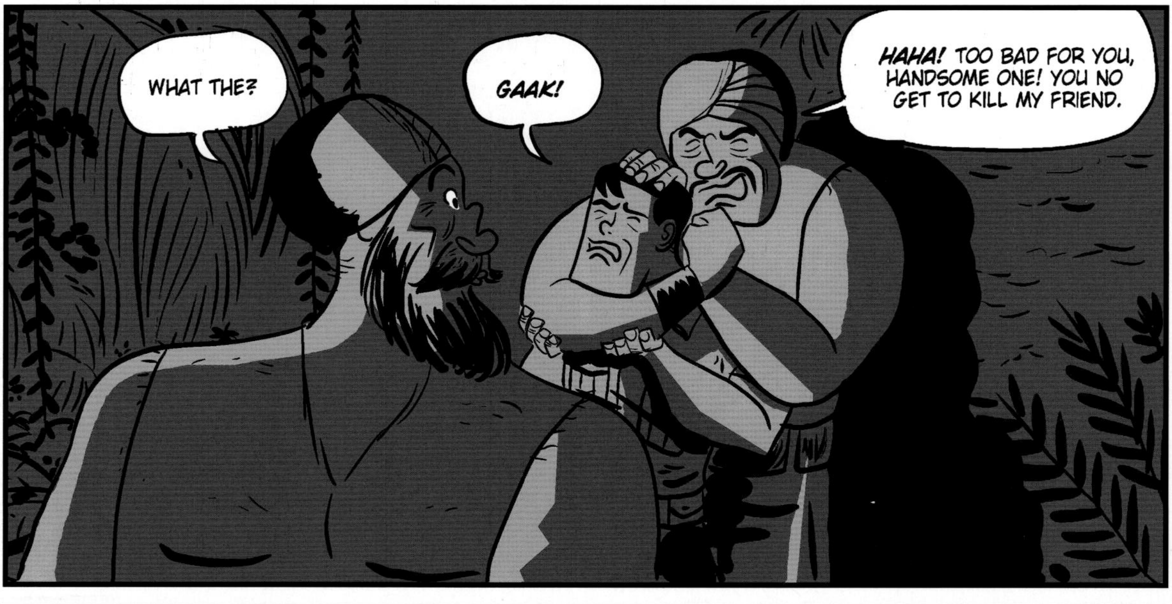
WHAT THE?
GAAK!
HAHA! TOO BAD FOR YOU, HANDSOME ONE! YOU NO GET TO KILL MY FRIEND.

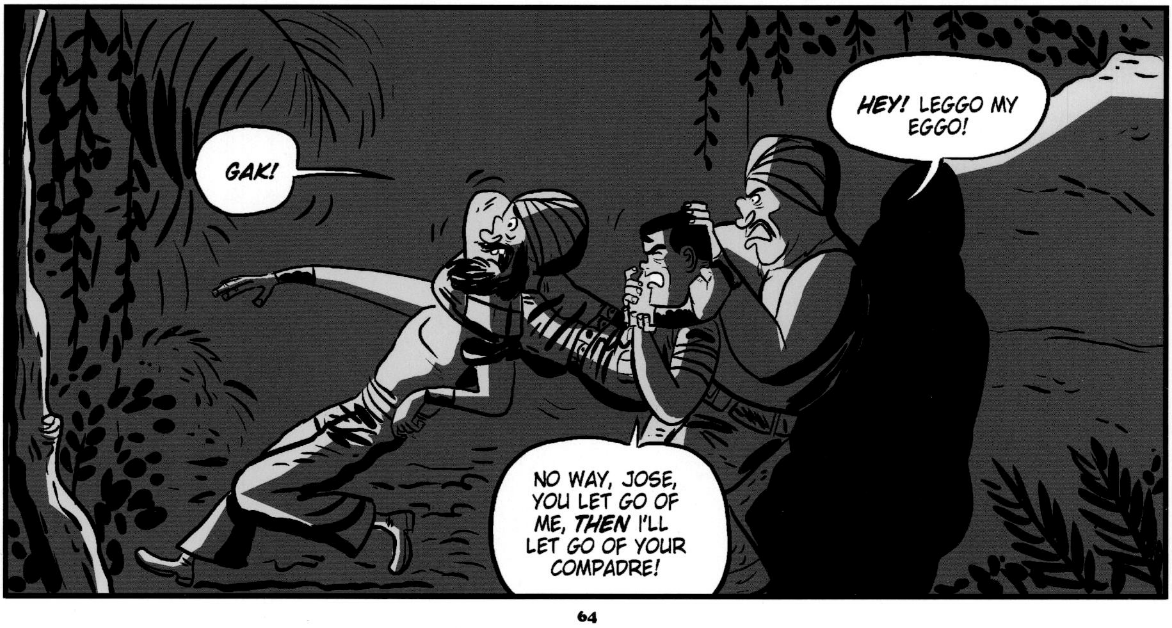
GAK!
HEY! LEGGO MY EGGO!
NO WAY, JOSE, YOU LET GO OF ME, THEN I'LL LET GO OF YOUR COMPADRE!

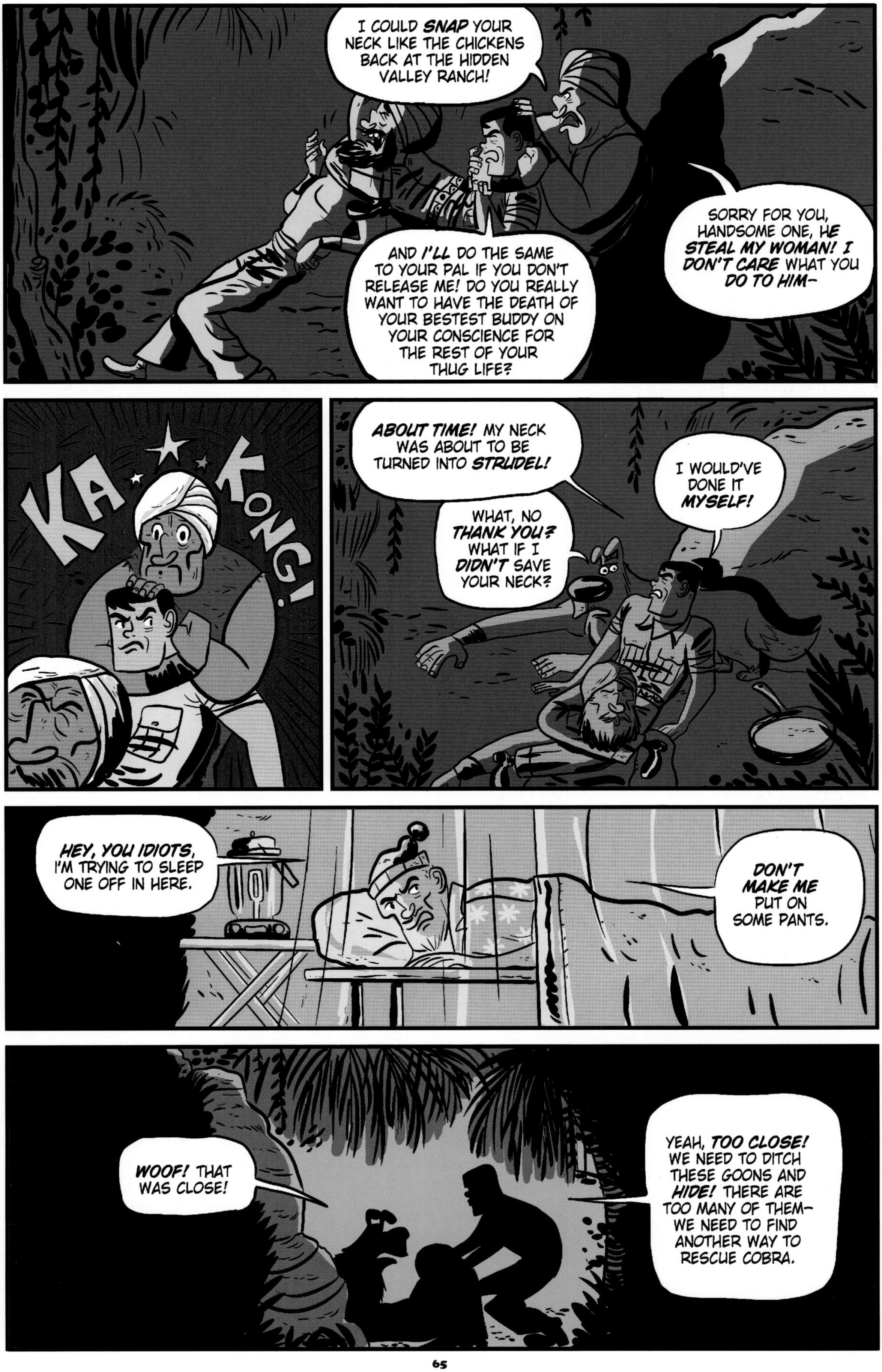
I COULD **SNAP** YOUR NECK LIKE THE CHICKENS BACK AT THE HIDDEN VALLEY RANCH!
AND **I'LL** DO THE SAME TO YOUR PAL IF YOU DON'T RELEASE ME! DO YOU REALLY WANT TO HAVE THE DEATH OF YOUR BESTEST BUDDY ON YOUR CONSCIENCE FOR THE REST OF YOUR THUG LIFE?
SORRY FOR YOU, HANDSOME ONE, **HE STEAL MY WOMAN! I DON'T CARE** WHAT YOU **DO TO HIM**–
KA-KONG!
ABOUT TIME! MY NECK WAS ABOUT TO BE TURNED INTO **STRUDEL!**
WHAT, NO **THANK YOU?** WHAT IF I **DIDN'T** SAVE YOUR NECK?
I WOULD'VE DONE IT **MYSELF!**
HEY, YOU IDIOTS, I'M TRYING TO SLEEP ONE OFF IN HERE.
DON'T MAKE ME PUT ON SOME PANTS.
WOOF! THAT WAS CLOSE!
YEAH, **TOO CLOSE!** WE NEED TO DITCH THESE GOONS AND **HIDE!** THERE ARE TOO MANY OF THEM– WE NEED TO FIND ANOTHER WAY TO RESCUE COBRA.

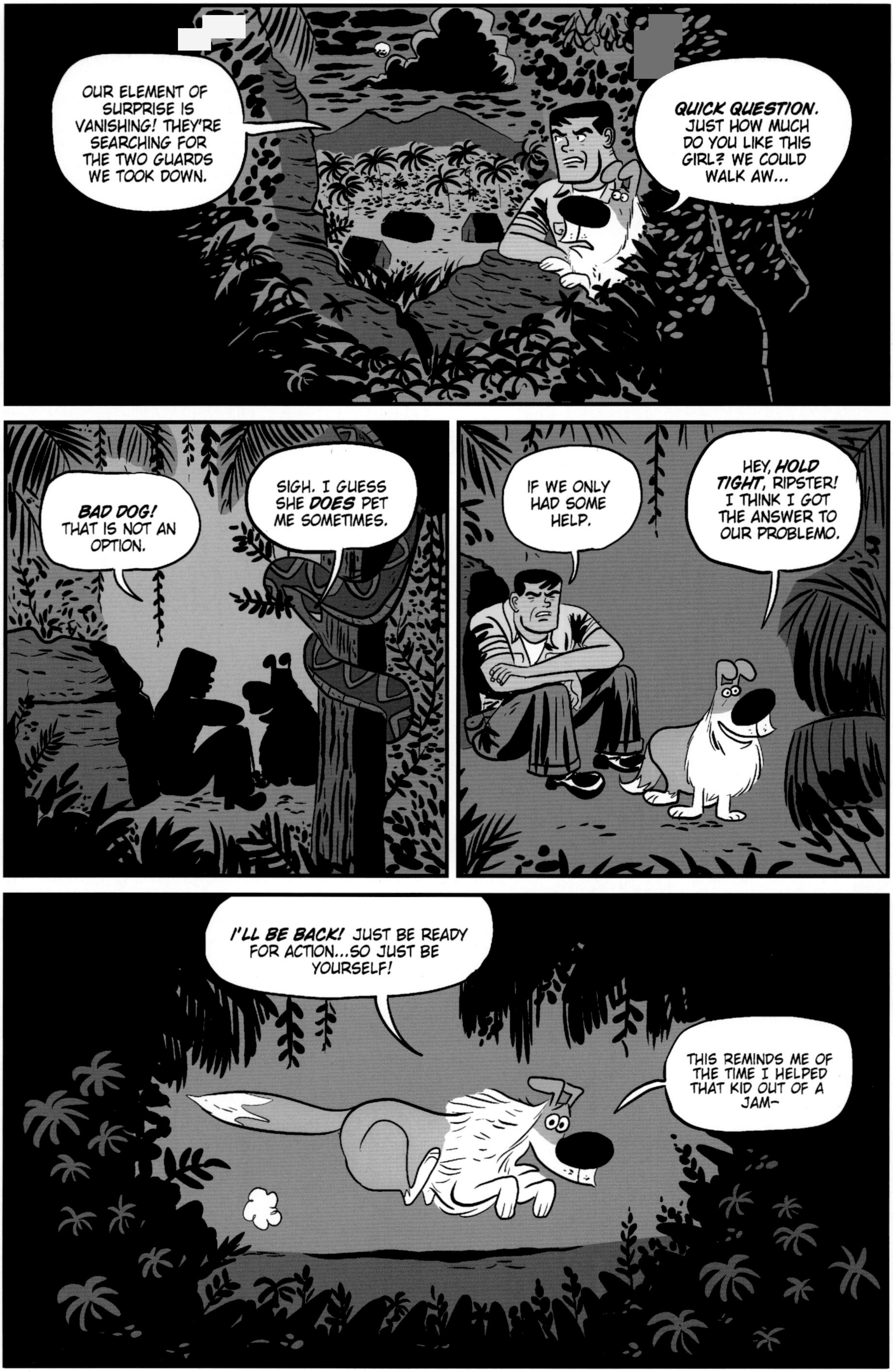
OUR ELEMENT OF SURPRISE IS VANISHING! THEY'RE SEARCHING FOR THE TWO GUARDS WE TOOK DOWN.
QUICK QUESTION. JUST HOW MUCH DO YOU LIKE THIS GIRL? WE COULD WALK AW...
BAD DOG! THAT IS NOT AN OPTION.
SIGH. I GUESS SHE DOES PET ME SOMETIMES.
IF WE ONLY HAD SOME HELP.
HEY, HOLD TIGHT, RIPSTER! I THINK I GOT THE ANSWER TO OUR PROBLEMO.
I'LL BE BACK! JUST BE READY FOR ACTION...SO JUST BE YOURSELF!
THIS REMINDS ME OF THE TIME I HELPED THAT KID OUT OF A JAM–

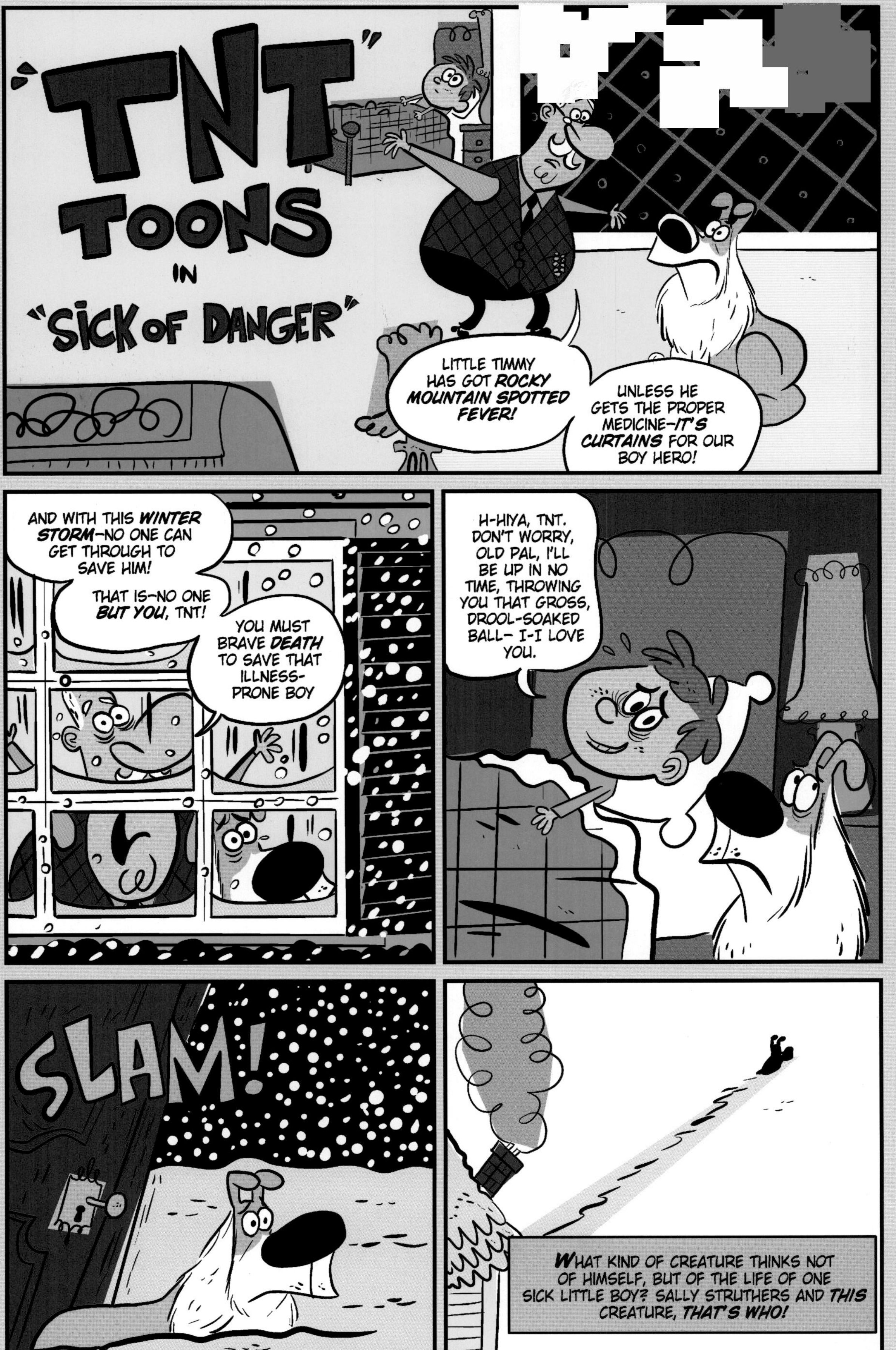
"TNT" TOONS
IN
"SICK OF DANGER"
LITTLE TIMMY HAS GOT ROCKY MOUNTAIN SPOTTED FEVER!
UNLESS HE GETS THE PROPER MEDICINE–IT'S CURTAINS FOR OUR BOY HERO!
AND WITH THIS WINTER STORM–NO ONE CAN GET THROUGH TO SAVE HIM!
THAT IS–NO ONE BUT YOU, TNT!
YOU MUST BRAVE DEATH TO SAVE THAT ILLNESS-PRONE BOY
H-HIYA, TNT. DON'T WORRY, OLD PAL, I'LL BE UP IN NO TIME, THROWING YOU THAT GROSS, DROOL-SOAKED BALL– I-I LOVE YOU.
SLAM!
WHAT KIND OF CREATURE THINKS NOT OF HIMSELF, BUT OF THE LIFE OF ONE SICK LITTLE BOY? SALLY STRUTHERS AND THIS CREATURE, THAT'S WHO!

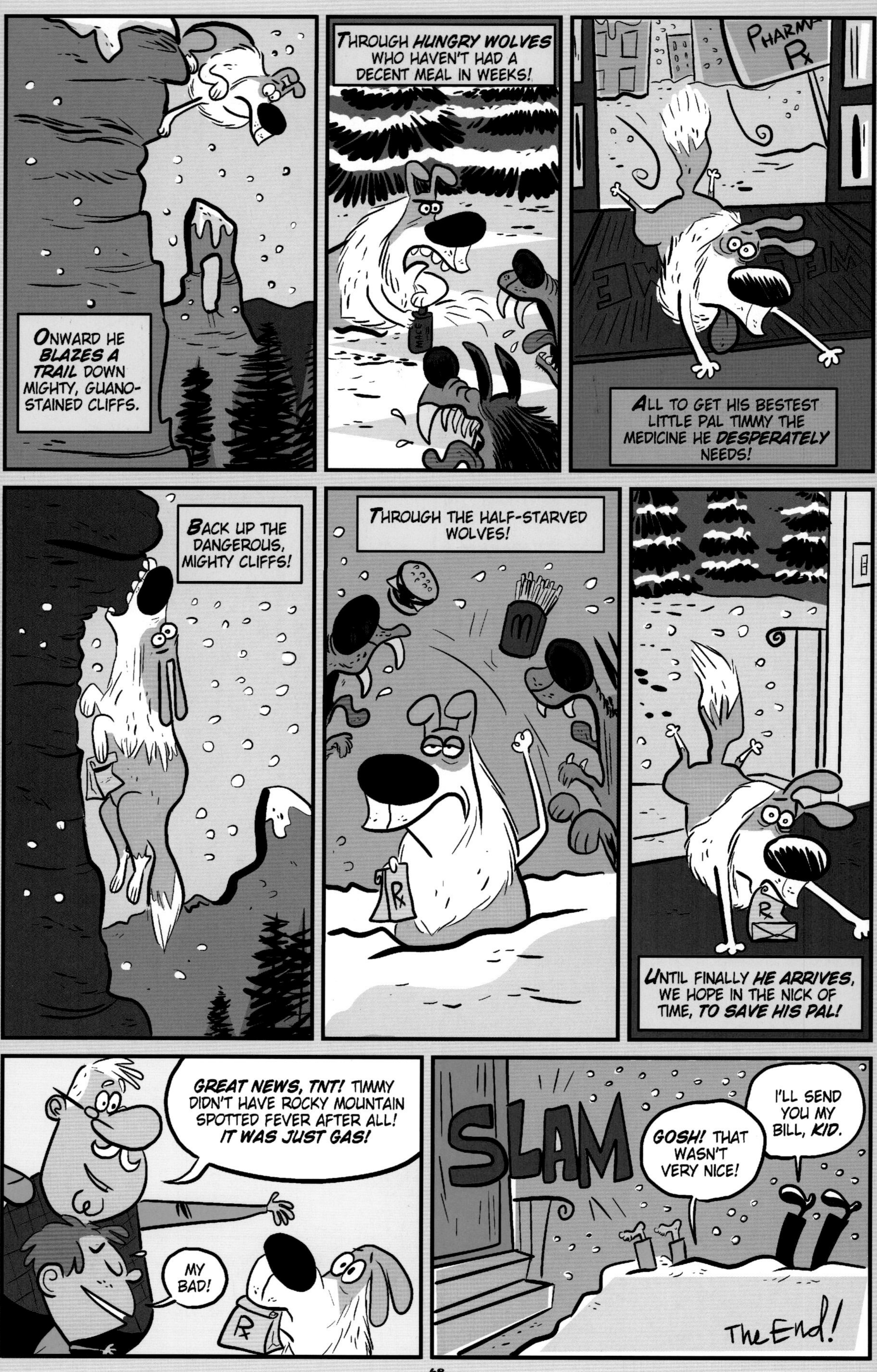
ONWARD HE BLAZES A TRAIL DOWN MIGHTY, GUANO-STAINED CLIFFS.
THROUGH HUNGRY WOLVES WHO HAVEN'T HAD A DECENT MEAL IN WEEKS!
ALL TO GET HIS BESTEST LITTLE PAL TIMMY THE MEDICINE HE DESPERATELY NEEDS!
BACK UP THE DANGEROUS, MIGHTY CLIFFS!
THROUGH THE HALF-STARVED WOLVES!
Rx
UNTIL FINALLY HE ARRIVES, WE HOPE IN THE NICK OF TIME, TO SAVE HIS PAL!
GREAT NEWS, TNT! TIMMY DIDN'T HAVE ROCKY MOUNTAIN SPOTTED FEVER AFTER ALL! IT WAS JUST GAS!
MY BAD!
Rx
SLAM
GOSH! THAT WASN'T VERY NICE!
I'LL SEND YOU MY BILL, KID.
The End!

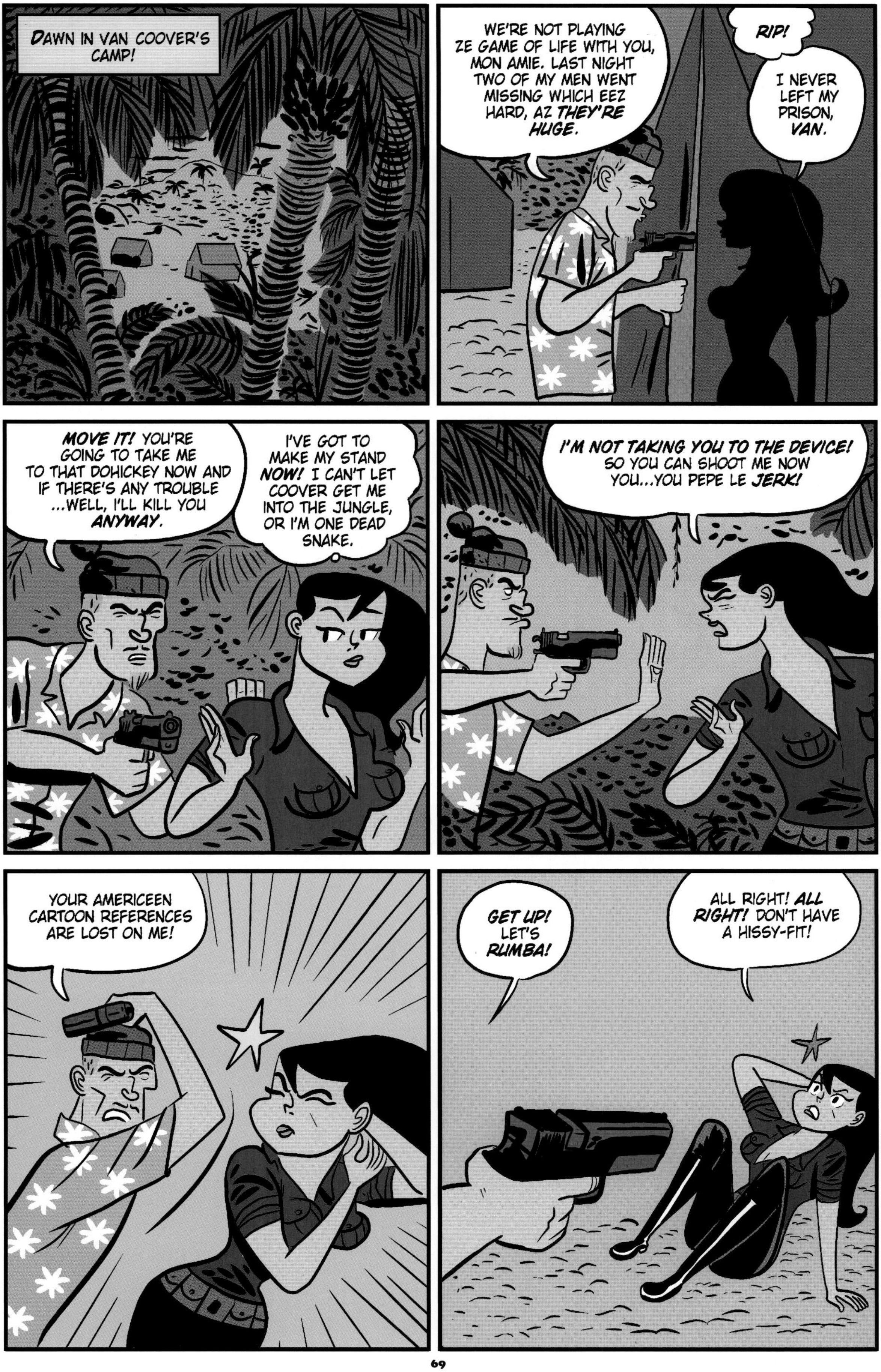
DAWN IN VAN COOVER'S CAMP!
WE'RE NOT PLAYING ZE GAME OF LIFE WITH YOU, MON AMIE. LAST NIGHT TWO OF MY MEN WENT MISSING WHICH EEZ HARD, AZ THEY'RE HUGE.
RIP!
I NEVER LEFT MY PRISON, VAN.
MOVE IT! YOU'RE GOING TO TAKE ME TO THAT DOHICKEY NOW AND IF THERE'S ANY TROUBLE ...WELL, I'LL KILL YOU ANYWAY.
I'VE GOT TO MAKE MY STAND NOW! I CAN'T LET COOVER GET ME INTO THE JUNGLE, OR I'M ONE DEAD SNAKE.
I'M NOT TAKING YOU TO THE DEVICE! SO YOU CAN SHOOT ME NOW YOU...YOU PEPE LE JERK!
YOUR AMERICEEN CARTOON REFERENCES ARE LOST ON ME!
GET UP! LET'S RUMBA!
ALL RIGHT! ALL RIGHT! DON'T HAVE A HISSY-FIT!

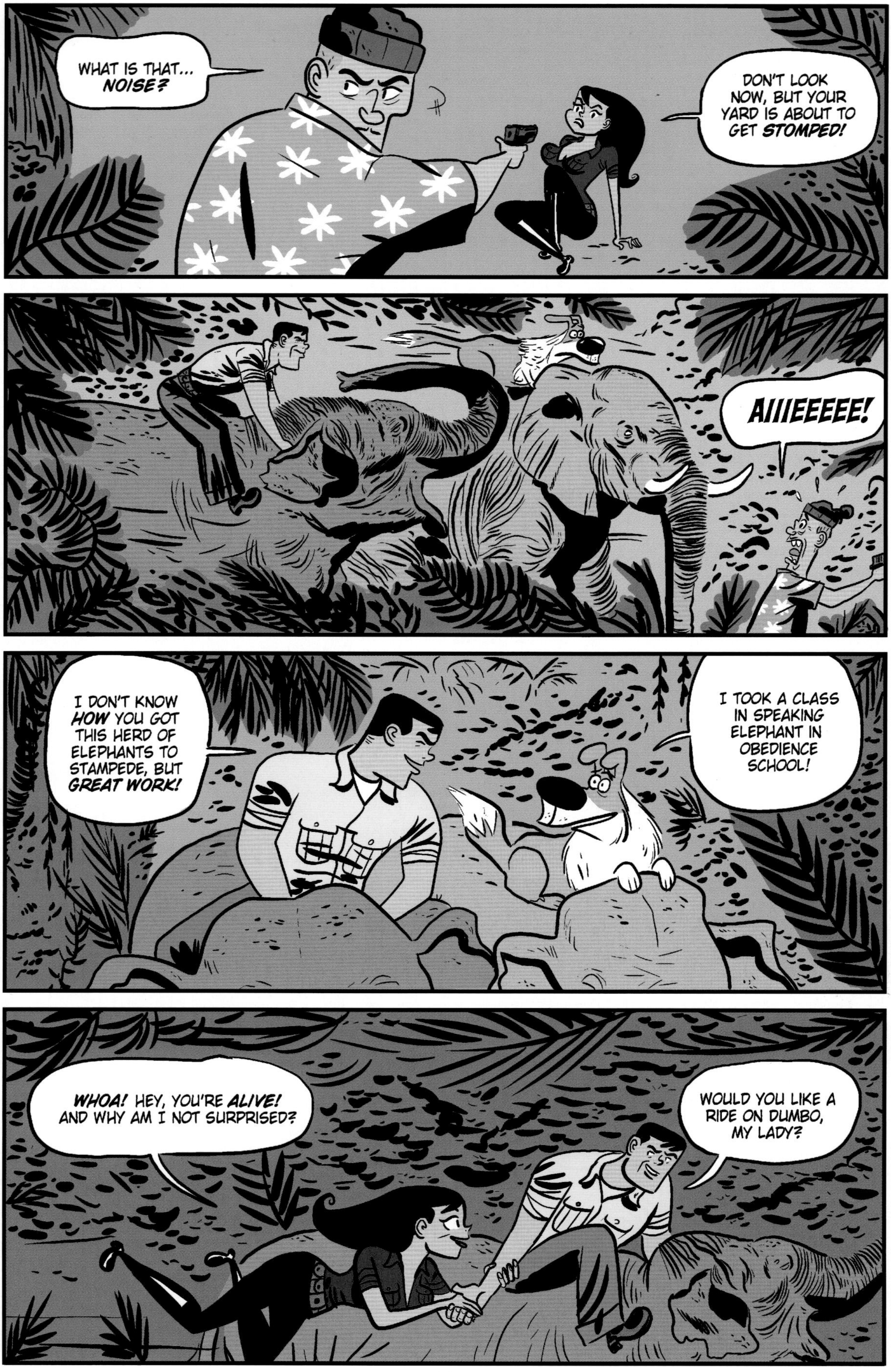

WHAT IS THAT... NOISE?
DON'T LOOK NOW, BUT YOUR YARD IS ABOUT TO GET STOMPED!
AIIIEEEEE!
I DON'T KNOW HOW YOU GOT THIS HERD OF ELEPHANTS TO STAMPEDE, BUT GREAT WORK!
I TOOK A CLASS IN SPEAKING ELEPHANT IN OBEDIENCE SCHOOL!
WHOA! HEY, YOU'RE ALIVE! AND WHY AM I NOT SURPRISED?
WOULD YOU LIKE A RIDE ON DUMBO, MY LADY?

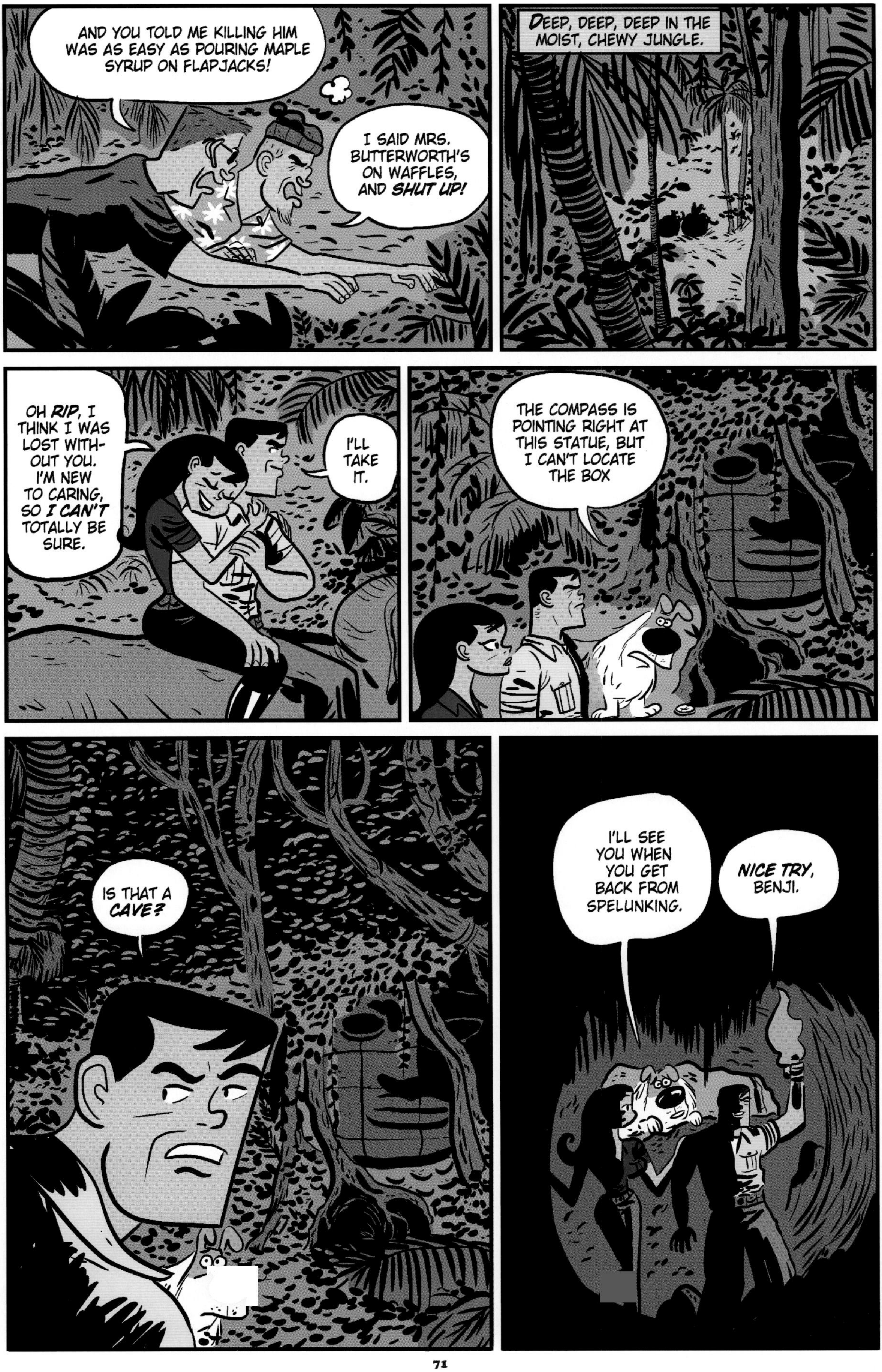
AND YOU TOLD ME KILLING HIM WAS AS EASY AS POURING MAPLE SYRUP ON FLAPJACKS!
I SAID MRS. BUTTERWORTH'S ON WAFFLES, AND SHUT UP!
DEEP, DEEP, DEEP IN THE MOIST, CHEWY JUNGLE.
OH RIP, I THINK I WAS LOST WITHOUT YOU. I'M NEW TO CARING, SO I CAN'T TOTALLY BE SURE.
I'LL TAKE IT.
THE COMPASS IS POINTING RIGHT AT THIS STATUE, BUT I CAN'T LOCATE THE BOX
IS THAT A CAVE?
I'LL SEE YOU WHEN YOU GET BACK FROM SPELUNKING.
NICE TRY, BENJI.

WELCOME TO MY FINAL RESTING PLACE!

I AM *SAMUEL LONGBEARD*.

BUT YOU CAN CALL ME SAMUEL LONG— YOU CAN ADDRESS ME AS SIR.

A-AREN'T YOU SUPPOSED TO WAIT FOR ME TO UN-UNLEASH YOU?

I FELT LIKE STRETCHING MY LEGS—

BESIDES, MY TWO BROTHERS POPPED IN AND TOLD ME YOU WERE COMING!

I AM TO WARN YOU OF WHAT IS TO BECOME OF YOU IF YOU FAIL TO RETURN THE TIKI GOD, TANGAROA, TO HIS TEMPLE.

EVERYONE WHO YOU LOVE *WILL LEAVE YOU!*

CRAVING CHINESE FOOD BUT *ALWAYS* BEING OUT OF DELIVERY RANGE!

SERIOUSLY, YOU'LL END UP LIKE AN UNDEAD GHOST, LONGING, SUFFERING ETC.—IT STINKS FOR *EVERYONE* INVOLVED!

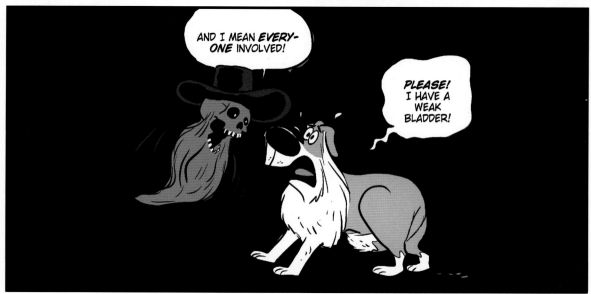

AND I MEAN *EVERY-ONE* INVOLVED!

PLEASE! I HAVE A WEAK BLADDER!

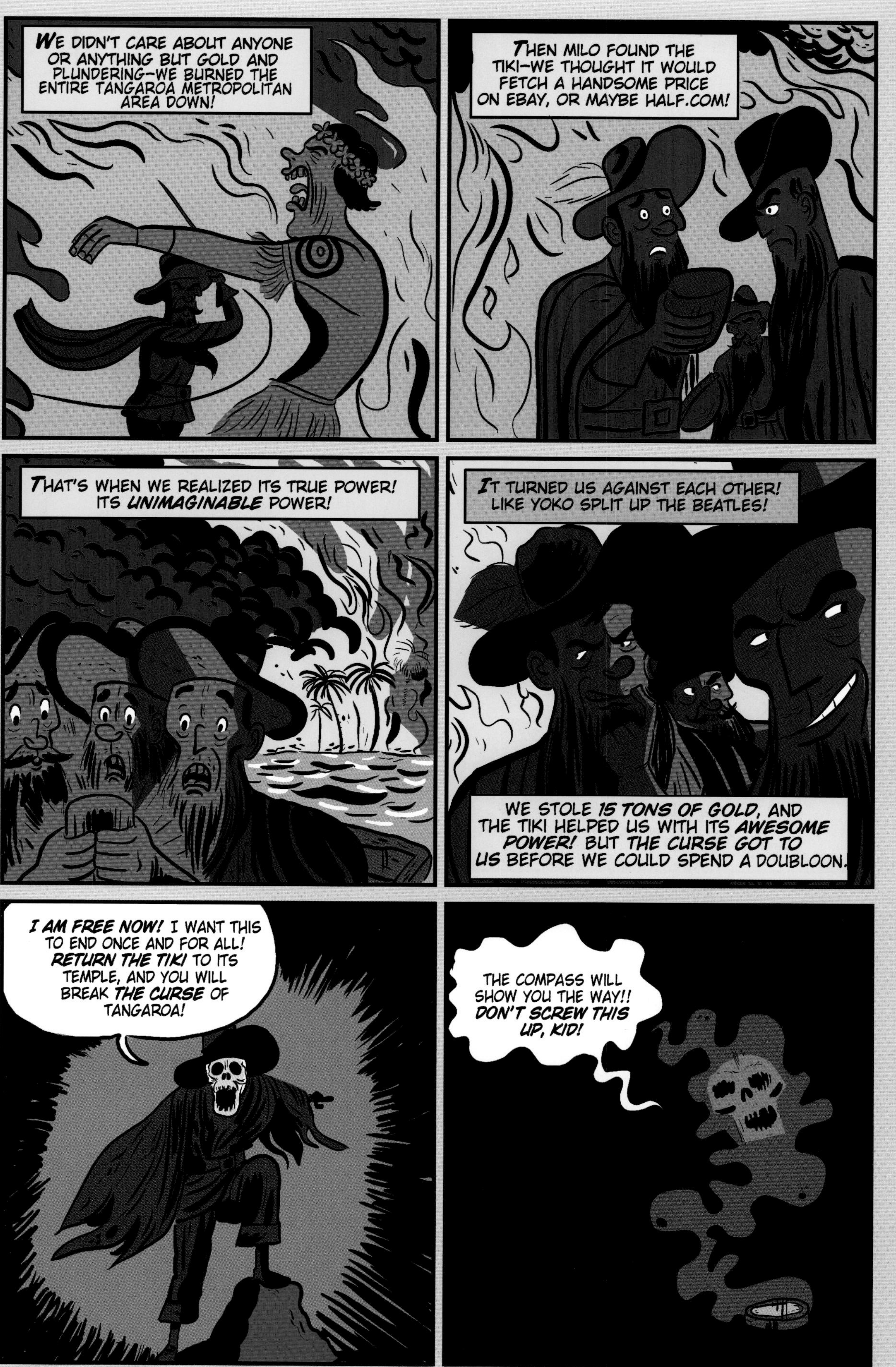
WE DIDN'T CARE ABOUT ANYONE OR ANYTHING BUT GOLD AND PLUNDERING—WE BURNED THE ENTIRE TANGAROA METROPOLITAN AREA DOWN!
THEN MILO FOUND THE TIKI—WE THOUGHT IT WOULD FETCH A HANDSOME PRICE ON EBAY, OR MAYBE HALF.COM!
THAT'S WHEN WE REALIZED ITS TRUE POWER! ITS UNIMAGINABLE POWER!
IT TURNED US AGAINST EACH OTHER! LIKE YOKO SPLIT UP THE BEATLES!
WE STOLE 15 TONS OF GOLD, AND THE TIKI HELPED US WITH ITS AWESOME POWER! BUT THE CURSE GOT TO US BEFORE WE COULD SPEND A DOUBLOON.
I AM FREE NOW! I WANT THIS TO END ONCE AND FOR ALL! RETURN THE TIKI TO ITS TEMPLE, AND YOU WILL BREAK THE CURSE OF TANGAROA!
THE COMPASS WILL SHOW YOU THE WAY!! DON'T SCREW THIS UP, KID!

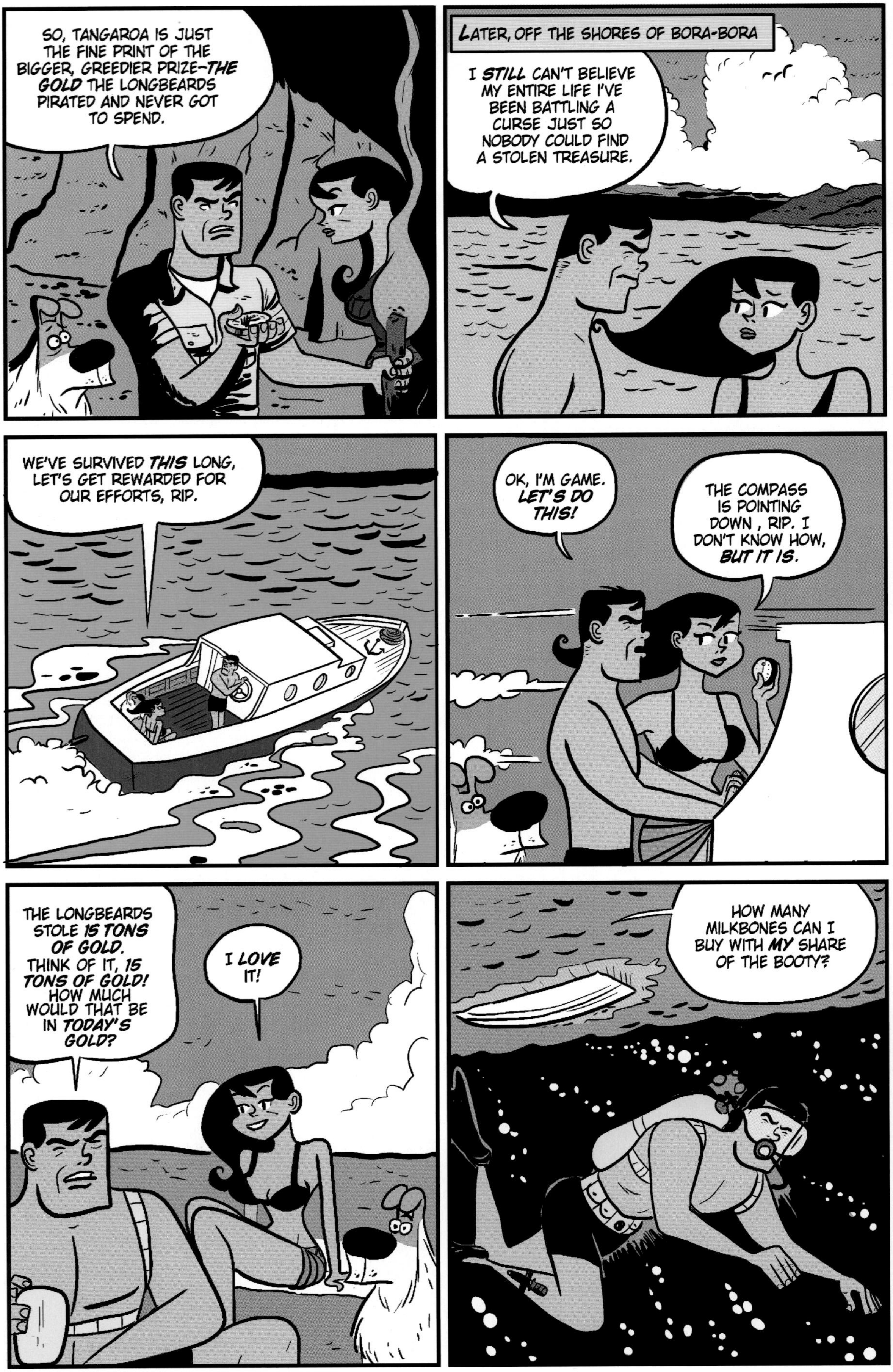
SO, TANGAROA IS JUST THE FINE PRINT OF THE BIGGER, GREEDIER PRIZE–THE GOLD THE LONGBEARDS PIRATED AND NEVER GOT TO SPEND.
LATER, OFF THE SHORES OF BORA-BORA
I STILL CAN'T BELIEVE MY ENTIRE LIFE I'VE BEEN BATTLING A CURSE JUST SO NOBODY COULD FIND A STOLEN TREASURE.
WE'VE SURVIVED THIS LONG, LET'S GET REWARDED FOR OUR EFFORTS, RIP.
OK, I'M GAME. LET'S DO THIS!
THE COMPASS IS POINTING DOWN , RIP. I DON'T KNOW HOW, BUT IT IS.
THE LONGBEARDS STOLE 15 TONS OF GOLD. THINK OF IT, 15 TONS OF GOLD! HOW MUCH WOULD THAT BE IN TODAY'S GOLD?
I LOVE IT!
HOW MANY MILKBONES CAN I BUY WITH MY SHARE OF THE BOOTY?

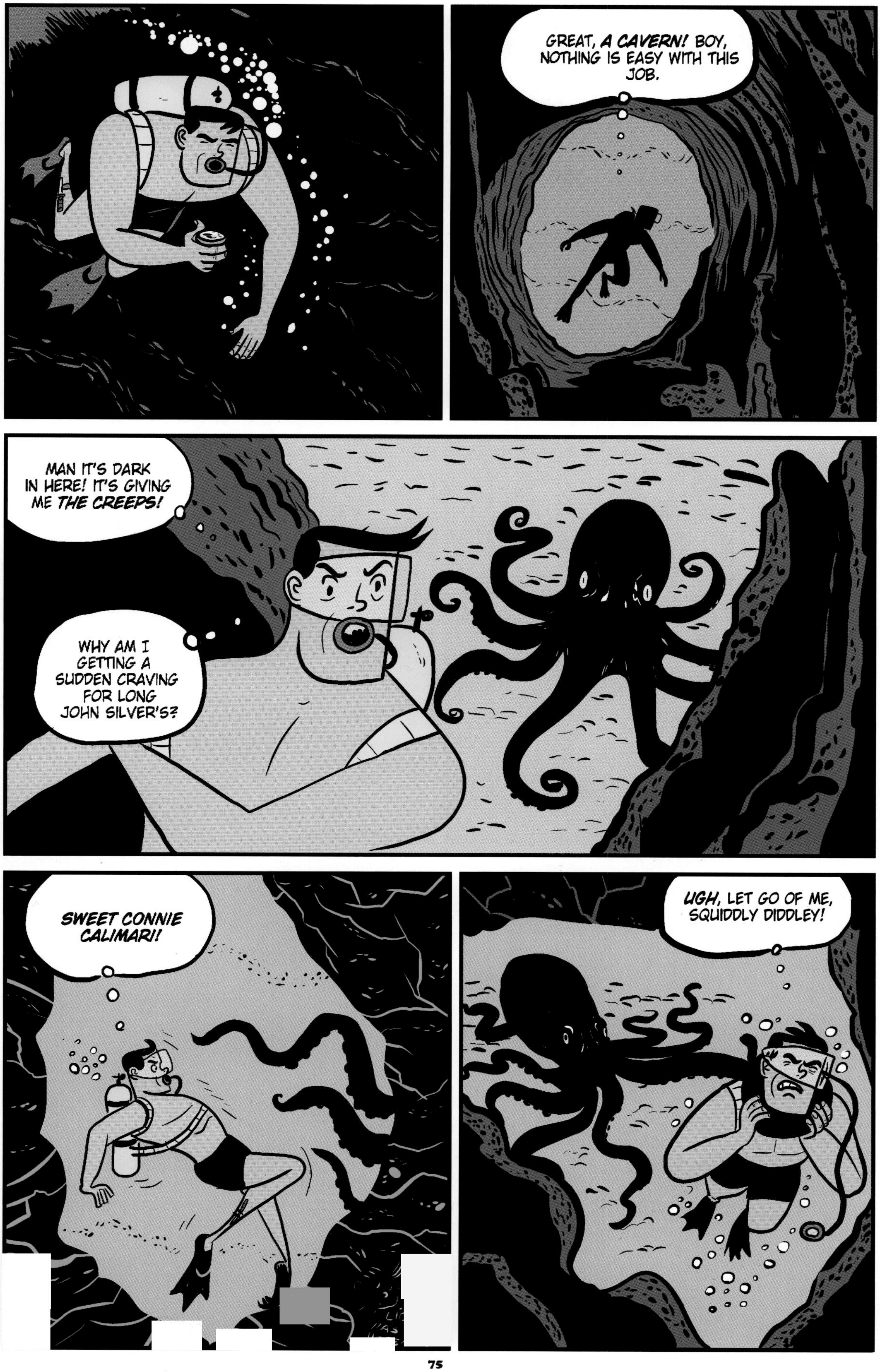
GREAT, A CAVERN! BOY, NOTHING IS EASY WITH THIS JOB.
MAN IT'S DARK IN HERE! IT'S GIVING ME THE CREEPS!
WHY AM I GETTING A SUDDEN CRAVING FOR LONG JOHN SILVER'S?
SWEET CONNIE CALIMARI!
UGH, LET GO OF ME, SQUIDDLY DIDDLEY!

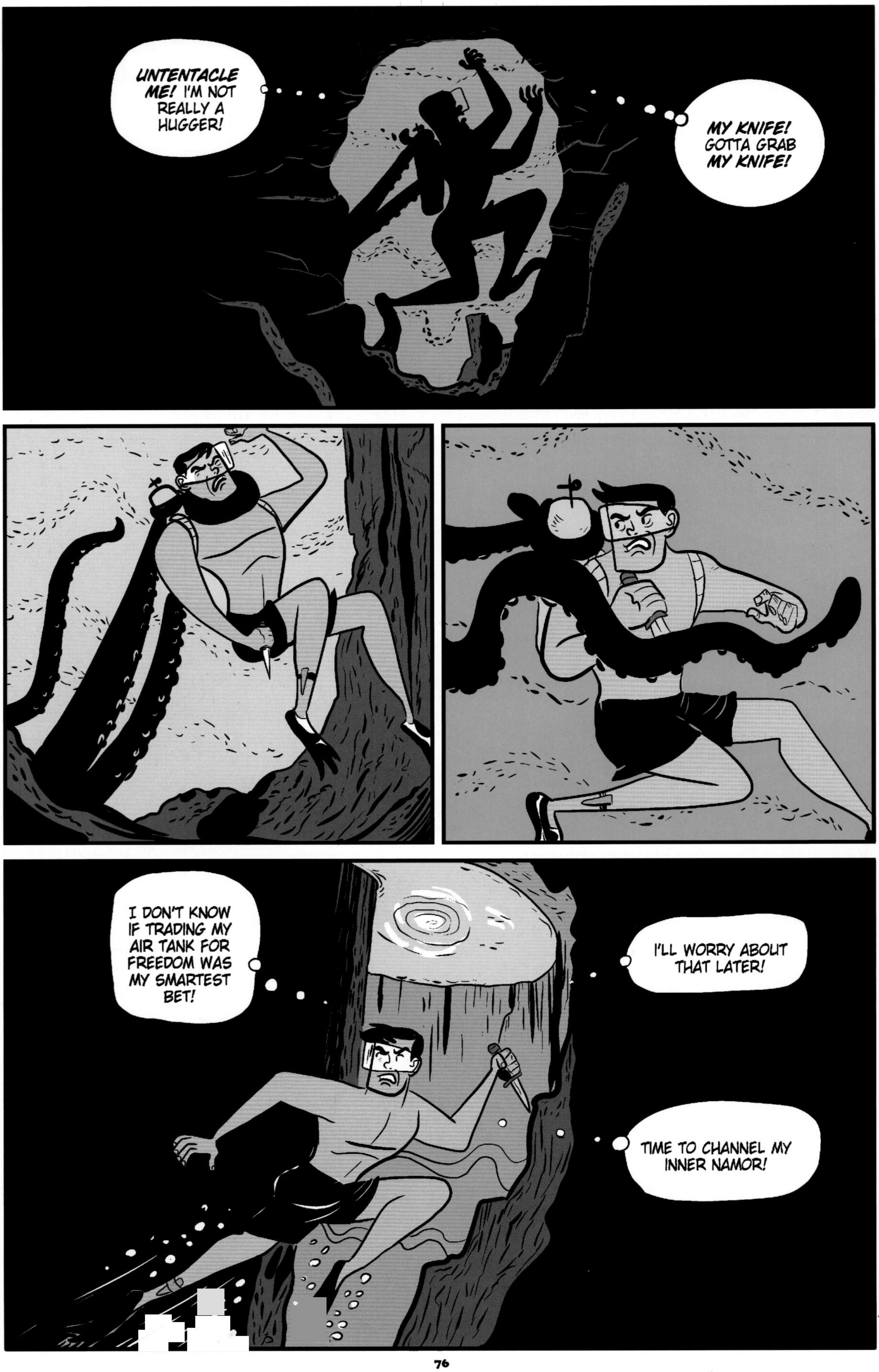
UNTENTACLE ME! I'M NOT REALLY A HUGGER!
MY KNIFE! GOTTA GRAB MY KNIFE!
I DON'T KNOW IF TRADING MY AIR TANK FOR FREEDOM WAS MY SMARTEST BET!
I'LL WORRY ABOUT THAT LATER!
TIME TO CHANNEL MY INNER NAMOR!

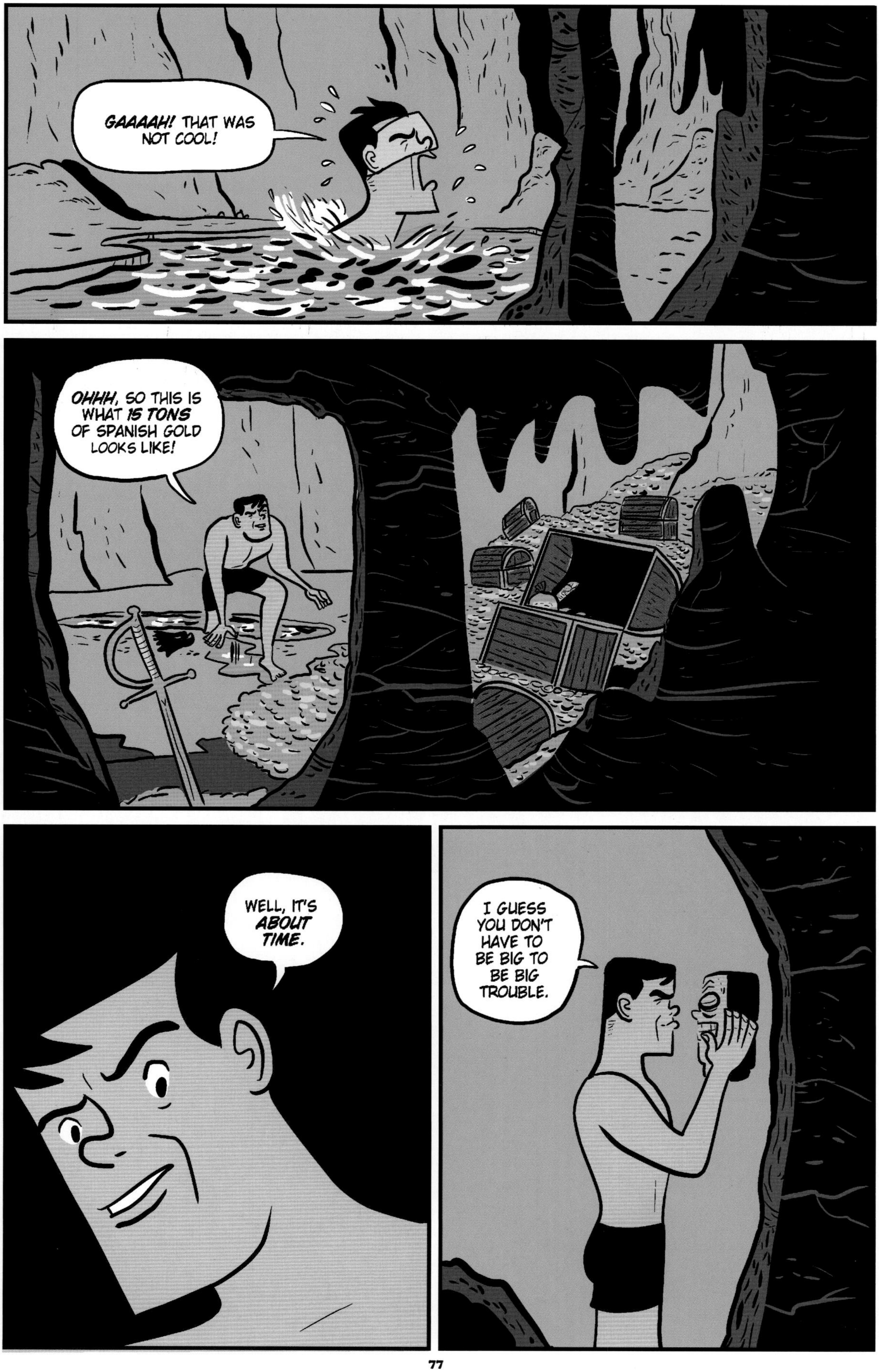
GAAAAH! THAT WAS NOT COOL!
OHHH, SO THIS IS WHAT 15 TONS OF SPANISH GOLD LOOKS LIKE!
WELL, IT'S ABOUT TIME.
I GUESS YOU DON'T HAVE TO BE BIG TO BE BIG TROUBLE.

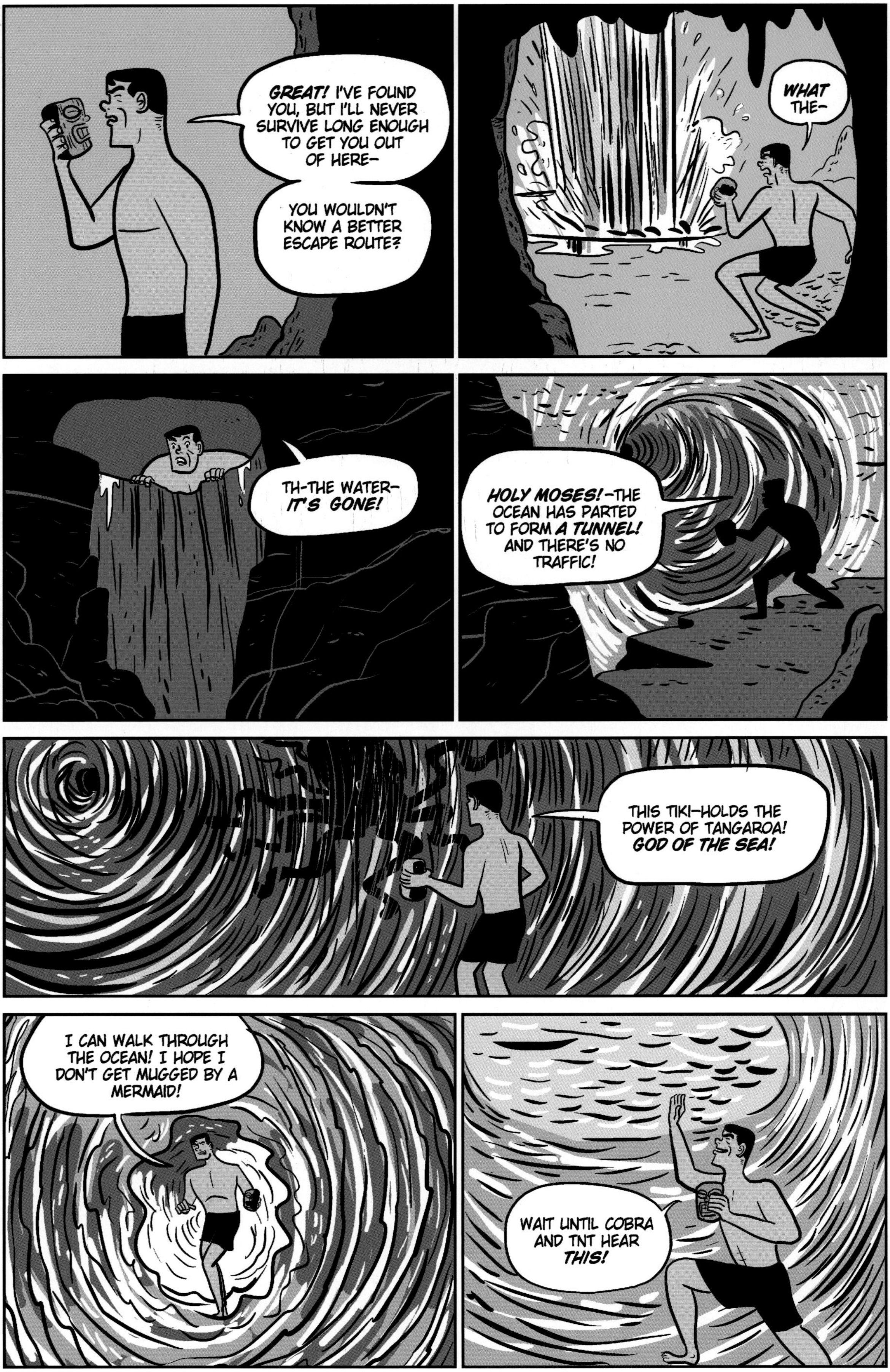
GREAT! I'VE FOUND YOU, BUT I'LL NEVER SURVIVE LONG ENOUGH TO GET YOU OUT OF HERE–
YOU WOULDN'T KNOW A BETTER ESCAPE ROUTE?
WHAT THE–
TH-THE WATER– IT'S GONE!
HOLY MOSES! –THE OCEAN HAS PARTED TO FORM A TUNNEL! AND THERE'S NO TRAFFIC!
THIS TIKI–HOLDS THE POWER OF TANGAROA! GOD OF THE SEA!
I CAN WALK THROUGH THE OCEAN! I HOPE I DON'T GET MUGGED BY A MERMAID!
WAIT UNTIL COBRA AND TNT HEAR THIS!

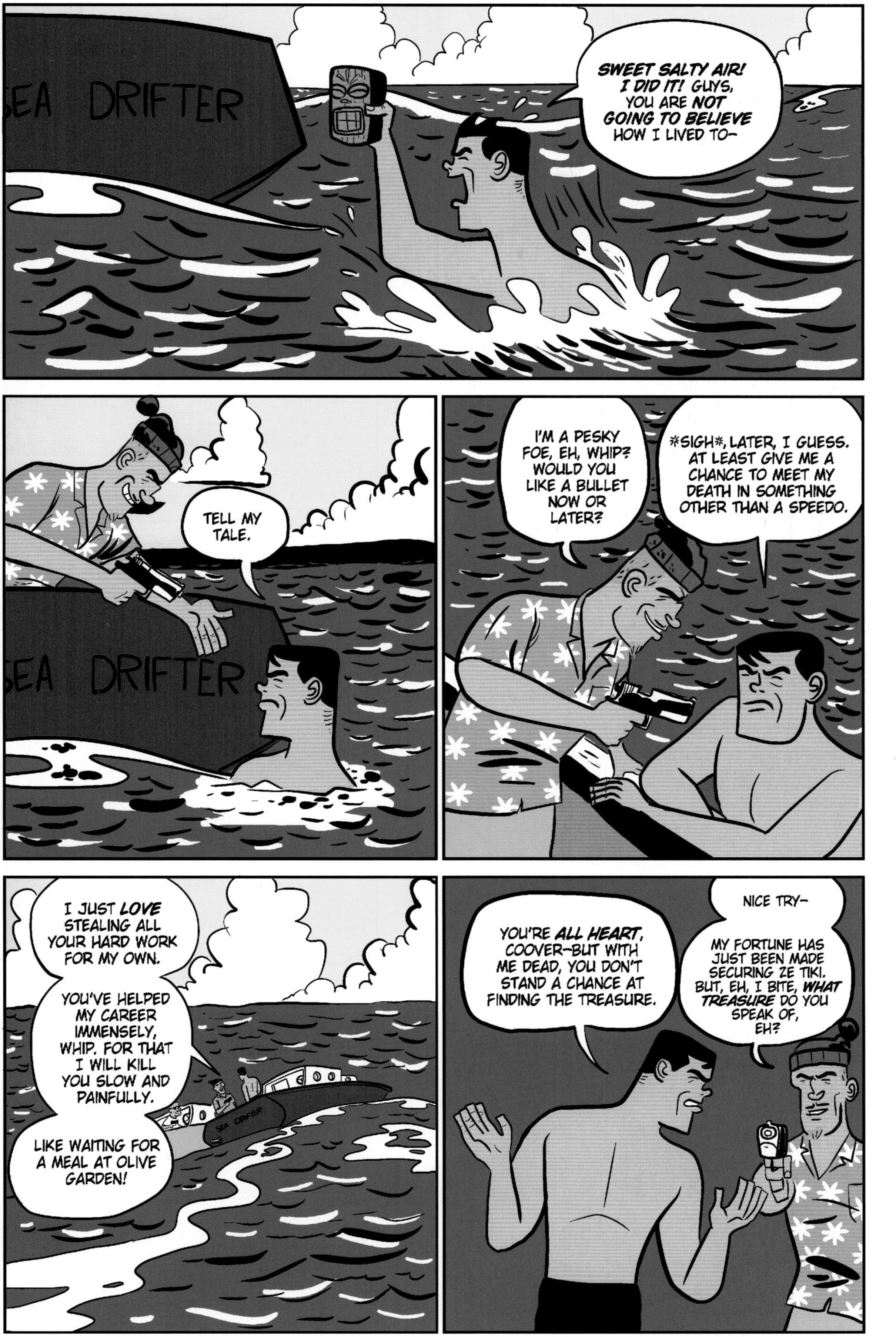
SWEET SALTY AIR! I DID IT! GUYS, YOU ARE NOT GOING TO BELIEVE HOW I LIVED TO-
SEA DRIFTER
TELL MY TALE.
SEA DRIFTER
I'M A PESKY FOE, EH, WHIP? WOULD YOU LIKE A BULLET NOW OR LATER?
SIGH, LATER, I GUESS. AT LEAST GIVE ME A CHANCE TO MEET MY DEATH IN SOMETHING OTHER THAN A SPEEDO.
I JUST LOVE STEALING ALL YOUR HARD WORK FOR MY OWN.
YOU'VE HELPED MY CAREER IMMENSELY, WHIP. FOR THAT I WILL KILL YOU SLOW AND PAINFULLY.
LIKE WAITING FOR A MEAL AT OLIVE GARDEN!
SEA DRIFTER
YOU'RE ALL HEART, COOVER-BUT WITH ME DEAD, YOU DON'T STAND A CHANCE AT FINDING THE TREASURE.
NICE TRY-
MY FORTUNE HAS JUST BEEN MADE SECURING ZE TIKI. BUT, EH, I BITE, WHAT TREASURE DO YOU SPEAK OF, EH?

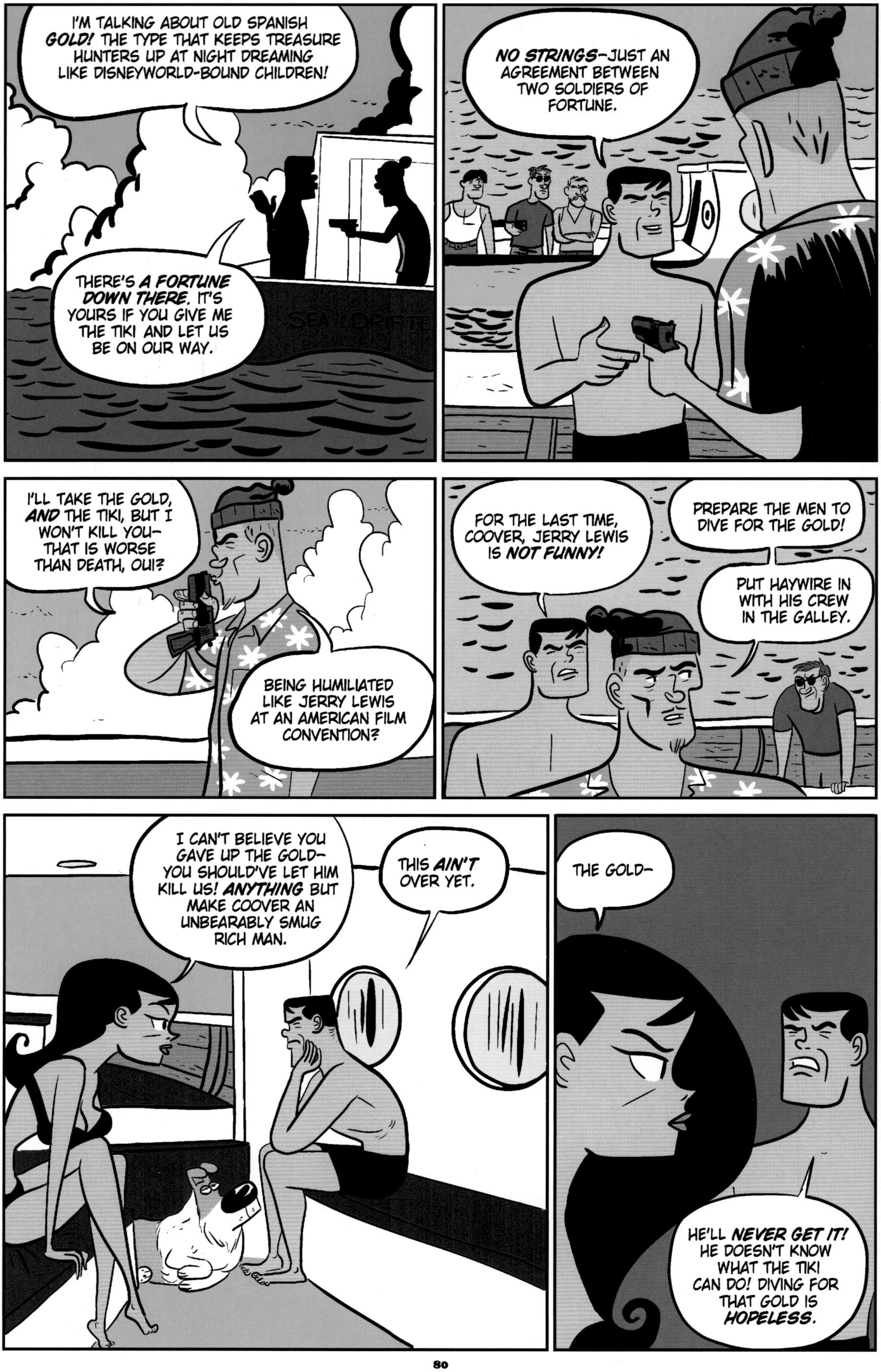
I'M TALKING ABOUT OLD SPANISH **GOLD!** THE TYPE THAT KEEPS TREASURE HUNTERS UP AT NIGHT DREAMING LIKE DISNEYWORLD-BOUND CHILDREN!
THERE'S **A FORTUNE DOWN THERE.** IT'S YOURS IF YOU GIVE ME THE TIKI AND LET US BE ON OUR WAY.
NO STRINGS—JUST AN AGREEMENT BETWEEN TWO SOLDIERS OF FORTUNE.
I'LL TAKE THE GOLD, **AND** THE TIKI, BUT I WON'T KILL YOU—THAT IS WORSE THAN DEATH, OUI?
BEING HUMILIATED LIKE JERRY LEWIS AT AN AMERICAN FILM CONVENTION?
FOR THE LAST TIME, COOVER, JERRY LEWIS IS **NOT FUNNY!**
PREPARE THE MEN TO DIVE FOR THE GOLD!
PUT HAYWIRE IN WITH HIS CREW IN THE GALLEY.
I CAN'T BELIEVE YOU GAVE UP THE GOLD—YOU SHOULD'VE LET HIM KILL US! **ANYTHING** BUT MAKE COOVER AN UNBEARABLY SMUG RICH MAN.
THIS **AIN'T** OVER YET.
THE GOLD—
HE'LL **NEVER GET IT!** HE DOESN'T KNOW WHAT THE TIKI CAN DO! DIVING FOR THAT GOLD IS **HOPELESS.**

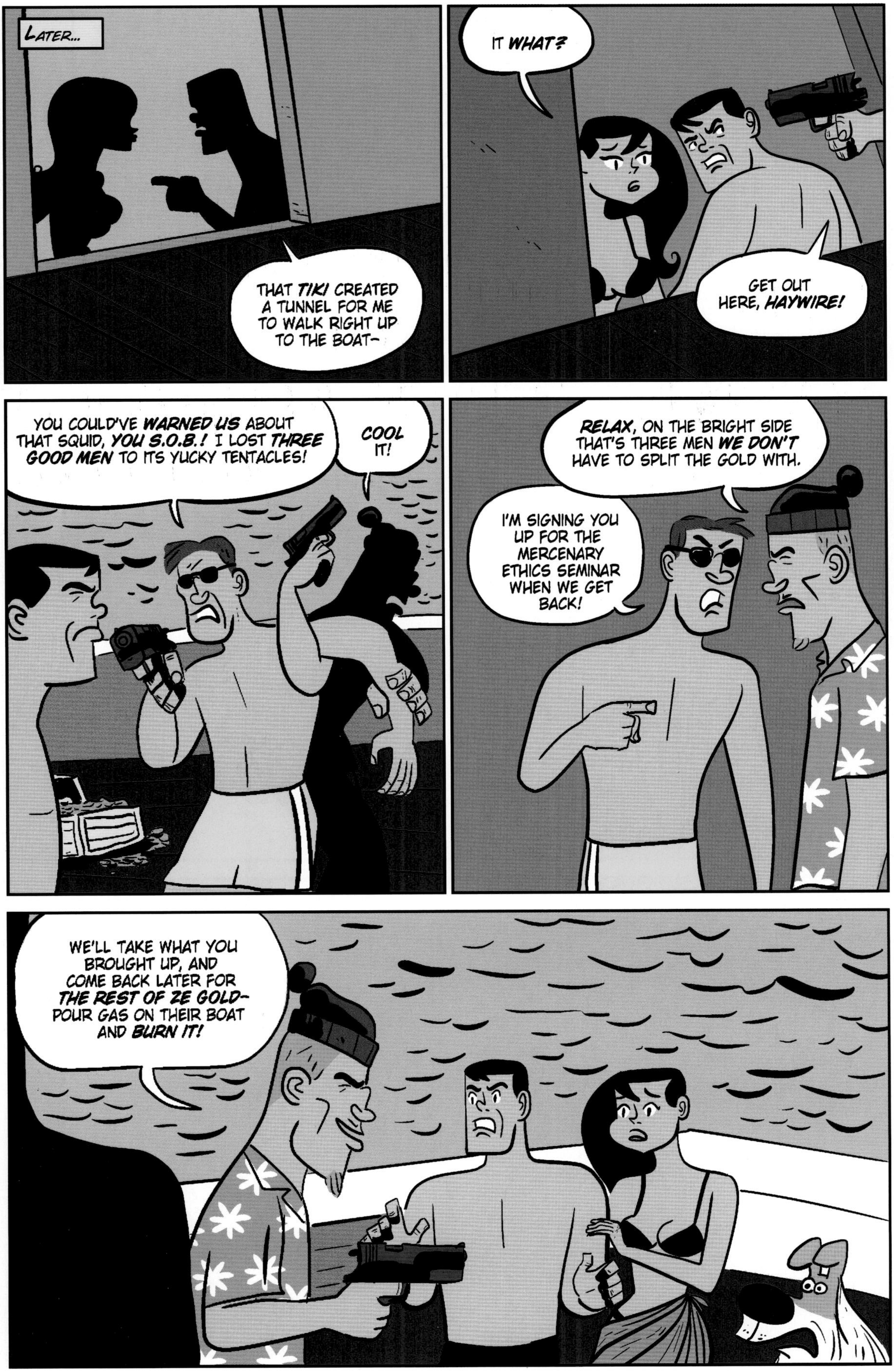

LATER...
THAT TIKI CREATED A TUNNEL FOR ME TO WALK RIGHT UP TO THE BOAT-
IT WHAT?
GET OUT HERE, HAYWIRE!
YOU COULD'VE WARNED US ABOUT THAT SQUID, YOU S.O.B.! I LOST THREE GOOD MEN TO ITS YUCKY TENTACLES!
COOL IT!
RELAX, ON THE BRIGHT SIDE THAT'S THREE MEN WE DON'T HAVE TO SPLIT THE GOLD WITH.
I'M SIGNING YOU UP FOR THE MERCENARY ETHICS SEMINAR WHEN WE GET BACK!
WE'LL TAKE WHAT YOU BROUGHT UP, AND COME BACK LATER FOR THE REST OF ZE GOLD- POUR GAS ON THEIR BOAT AND BURN IT!

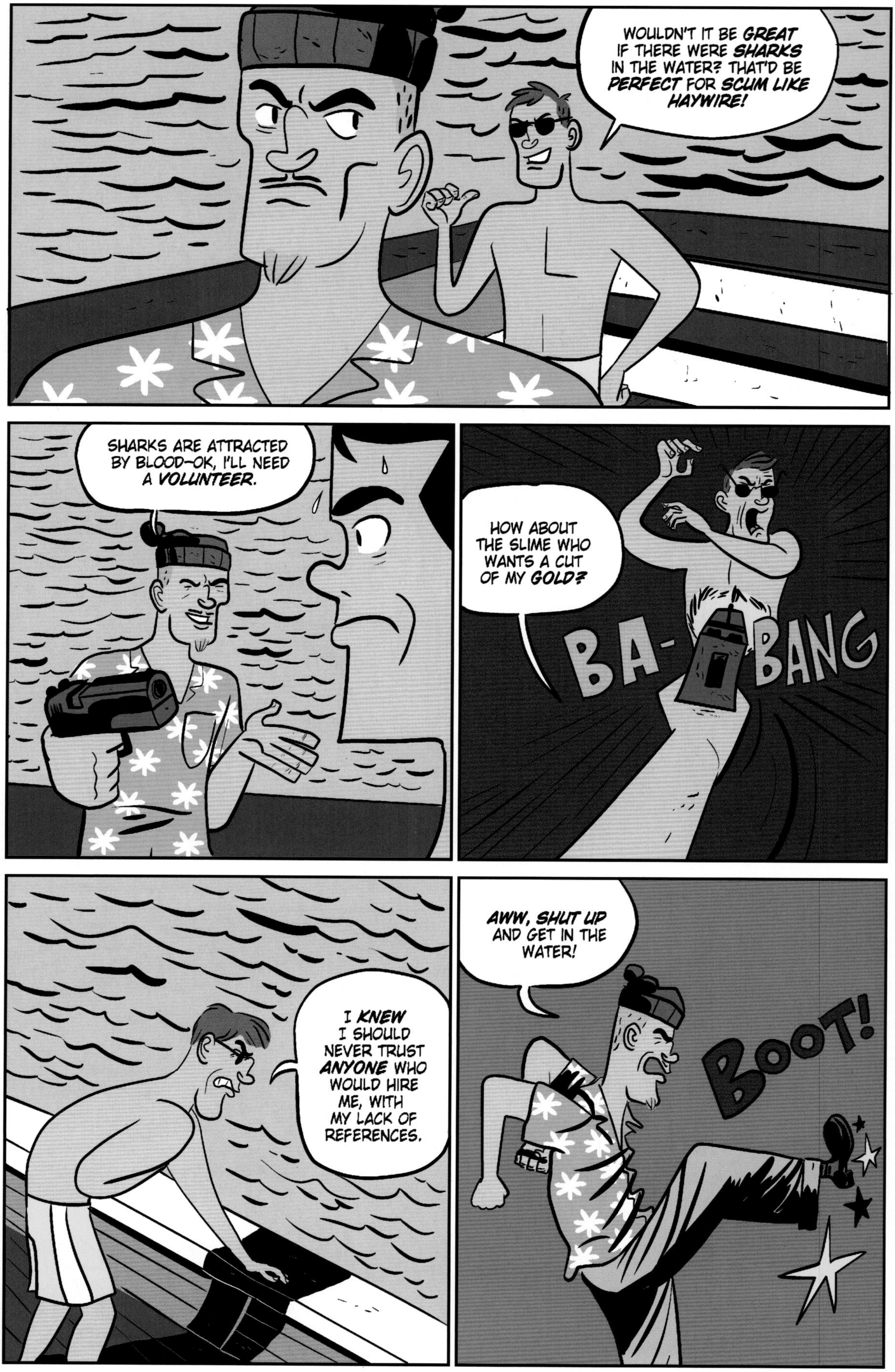
WOULDN'T IT BE GREAT IF THERE WERE SHARKS IN THE WATER? THAT'D BE PERFECT FOR SCUM LIKE HAYWIRE!
SHARKS ARE ATTRACTED BY BLOOD—OK, I'LL NEED A VOLUNTEER.
HOW ABOUT THE SLIME WHO WANTS A CUT OF MY GOLD?
BA-BANG
I KNEW I SHOULD NEVER TRUST ANYONE WHO WOULD HIRE ME, WITH MY LACK OF REFERENCES.
AWW, SHUT UP AND GET IN THE WATER!
BOOT!

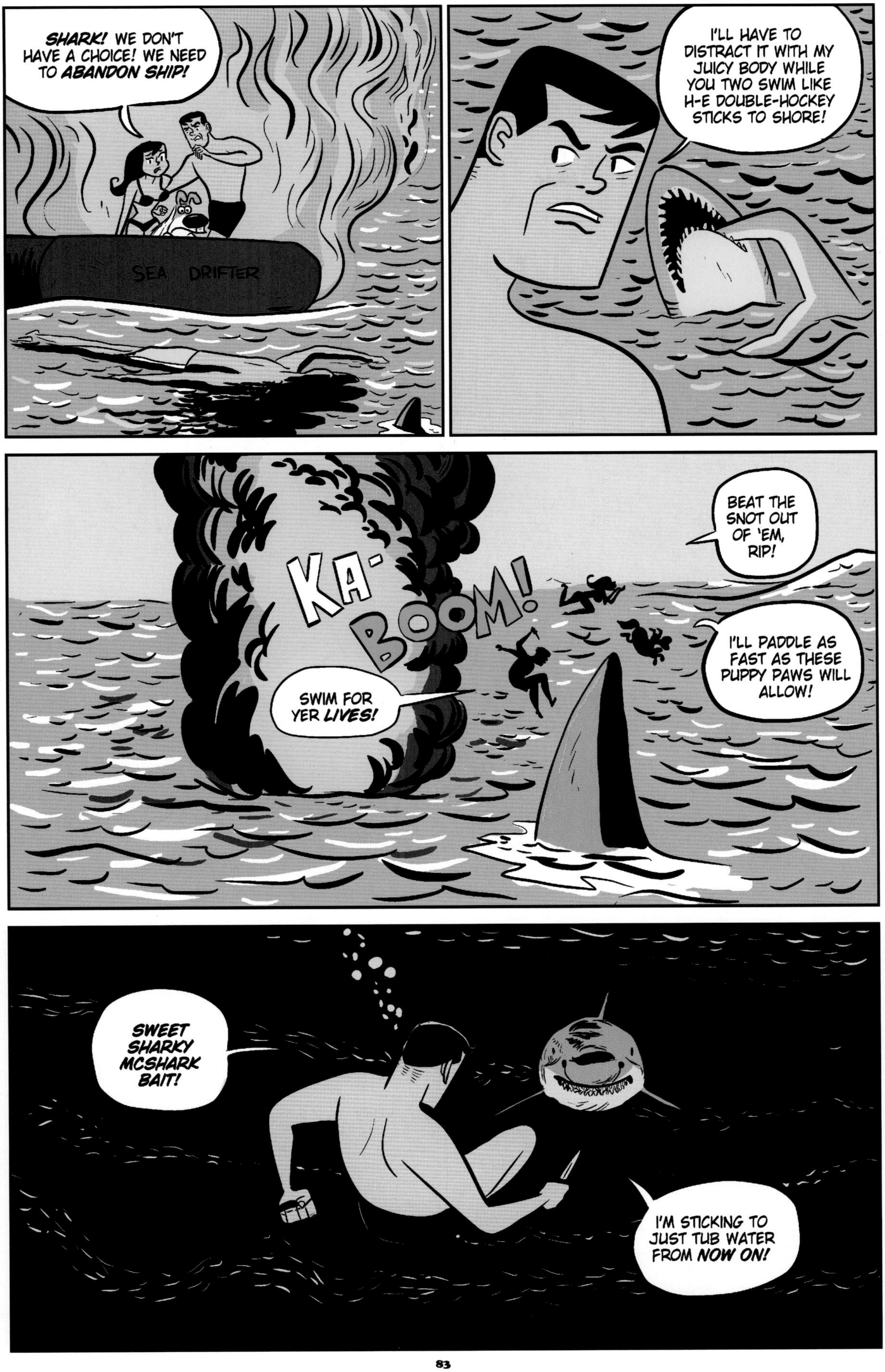

SHARK! WE DON'T HAVE A CHOICE! WE NEED TO ABANDON SHIP!
SEA DRIFTER
I'LL HAVE TO DISTRACT IT WITH MY JUICY BODY WHILE YOU TWO SWIM LIKE H-E DOUBLE-HOCKEY STICKS TO SHORE!
KA-BOOM!
SWIM FOR YER LIVES!
BEAT THE SNOT OUT OF 'EM, RIP!
I'LL PADDLE AS FAST AS THESE PUPPY PAWS WILL ALLOW!
SWEET SHARKY MCSHARK BAIT!
I'M STICKING TO JUST TUB WATER FROM NOW ON!

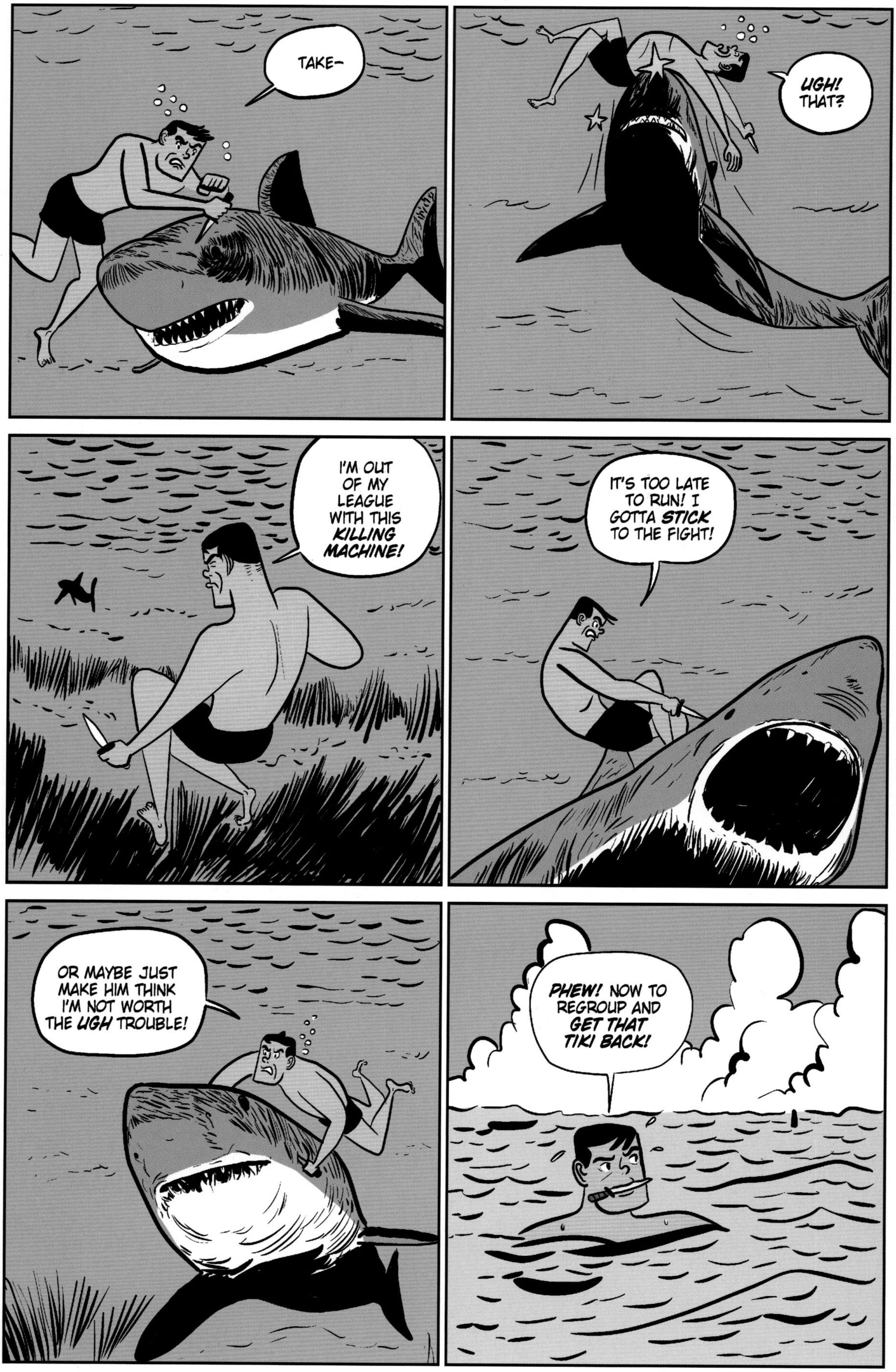
TAKE-
UGH! THAT?
I'M OUT OF MY LEAGUE WITH THIS KILLING MACHINE!
IT'S TOO LATE TO RUN! I GOTTA STICK TO THE FIGHT!
OR MAYBE JUST MAKE HIM THINK I'M NOT WORTH THE UGH TROUBLE!
PHEW! NOW TO REGROUP AND GET THAT TIKI BACK!

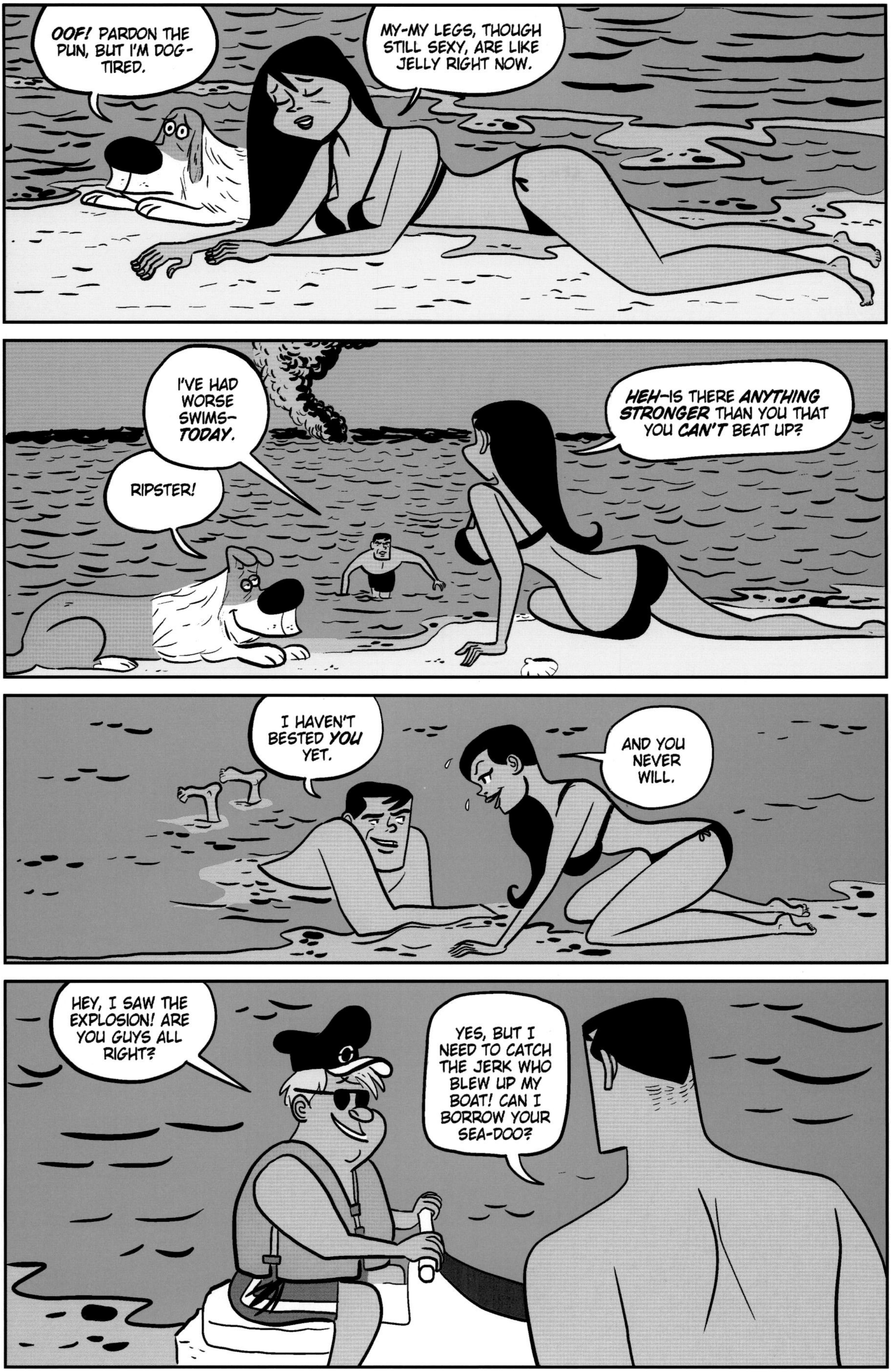
OOF! PARDON THE PUN, BUT I'M DOG-TIRED.
MY-MY LEGS, THOUGH STILL SEXY, ARE LIKE JELLY RIGHT NOW.
I'VE HAD WORSE SWIMS-TODAY.
RIPSTER!
HEH-IS THERE ANYTHING STRONGER THAN YOU THAT YOU CAN'T BEAT UP?
I HAVEN'T BESTED YOU YET.
AND YOU NEVER WILL.
HEY, I SAW THE EXPLOSION! ARE YOU GUYS ALL RIGHT?
YES, BUT I NEED TO CATCH THE JERK WHO BLEW UP MY BOAT! CAN I BORROW YOUR SEA-DOO?

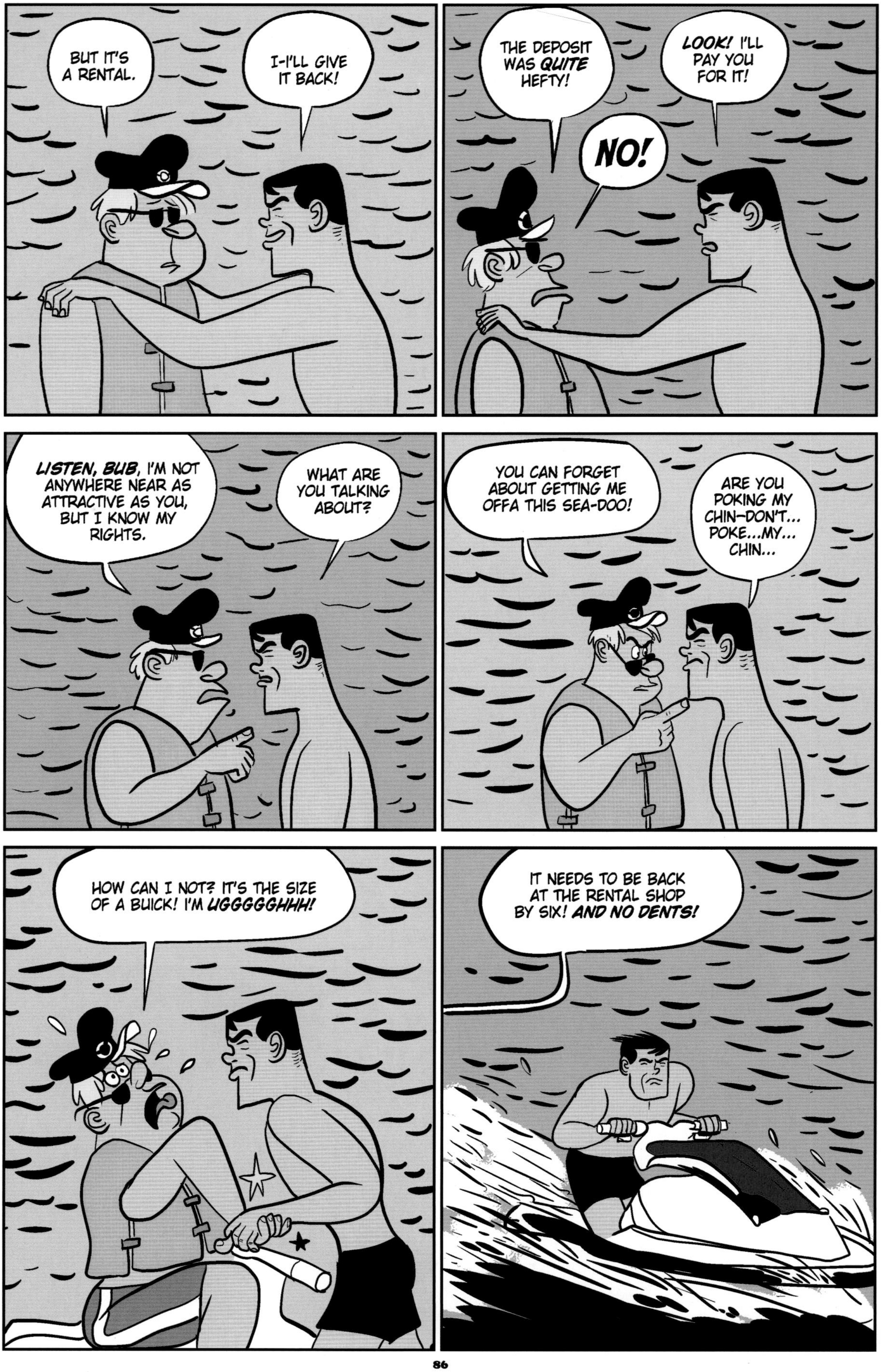
BUT IT'S A RENTAL.
I-I'LL GIVE IT BACK!
THE DEPOSIT WAS QUITE HEFTY!
LOOK! I'LL PAY YOU FOR IT!
NO!
LISTEN, BUB, I'M NOT ANYWHERE NEAR AS ATTRACTIVE AS YOU, BUT I KNOW MY RIGHTS.
WHAT ARE YOU TALKING ABOUT?
YOU CAN FORGET ABOUT GETTING ME OFFA THIS SEA-DOO!
ARE YOU POKING MY CHIN–DON'T... POKE...MY... CHIN...
HOW CAN I NOT? IT'S THE SIZE OF A BUICK! I'M UGGGGGHHH!
IT NEEDS TO BE BACK AT THE RENTAL SHOP BY SIX! AND NO DENTS!

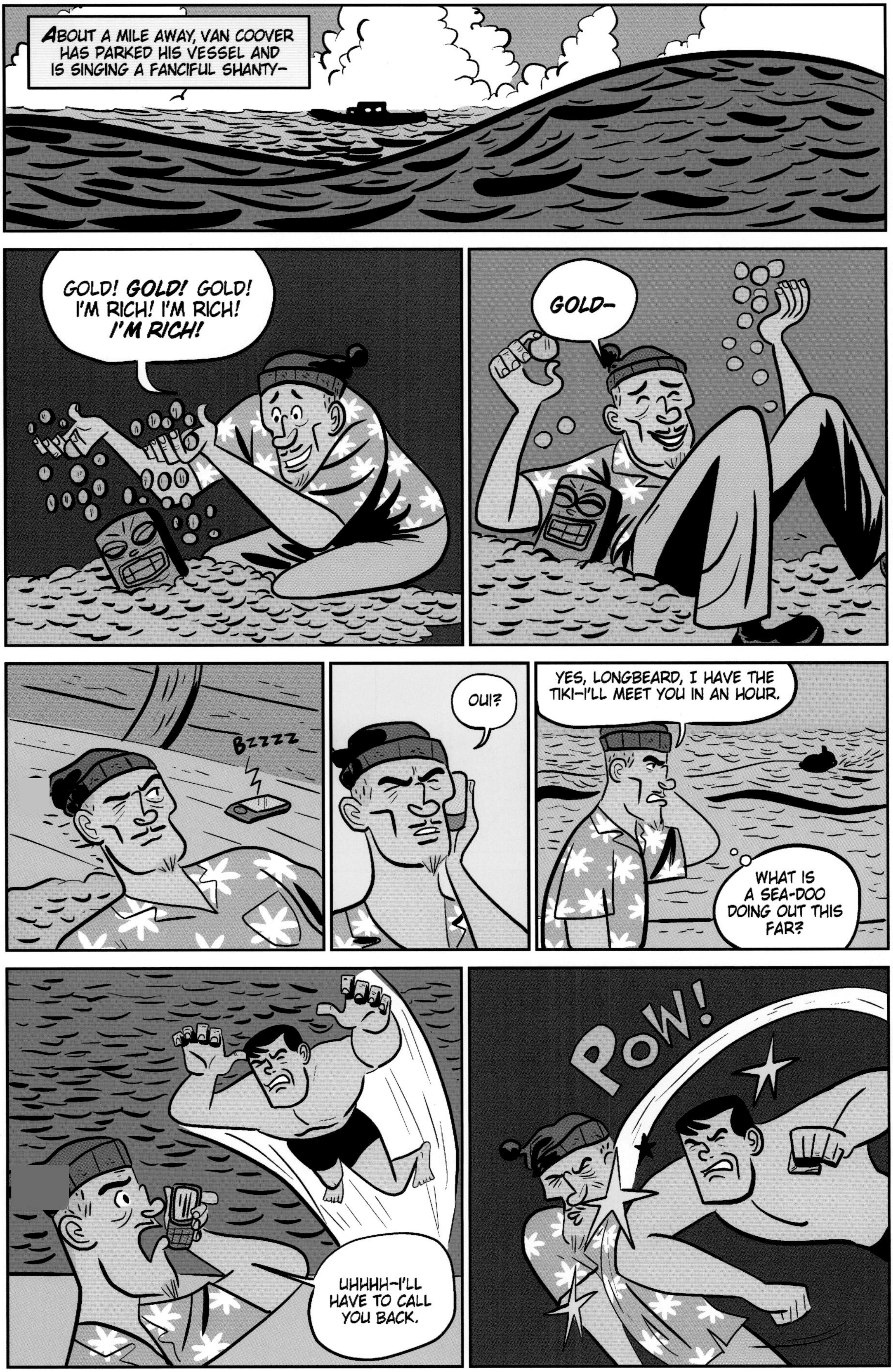
ABOUT A MILE AWAY, VAN COOVER HAS PARKED HIS VESSEL AND IS SINGING A FANCIFUL SHANTY–
GOLD! GOLD! GOLD! I'M RICH! I'M RICH! I'M RICH!
GOLD–
BZZZZ
OUI?
YES, LONGBEARD, I HAVE THE TIKI–I'LL MEET YOU IN AN HOUR.
WHAT IS A SEA-DOO DOING OUT THIS FAR?
UHHHH–I'LL HAVE TO CALL YOU BACK.
POW!

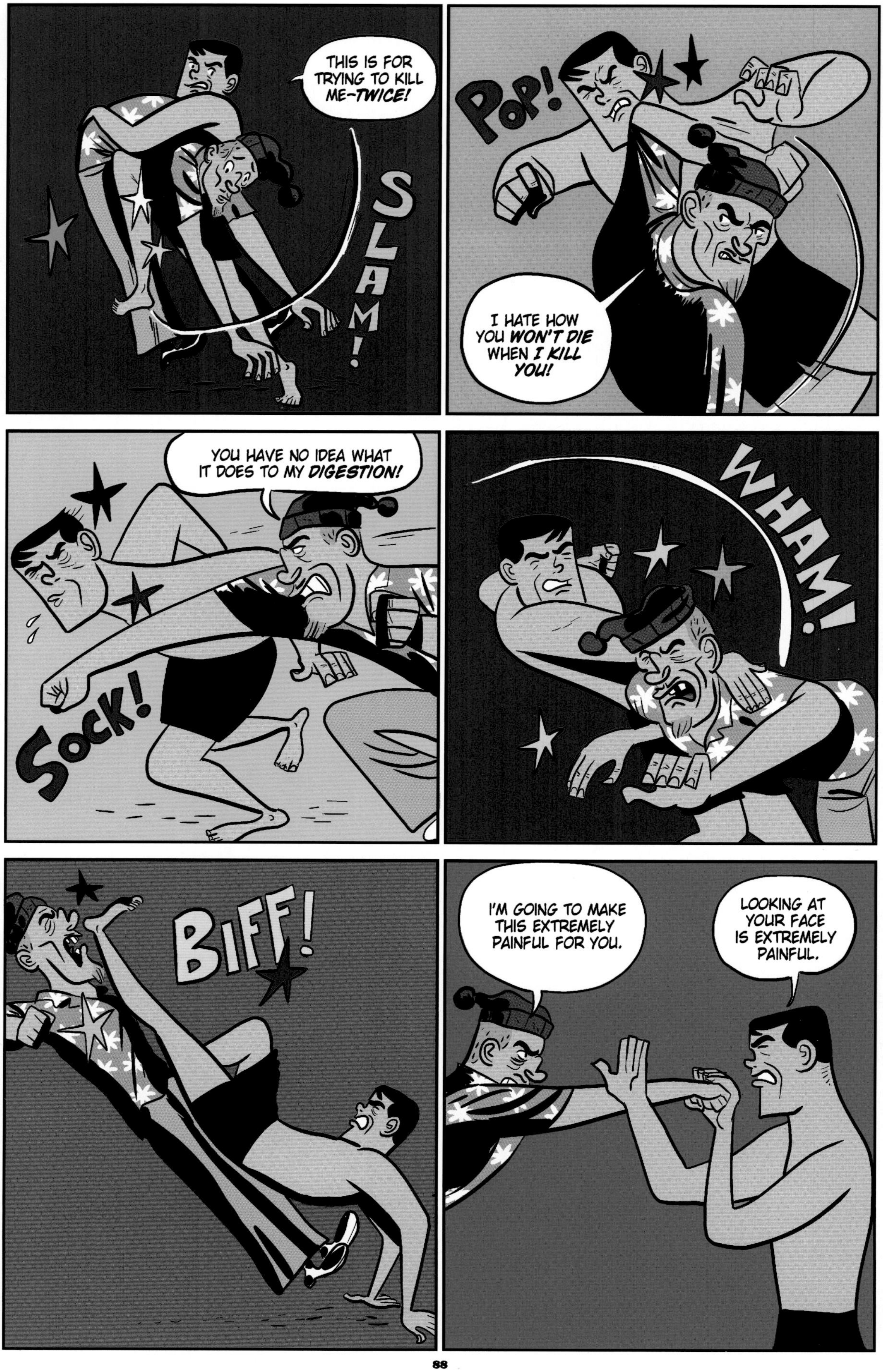
THIS IS FOR TRYING TO KILL ME—*TWICE!*
SLAM!
POP!
I HATE HOW YOU ***WON'T DIE*** WHEN ***I KILL YOU!***
YOU HAVE NO IDEA WHAT IT DOES TO MY ***DIGESTION!***
SOCK!
WHAM!
BIFF!
I'M GOING TO MAKE THIS EXTREMELY PAINFUL FOR YOU.
LOOKING AT YOUR FACE IS EXTREMELY PAINFUL.

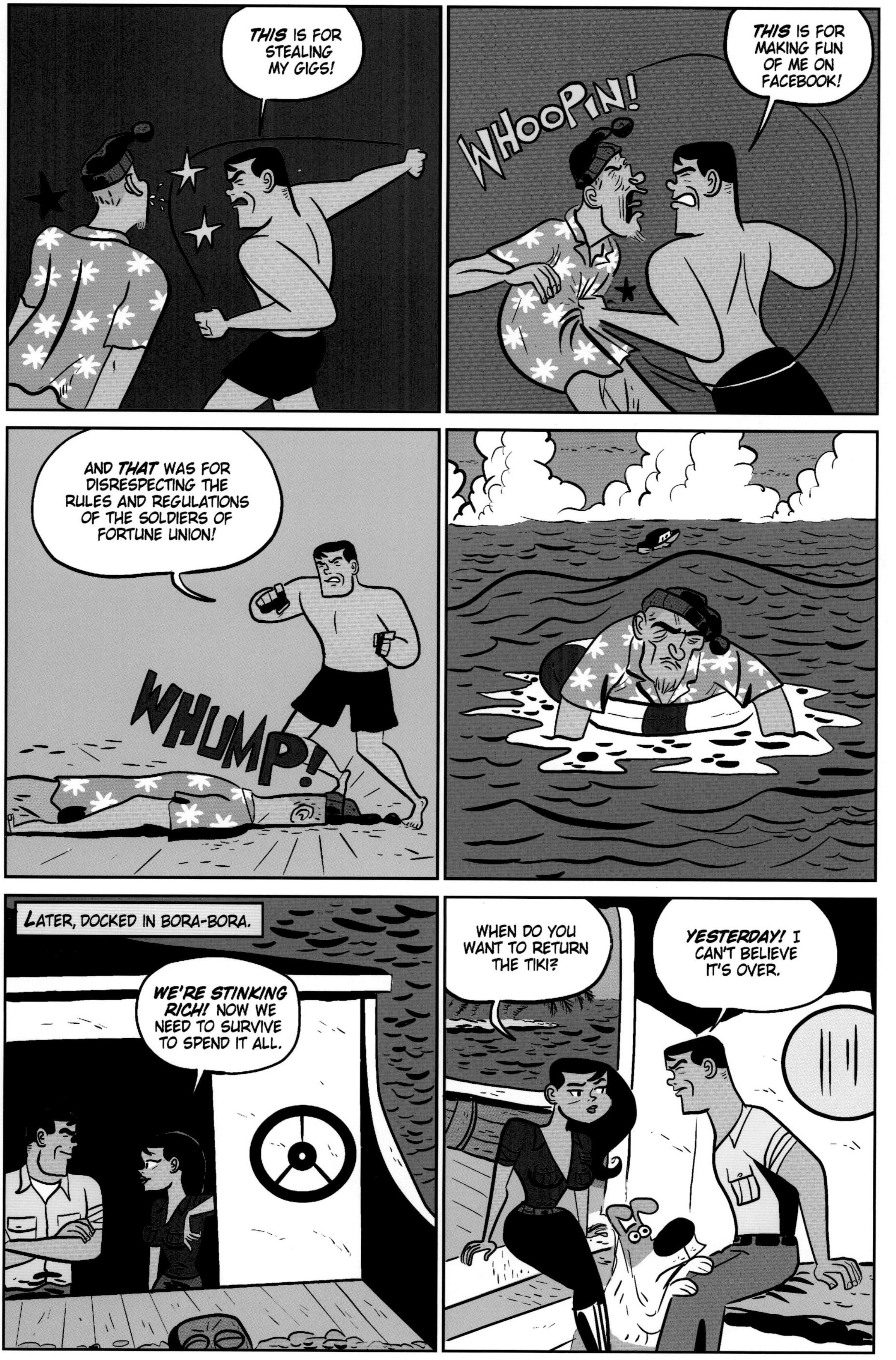
THIS IS FOR STEALING MY GIGS!
WHOOPIN!
THIS IS FOR MAKING FUN OF ME ON FACEBOOK!
AND THAT WAS FOR DISRESPECTING THE RULES AND REGULATIONS OF THE SOLDIERS OF FORTUNE UNION!
WHUMP!
LATER, DOCKED IN BORA-BORA.
WE'RE STINKING RICH! NOW WE NEED TO SURVIVE TO SPEND IT ALL.
WHEN DO YOU WANT TO RETURN THE TIKI?
YESTERDAY! I CAN'T BELIEVE IT'S OVER.

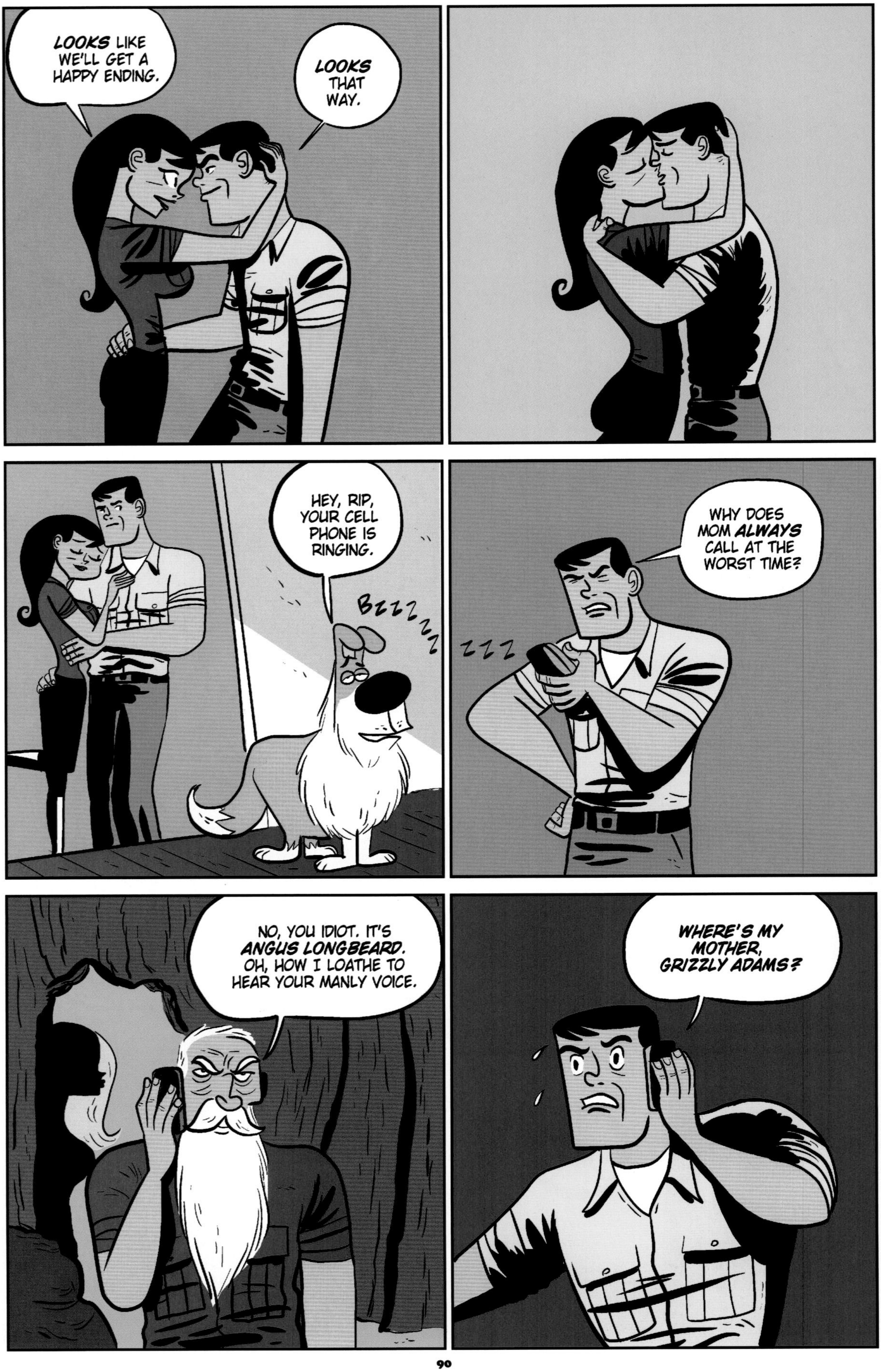
LOOKS LIKE WE'LL GET A HAPPY ENDING.
LOOKS THAT WAY.
HEY, RIP, YOUR CELL PHONE IS RINGING.
BZZZZ
ZZZ
WHY DOES MOM ALWAYS CALL AT THE WORST TIME?
NO, YOU IDIOT. IT'S ANGUS LONGBEARD. OH, HOW I LOATHE TO HEAR YOUR MANLY VOICE.
WHERE'S MY MOTHER, GRIZZLY ADAMS?

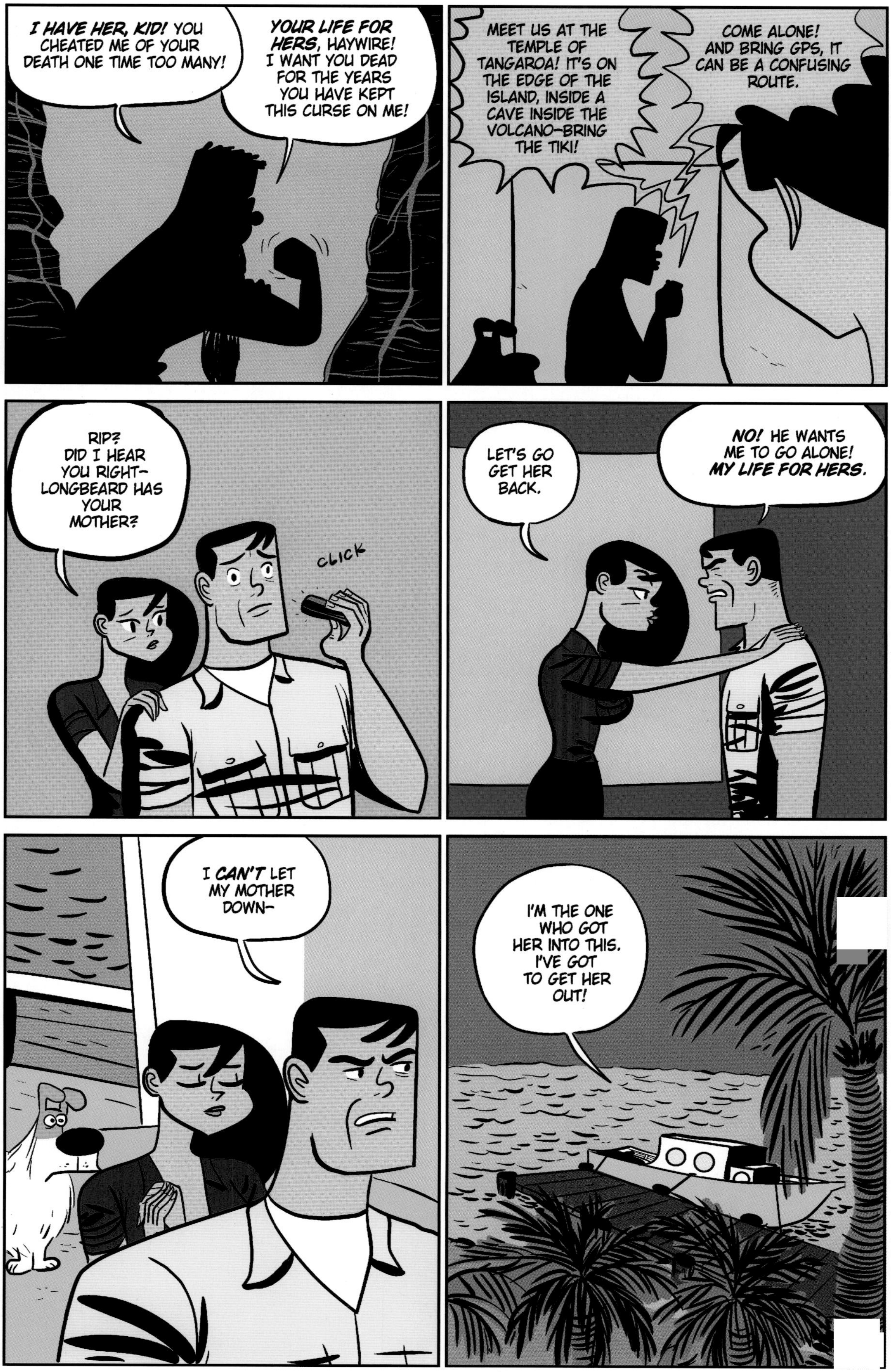
I HAVE HER, KID! YOU CHEATED ME OF YOUR DEATH ONE TIME TOO MANY!
YOUR LIFE FOR HERS, HAYWIRE! I WANT YOU DEAD FOR THE YEARS YOU HAVE KEPT THIS CURSE ON ME!
MEET US AT THE TEMPLE OF TANGAROA! IT'S ON THE EDGE OF THE ISLAND, INSIDE A CAVE INSIDE THE VOLCANO—BRING THE TIKI!
COME ALONE! AND BRING GPS, IT CAN BE A CONFUSING ROUTE.
RIP? DID I HEAR YOU RIGHT— LONGBEARD HAS YOUR MOTHER?
CLICK
LET'S GO GET HER BACK.
NO! HE WANTS ME TO GO ALONE! MY LIFE FOR HERS.
I CAN'T LET MY MOTHER DOWN—
I'M THE ONE WHO GOT HER INTO THIS. I'VE GOT TO GET HER OUT!

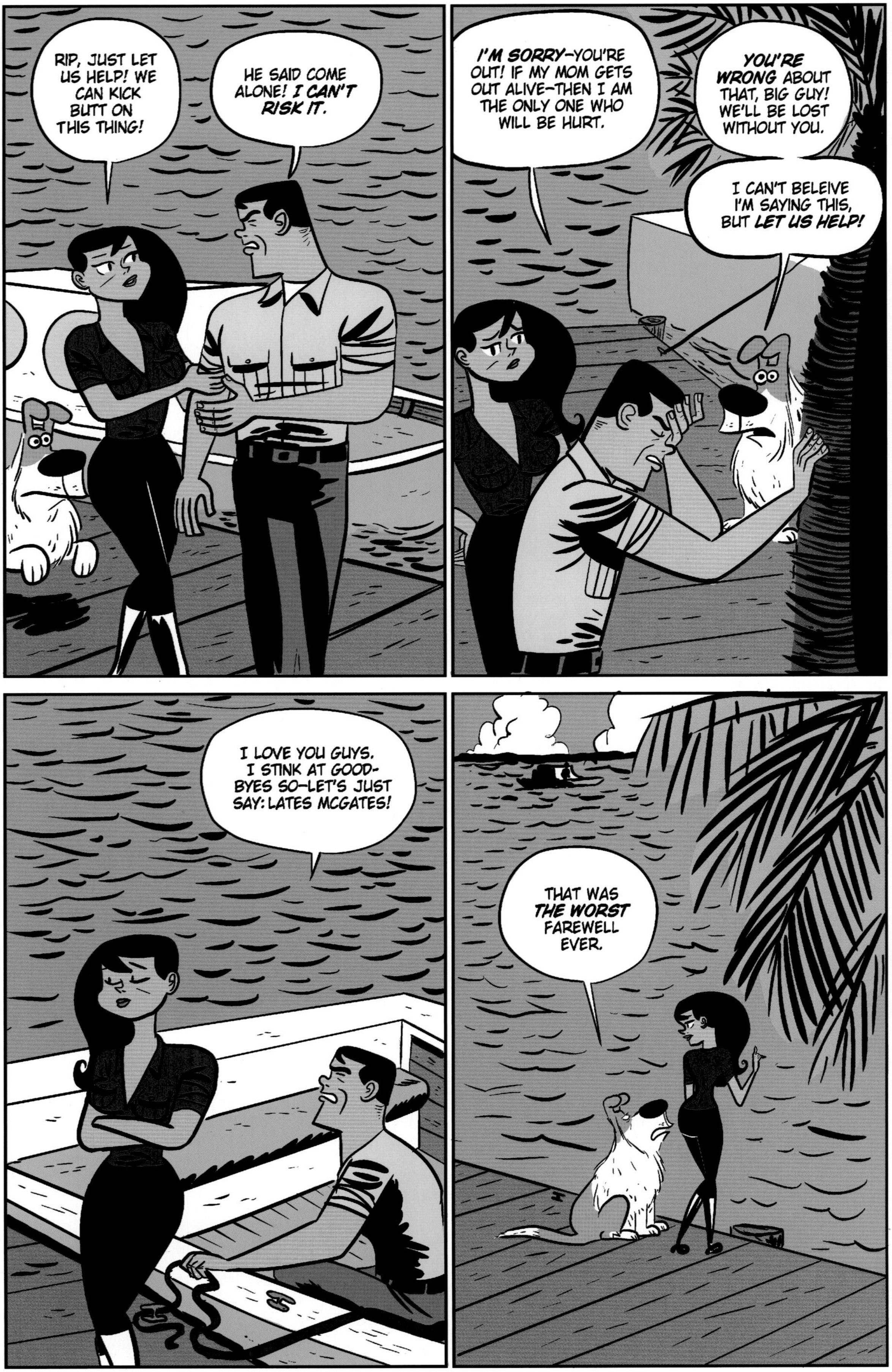
RIP, JUST LET US HELP! WE CAN KICK BUTT ON THIS THING!
HE SAID COME ALONE! I CAN'T RISK IT.
I'M SORRY–YOU'RE OUT! IF MY MOM GETS OUT ALIVE–THEN I AM THE ONLY ONE WHO WILL BE HURT.
YOU'RE WRONG ABOUT THAT, BIG GUY! WE'LL BE LOST WITHOUT YOU.
I CAN'T BELEIVE I'M SAYING THIS, BUT LET US HELP!
I LOVE YOU GUYS. I STINK AT GOOD-BYES SO–LET'S JUST SAY: LATES MCGATES!
THAT WAS THE WORST FAREWELL EVER.

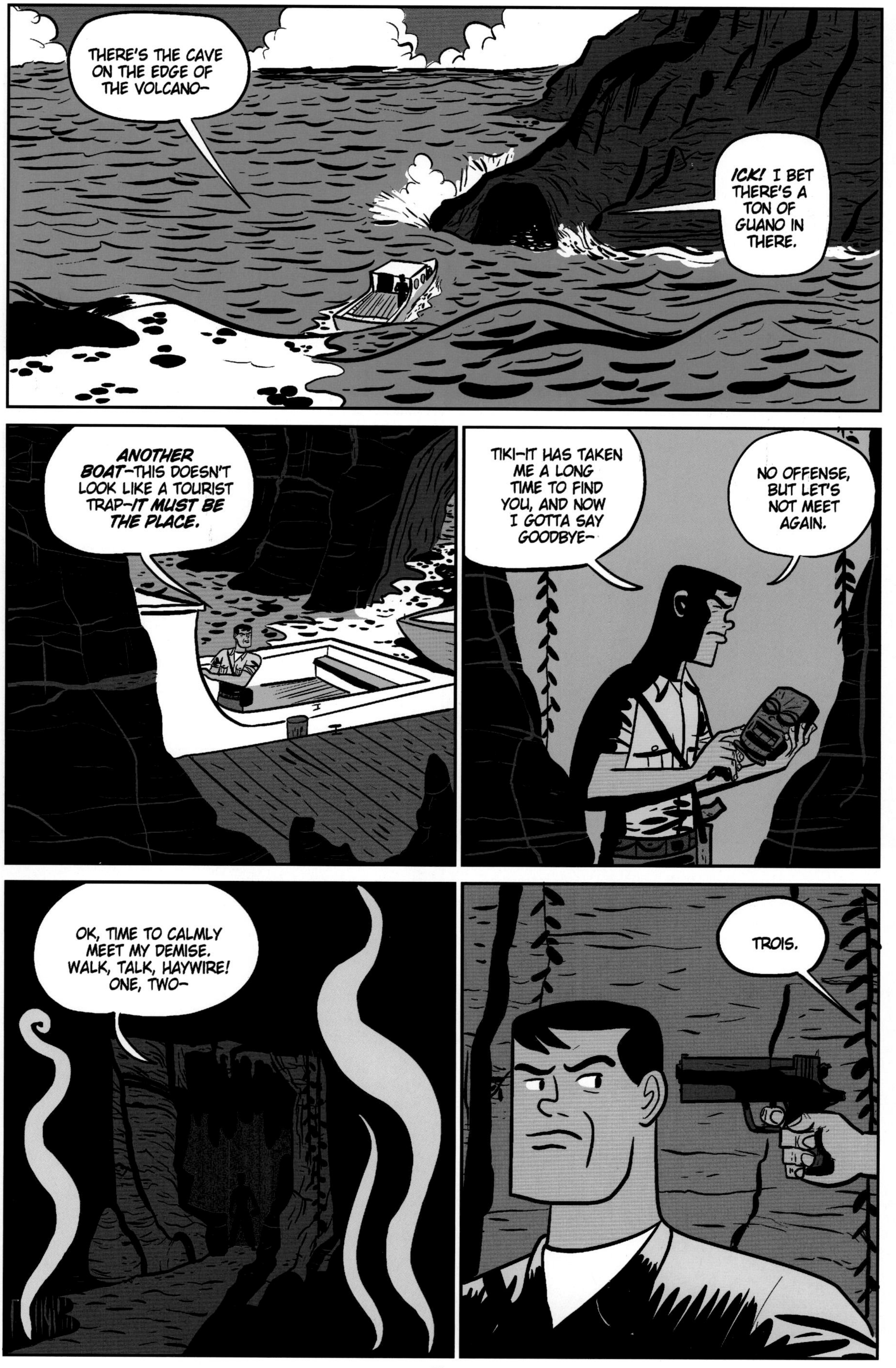
THERE'S THE CAVE ON THE EDGE OF THE VOLCANO-
ICK! I BET THERE'S A TON OF GUANO IN THERE.
ANOTHER BOAT-THIS DOESN'T LOOK LIKE A TOURIST TRAP-IT MUST BE THE PLACE.
TIKI-IT HAS TAKEN ME A LONG TIME TO FIND YOU, AND NOW I GOTTA SAY GOODBYE-
NO OFFENSE, BUT LET'S NOT MEET AGAIN.
OK, TIME TO CALMLY MEET MY DEMISE. WALK, TALK, HAYWIRE! ONE, TWO-
TROIS.

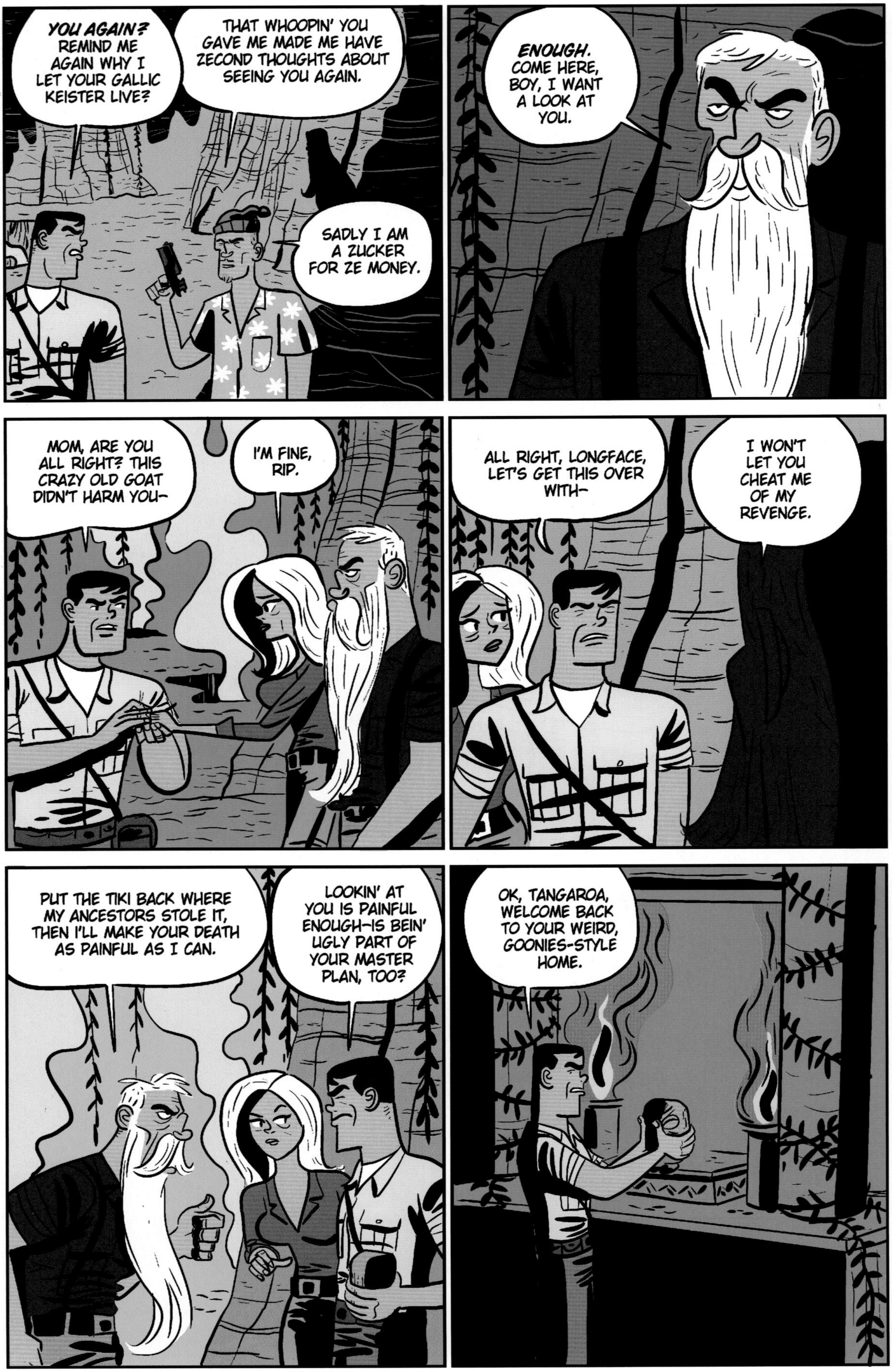
YOU AGAIN? REMIND ME AGAIN WHY I LET YOUR GALLIC KEISTER LIVE?
THAT WHOOPIN' YOU GAVE ME MADE ME HAVE ZECOND THOUGHTS ABOUT SEEING YOU AGAIN.
SADLY I AM A ZUCKER FOR ZE MONEY.
ENOUGH. COME HERE, BOY, I WANT A LOOK AT YOU.
MOM, ARE YOU ALL RIGHT? THIS CRAZY OLD GOAT DIDN'T HARM YOU–
I'M FINE, RIP.
ALL RIGHT, LONGFACE, LET'S GET THIS OVER WITH–
I WON'T LET YOU CHEAT ME OF MY REVENGE.
PUT THE TIKI BACK WHERE MY ANCESTORS STOLE IT, THEN I'LL MAKE YOUR DEATH AS PAINFUL AS I CAN.
LOOKIN' AT YOU IS PAINFUL ENOUGH–IS BEIN' UGLY PART OF YOUR MASTER PLAN, TOO?
OK, TANGAROA, WELCOME BACK TO YOUR WEIRD, GOONIES-STYLE HOME.

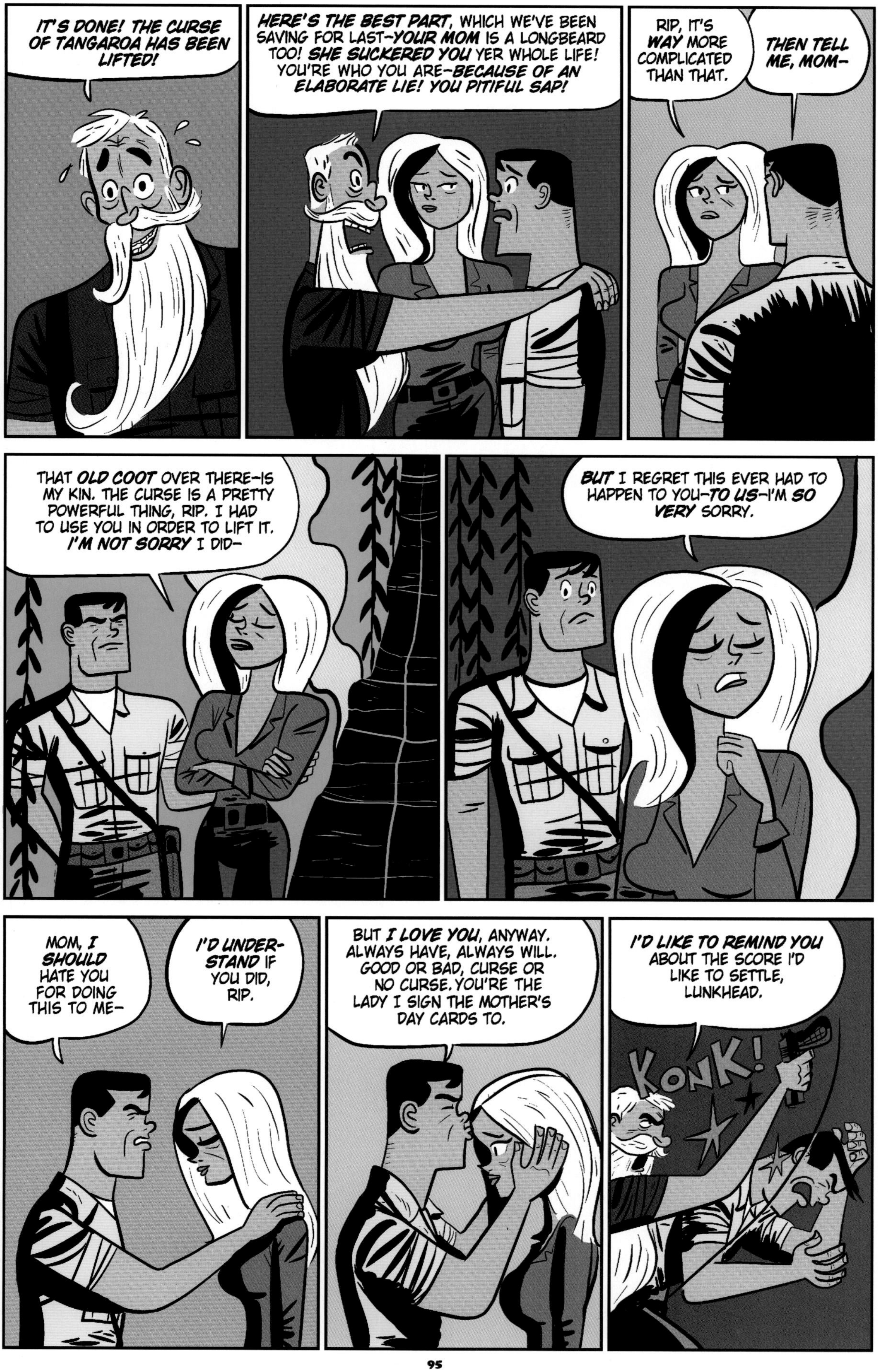
IT'S DONE! THE CURSE OF TANGAROA HAS BEEN LIFTED!
HERE'S THE BEST PART, WHICH WE'VE BEEN SAVING FOR LAST–YOUR MOM IS A LONGBEARD TOO! SHE SUCKERED YOU YER WHOLE LIFE! YOU'RE WHO YOU ARE–BECAUSE OF AN ELABORATE LIE! YOU PITIFUL SAP!
RIP, IT'S WAY MORE COMPLICATED THAN THAT.
THEN TELL ME, MOM–
THAT OLD COOT OVER THERE–IS MY KIN. THE CURSE IS A PRETTY POWERFUL THING, RIP. I HAD TO USE YOU IN ORDER TO LIFT IT. I'M NOT SORRY I DID–
BUT I REGRET THIS EVER HAD TO HAPPEN TO YOU–TO US–I'M SO VERY SORRY.
MOM, I SHOULD HATE YOU FOR DOING THIS TO ME–
I'D UNDERSTAND IF YOU DID, RIP.
BUT I LOVE YOU, ANYWAY. ALWAYS HAVE, ALWAYS WILL. GOOD OR BAD, CURSE OR NO CURSE. YOU'RE THE LADY I SIGN THE MOTHER'S DAY CARDS TO.
I'D LIKE TO REMIND YOU ABOUT THE SCORE I'D LIKE TO SETTLE, LUNKHEAD.
KONK!

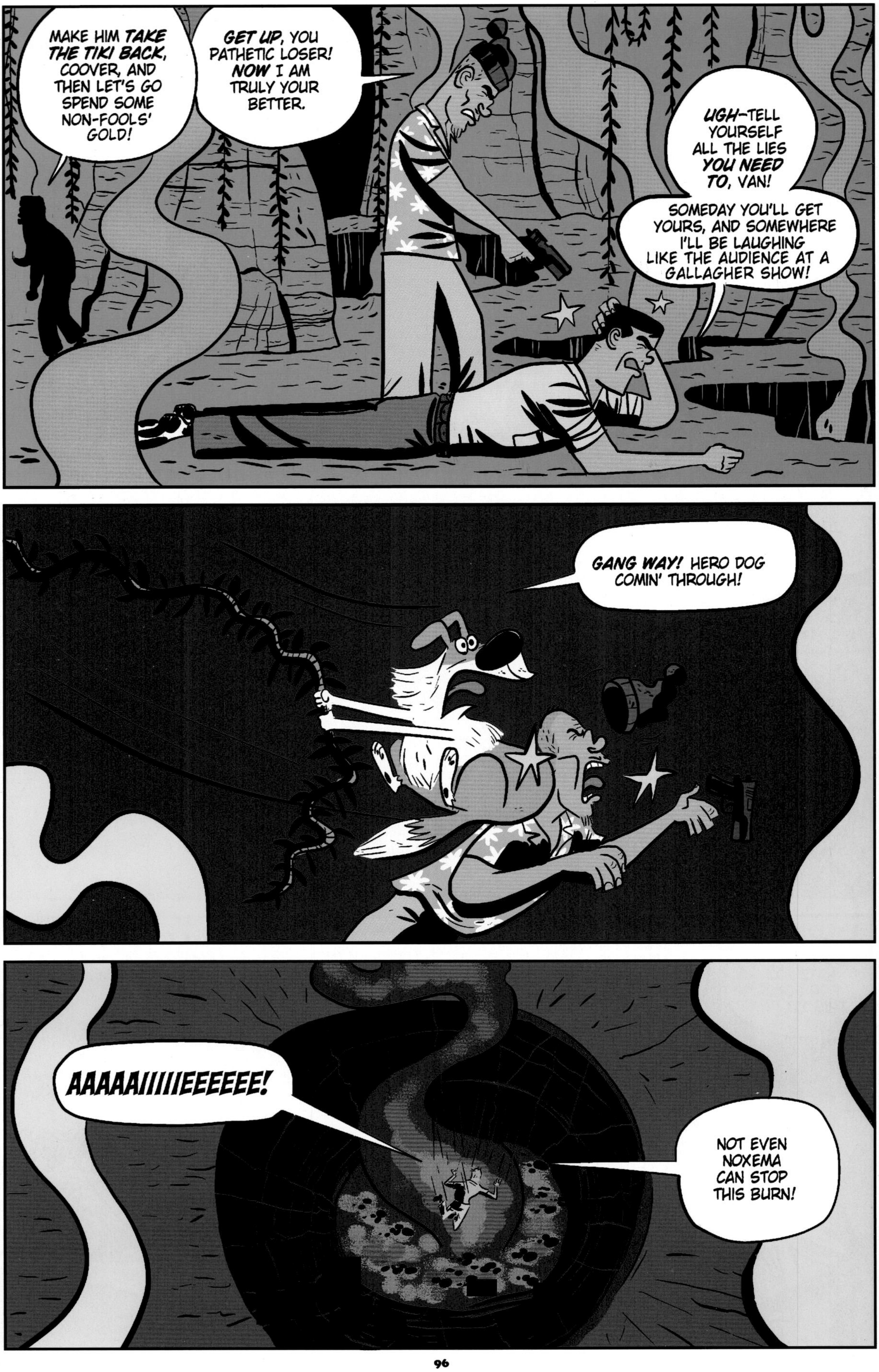
MAKE HIM TAKE THE TIKI BACK, COOVER, AND THEN LET'S GO SPEND SOME NON-FOOLS' GOLD!
GET UP, YOU PATHETIC LOSER! NOW I AM TRULY YOUR BETTER.
UGH–TELL YOURSELF ALL THE LIES YOU NEED TO, VAN!
SOMEDAY YOU'LL GET YOURS, AND SOMEWHERE I'LL BE LAUGHING LIKE THE AUDIENCE AT A GALLAGHER SHOW!
GANG WAY! HERO DOG COMIN' THROUGH!
AAAAAIIIIIIEEEEEE!
NOT EVEN NOXEMA CAN STOP THIS BURN!

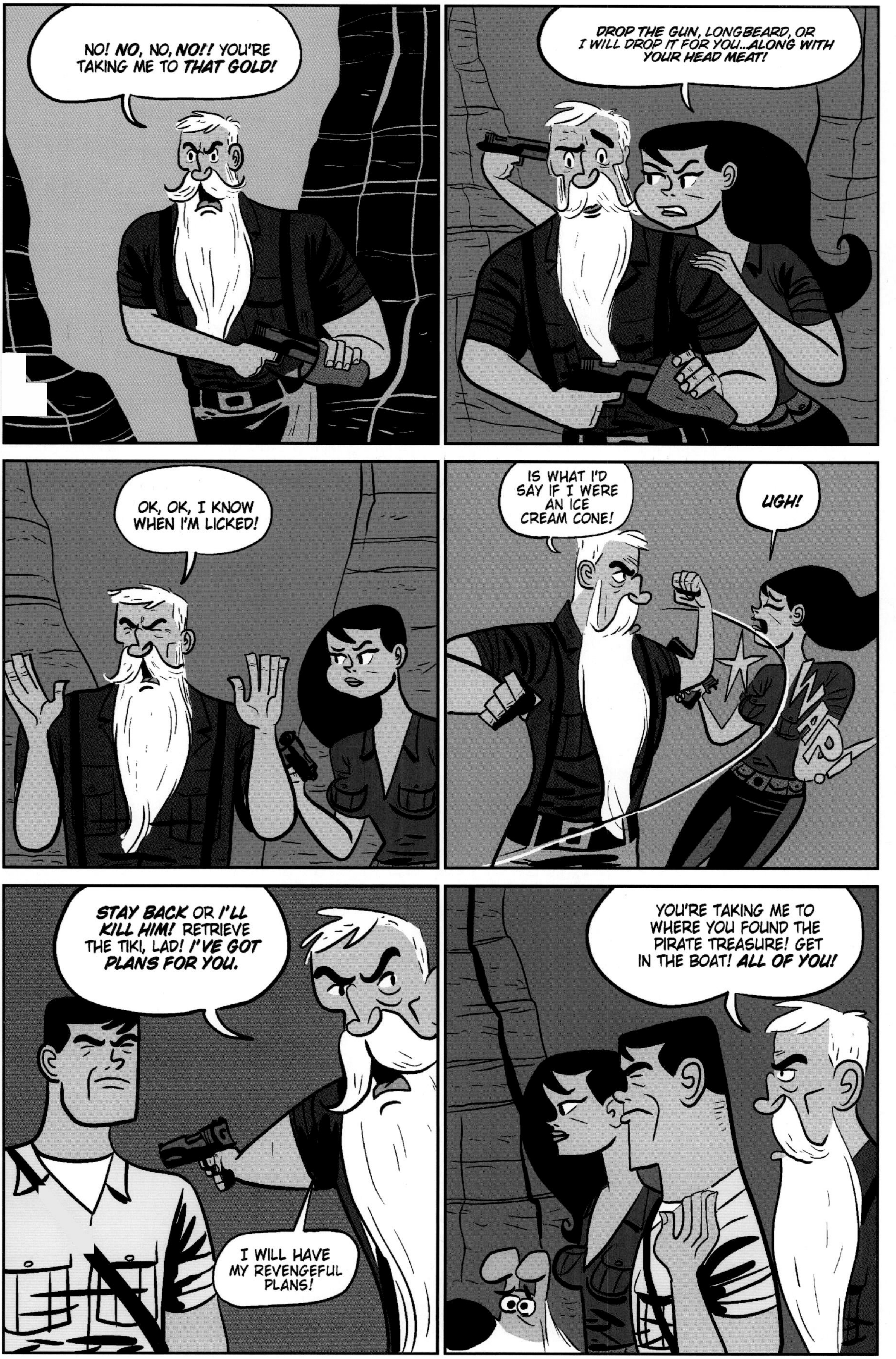
NO! NO, NO, NO!! YOU'RE TAKING ME TO THAT GOLD!
DROP THE GUN, LONGBEARD, OR I WILL DROP IT FOR YOU...ALONG WITH YOUR HEAD MEAT!
OK, OK, I KNOW WHEN I'M LICKED!
IS WHAT I'D SAY IF I WERE AN ICE CREAM CONE!
UGH!
STAY BACK OR I'LL KILL HIM! RETRIEVE THE TIKI, LAD! I'VE GOT PLANS FOR YOU.
I WILL HAVE MY REVENGEFUL PLANS!
YOU'RE TAKING ME TO WHERE YOU FOUND THE PIRATE TREASURE! GET IN THE BOAT! ALL OF YOU!

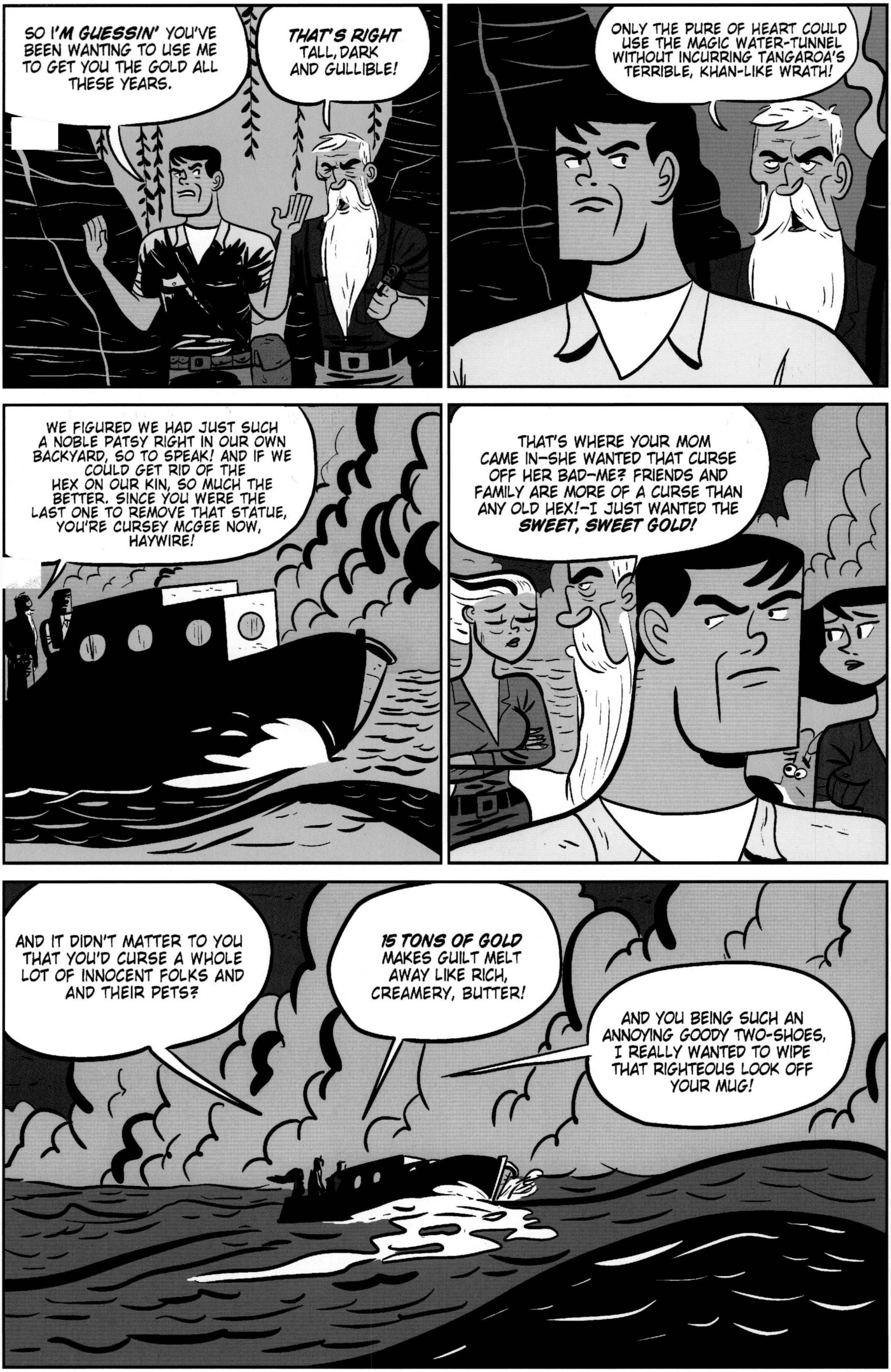
SO I'M GUESSIN' YOU'VE BEEN WANTING TO USE ME TO GET YOU THE GOLD ALL THESE YEARS.
THAT'S RIGHT TALL, DARK AND GULLIBLE!
ONLY THE PURE OF HEART COULD USE THE MAGIC WATER-TUNNEL WITHOUT INCURRING TANGAROA'S TERRIBLE, KHAN-LIKE WRATH!
WE FIGURED WE HAD JUST SUCH A NOBLE PATSY RIGHT IN OUR OWN BACKYARD, SO TO SPEAK! AND IF WE COULD GET RID OF THE HEX ON OUR KIN, SO MUCH THE BETTER. SINCE YOU WERE THE LAST ONE TO REMOVE THAT STATUE, YOU'RE CURSEY MCGEE NOW, HAYWIRE!
THAT'S WHERE YOUR MOM CAME IN—SHE WANTED THAT CURSE OFF HER BAD-ME? FRIENDS AND FAMILY ARE MORE OF A CURSE THAN ANY OLD HEX!—I JUST WANTED THE SWEET, SWEET GOLD!
AND IT DIDN'T MATTER TO YOU THAT YOU'D CURSE A WHOLE LOT OF INNOCENT FOLKS AND AND THEIR PETS?
15 TONS OF GOLD MAKES GUILT MELT AWAY LIKE RICH, CREAMERY, BUTTER!
AND YOU BEING SUCH AN ANNOYING GOODY TWO-SHOES, I REALLY WANTED TO WIPE THAT RIGHTEOUS LOOK OFF YOUR MUG!

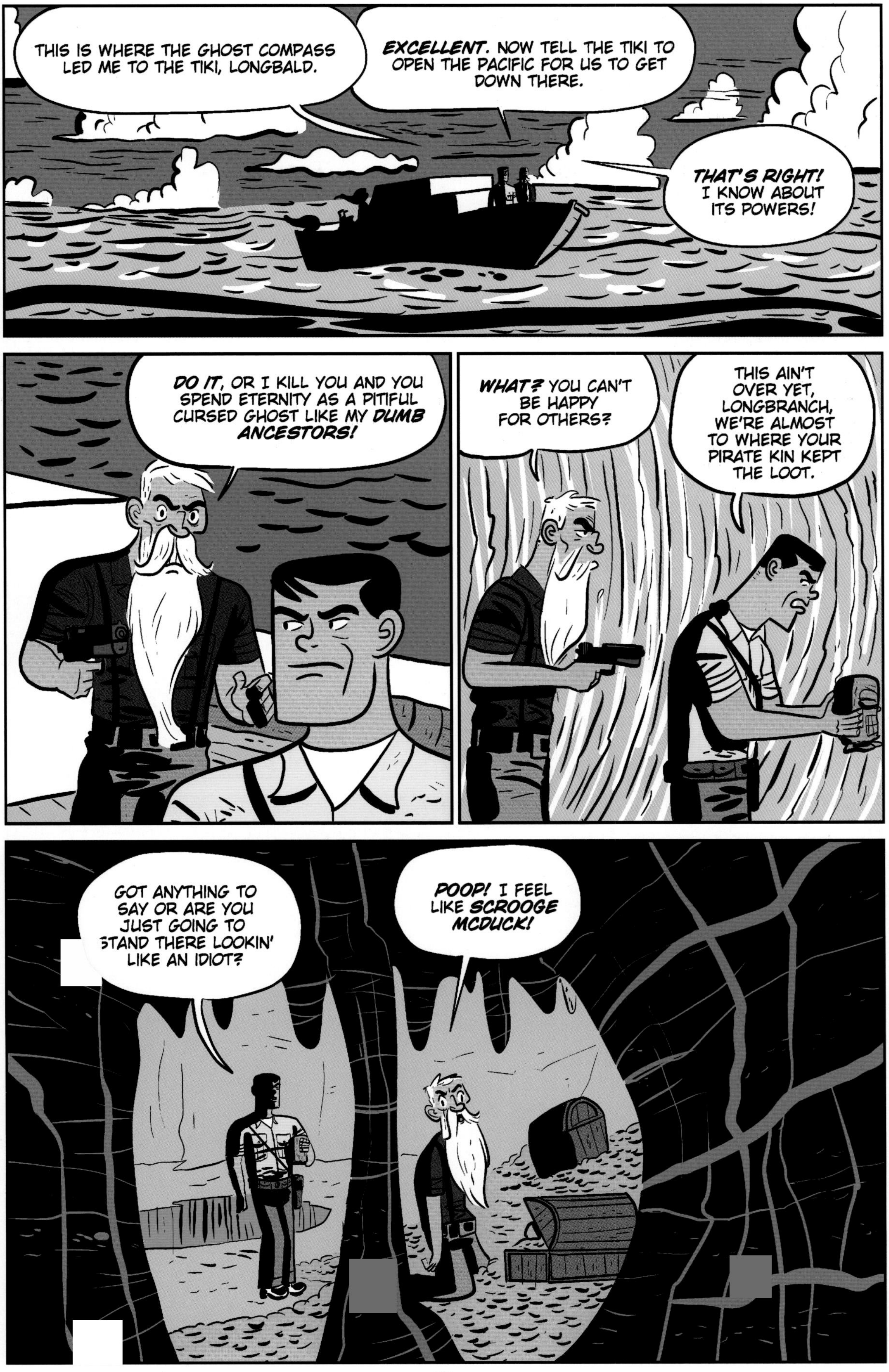
THIS IS WHERE THE GHOST COMPASS LED ME TO THE TIKI, LONGBALD.
EXCELLENT. NOW TELL THE TIKI TO OPEN THE PACIFIC FOR US TO GET DOWN THERE.
THAT'S RIGHT! I KNOW ABOUT ITS POWERS!
DO IT, OR I KILL YOU AND YOU SPEND ETERNITY AS A PITIFUL CURSED GHOST LIKE MY DUMB ANCESTORS!
WHAT? YOU CAN'T BE HAPPY FOR OTHERS?
THIS AIN'T OVER YET, LONGBRANCH, WE'RE ALMOST TO WHERE YOUR PIRATE KIN KEPT THE LOOT.
GOT ANYTHING TO SAY OR ARE YOU JUST GOING TO STAND THERE LOOKIN' LIKE AN IDIOT?
POOP! I FEEL LIKE SCROOGE MCDUCK!

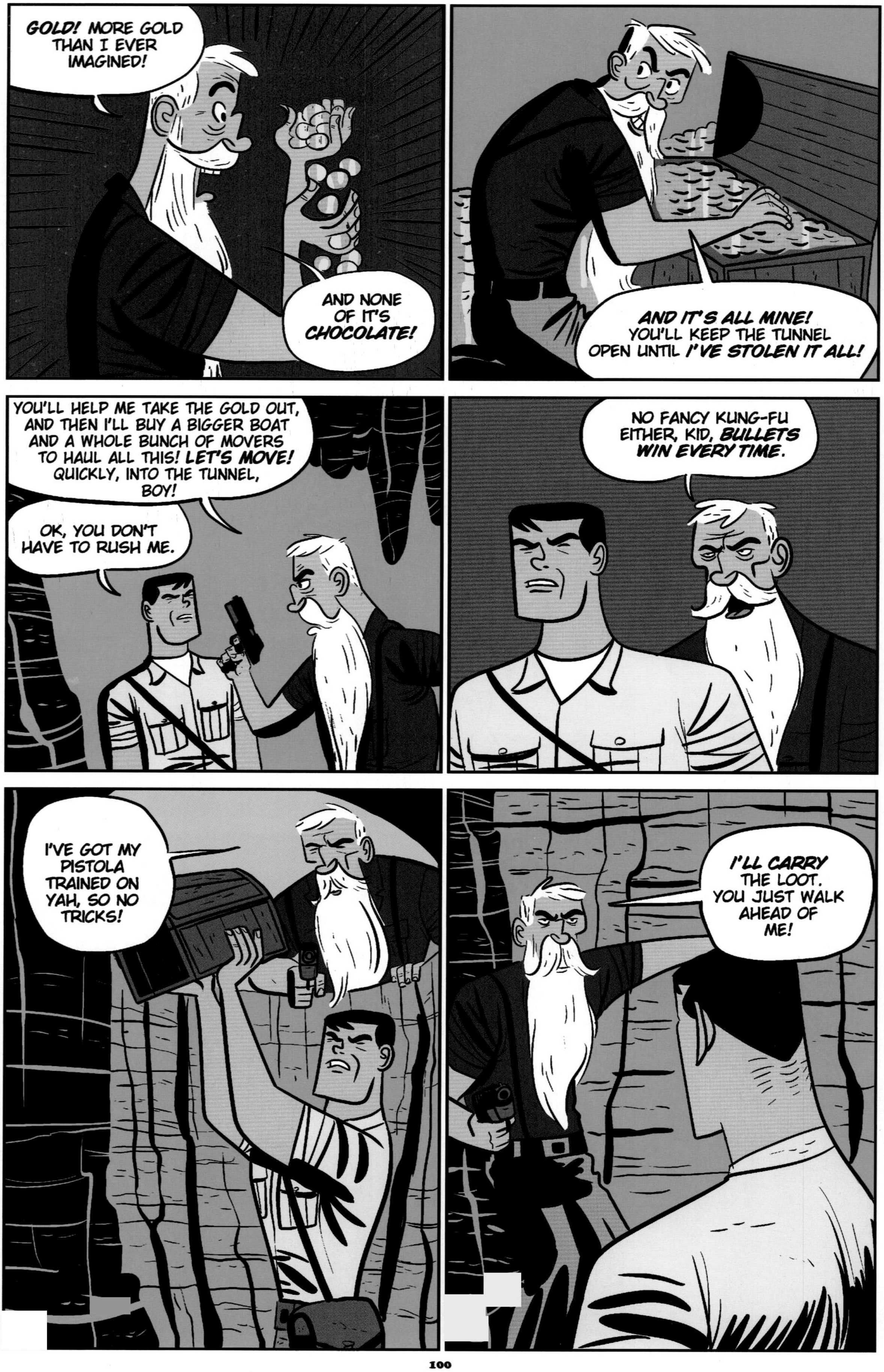
GOLD! MORE GOLD THAN I EVER IMAGINED!
AND NONE OF IT'S CHOCOLATE!
AND IT'S ALL MINE! YOU'LL KEEP THE TUNNEL OPEN UNTIL I'VE STOLEN IT ALL!
YOU'LL HELP ME TAKE THE GOLD OUT, AND THEN I'LL BUY A BIGGER BOAT AND A WHOLE BUNCH OF MOVERS TO HAUL ALL THIS! LET'S MOVE! QUICKLY, INTO THE TUNNEL, BOY!
OK, YOU DON'T HAVE TO RUSH ME.
NO FANCY KUNG-FU EITHER, KID, BULLETS WIN EVERY TIME.
I'VE GOT MY PISTOLA TRAINED ON YAH, SO NO TRICKS!
I'LL CARRY THE LOOT. YOU JUST WALK AHEAD OF ME!

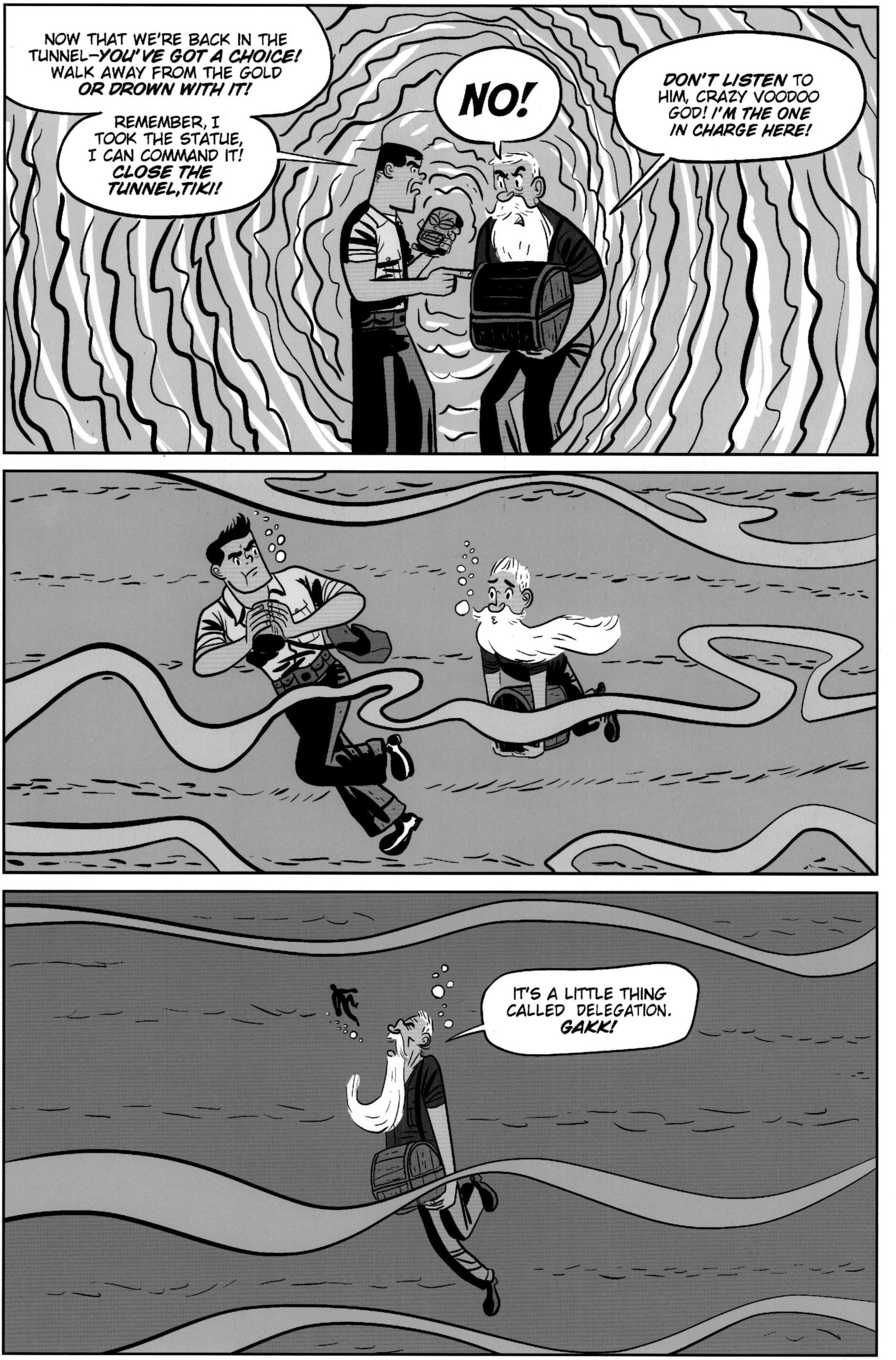
NOW THAT WE'RE BACK IN THE TUNNEL–YOU'VE GOT A CHOICE! WALK AWAY FROM THE GOLD OR DROWN WITH IT!
REMEMBER, I TOOK THE STATUE, I CAN COMMAND IT! CLOSE THE TUNNEL,TIKI!
NO!
DON'T LISTEN TO HIM, CRAZY VOODOO GOD! I'M THE ONE IN CHARGE HERE!
IT'S A LITTLE THING CALLED DELEGATION. GAKK!

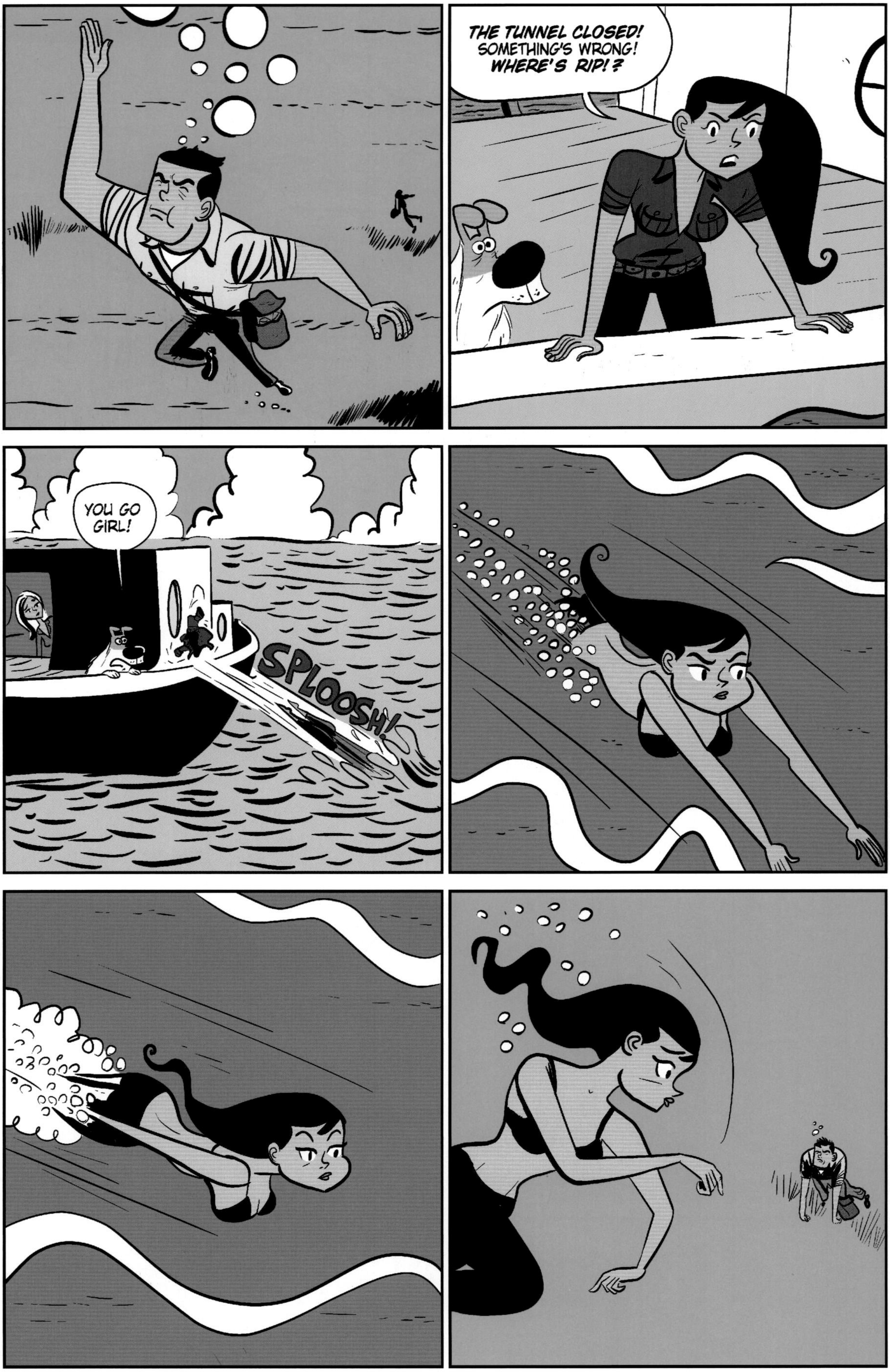
THE TUNNEL CLOSED! SOMETHING'S WRONG! WHERE'S RIP!?
YOU GO GIRL!
SPLOOSH!

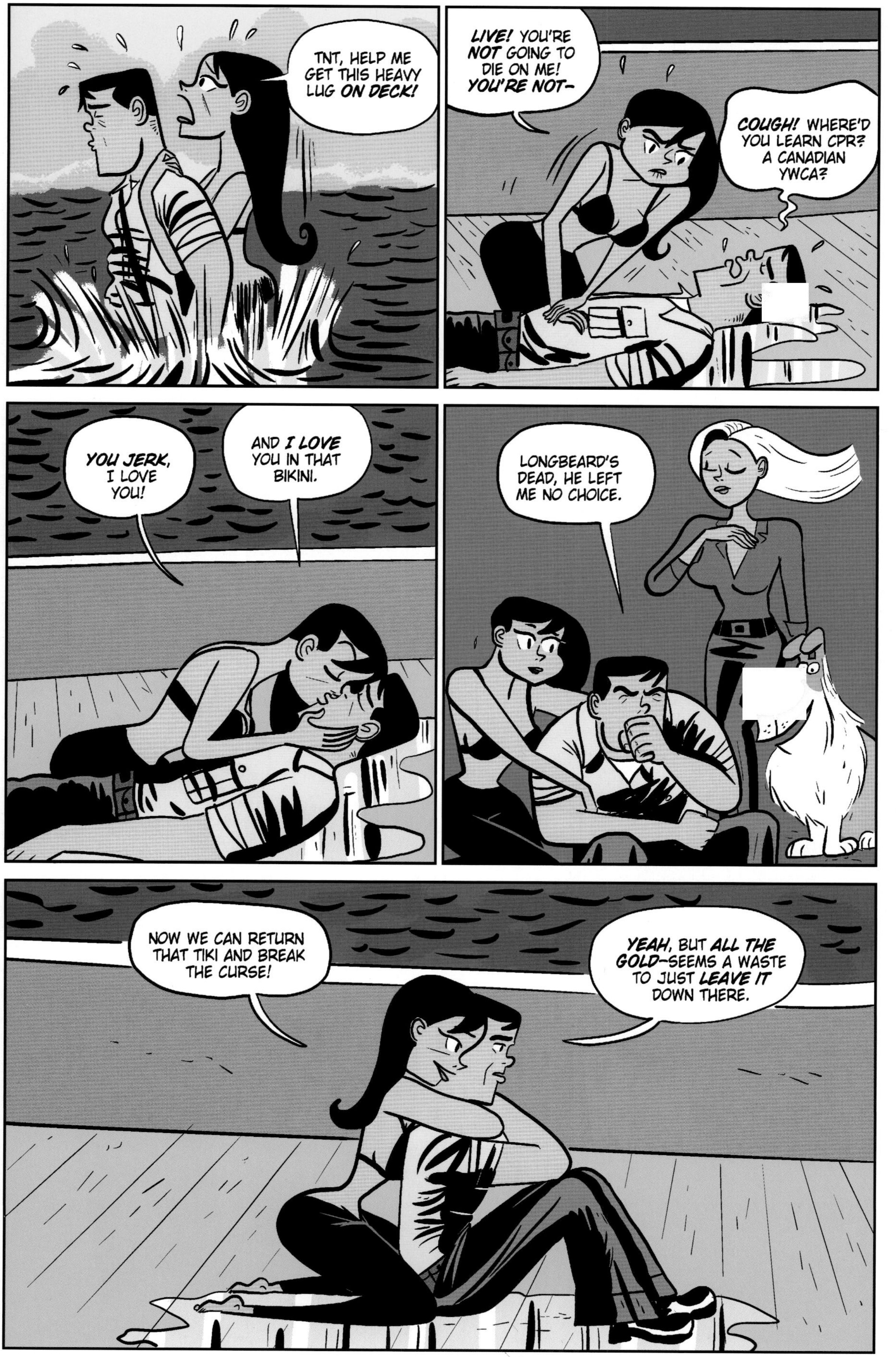
TNT, HELP ME GET THIS HEAVY LUG ON DECK!
LIVE! YOU'RE NOT GOING TO DIE ON ME! YOU'RE NOT-
COUGH! WHERE'D YOU LEARN CPR? A CANADIAN YWCA?
YOU JERK, I LOVE YOU!
AND I LOVE YOU IN THAT BIKINI.
LONGBEARD'S DEAD, HE LEFT ME NO CHOICE.
NOW WE CAN RETURN THAT TIKI AND BREAK THE CURSE!
YEAH, BUT ALL THE GOLD-SEEMS A WASTE TO JUST LEAVE IT DOWN THERE.

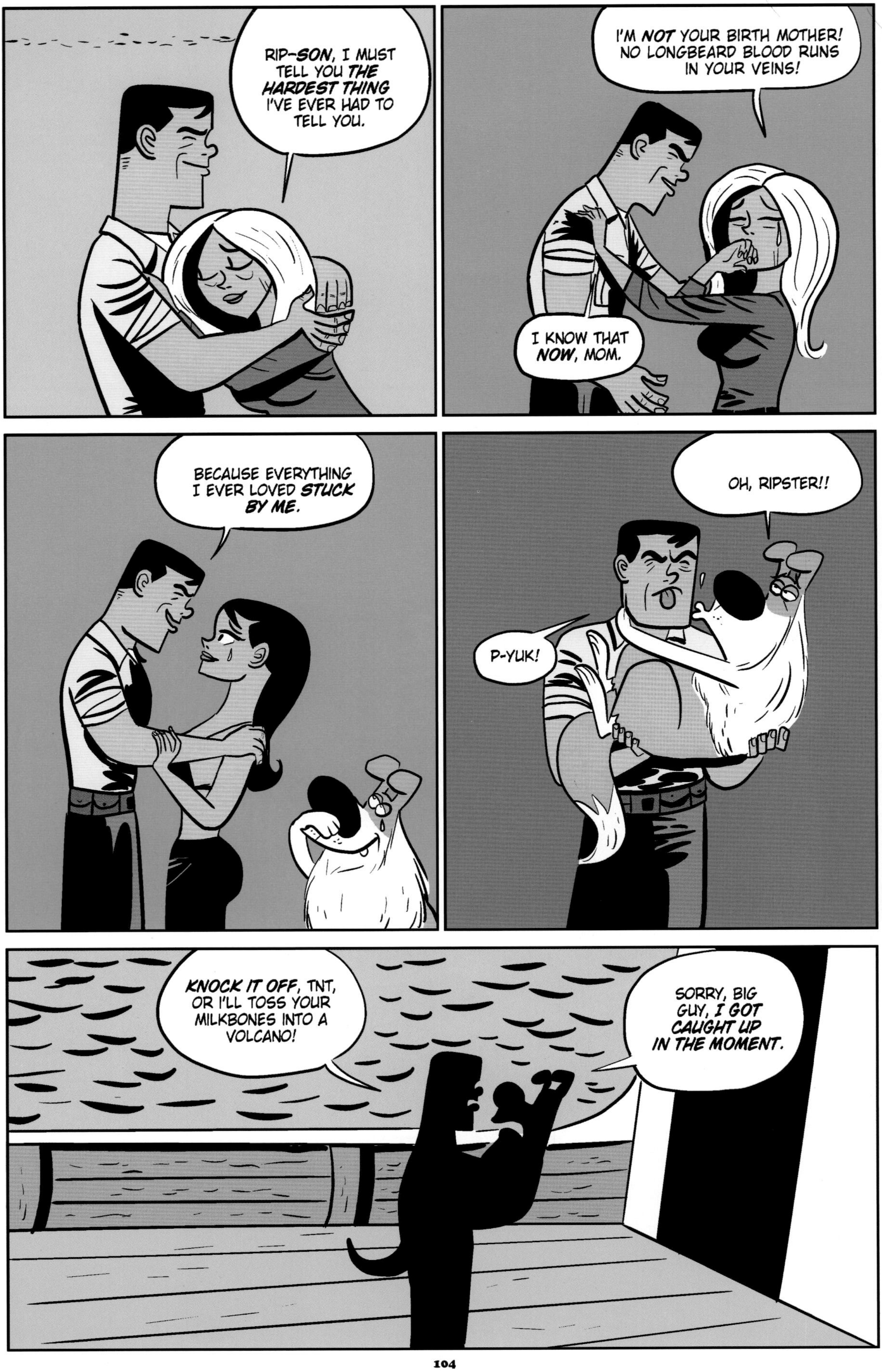
RIP-SON, I MUST TELL YOU THE HARDEST THING I'VE EVER HAD TO TELL YOU.
I'M NOT YOUR BIRTH MOTHER! NO LONGBEARD BLOOD RUNS IN YOUR VEINS!
I KNOW THAT NOW, MOM.
BECAUSE EVERYTHING I EVER LOVED STUCK BY ME.
OH, RIPSTER!!
P-YUK!
KNOCK IT OFF, TNT, OR I'LL TOSS YOUR MILKBONES INTO A VOLCANO!
SORRY, BIG GUY, I GOT CAUGHT UP IN THE MOMENT.

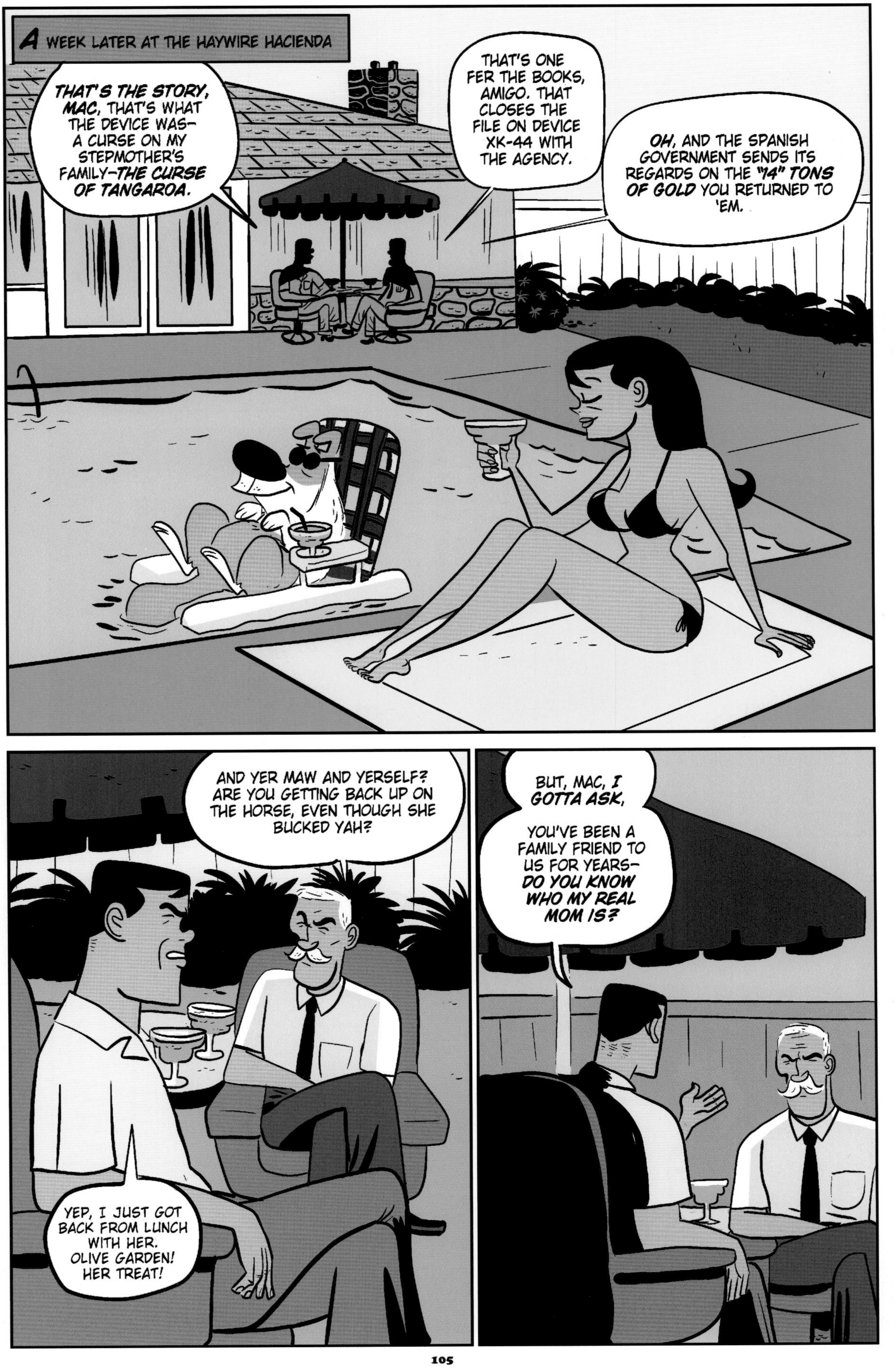
A WEEK LATER AT THE HAYWIRE HACIENDA
THAT'S THE STORY, MAC, THAT'S WHAT THE DEVICE WAS– A CURSE ON MY STEPMOTHER'S FAMILY–THE CURSE OF TANGAROA.
THAT'S ONE FER THE BOOKS, AMIGO. THAT CLOSES THE FILE ON DEVICE XK-44 WITH THE AGENCY.
OH, AND THE SPANISH GOVERNMENT SENDS ITS REGARDS ON THE "14" TONS OF GOLD YOU RETURNED TO 'EM.
AND YER MAW AND YERSELF? ARE YOU GETTING BACK UP ON THE HORSE, EVEN THOUGH SHE BUCKED YAH?
YEP, I JUST GOT BACK FROM LUNCH WITH HER. OLIVE GARDEN! HER TREAT!
BUT, MAC, I GOTTA ASK,
YOU'VE BEEN A FAMILY FRIEND TO US FOR YEARS– DO YOU KNOW WHO MY REAL MOM IS?

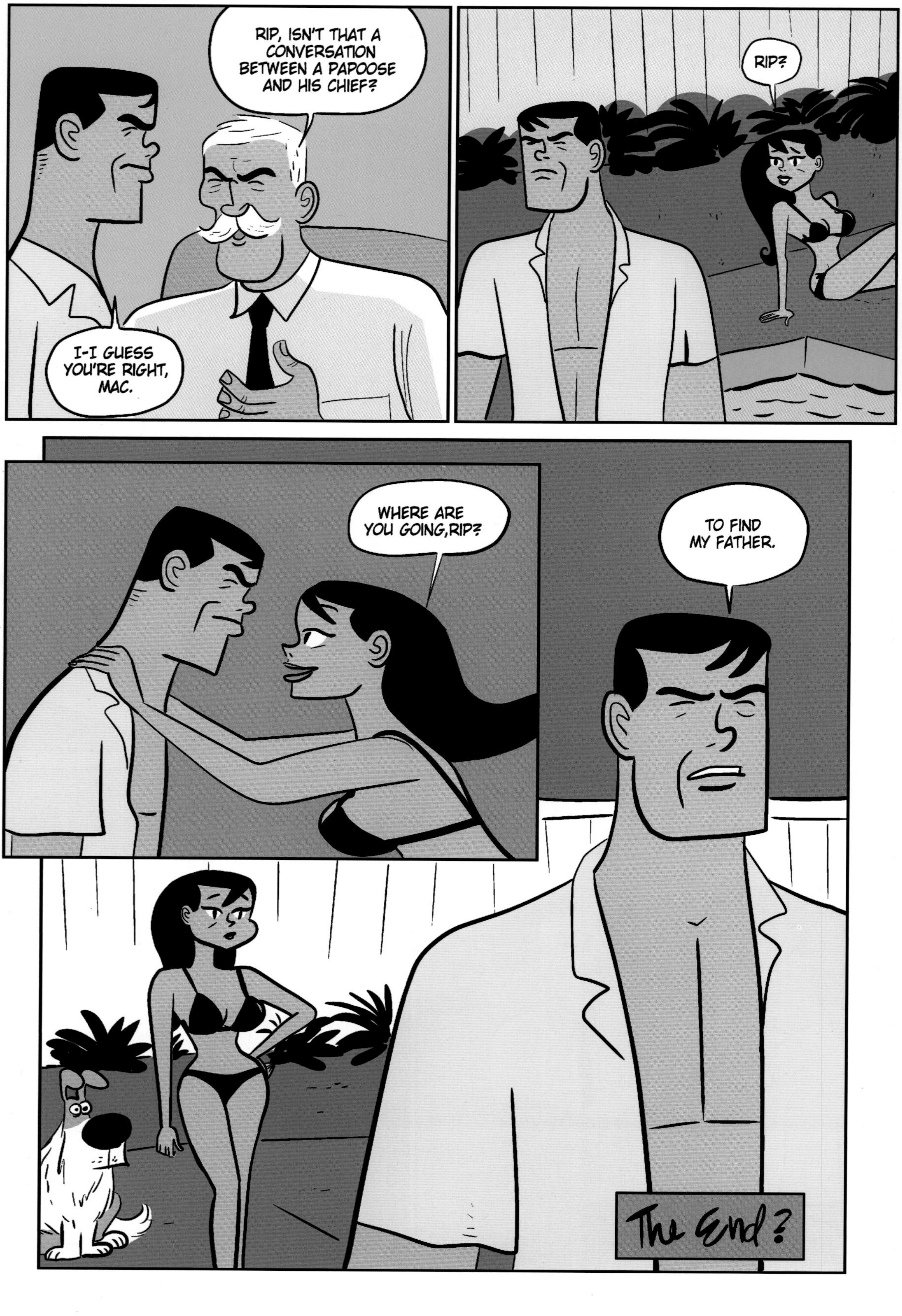
RIP, ISN'T THAT A CONVERSATION BETWEEN A PAPOOSE AND HIS CHIEF?
I-I GUESS YOU'RE RIGHT, MAC.
RIP?
WHERE ARE YOU GOING, RIP?
TO FIND MY FATHER.
The End?

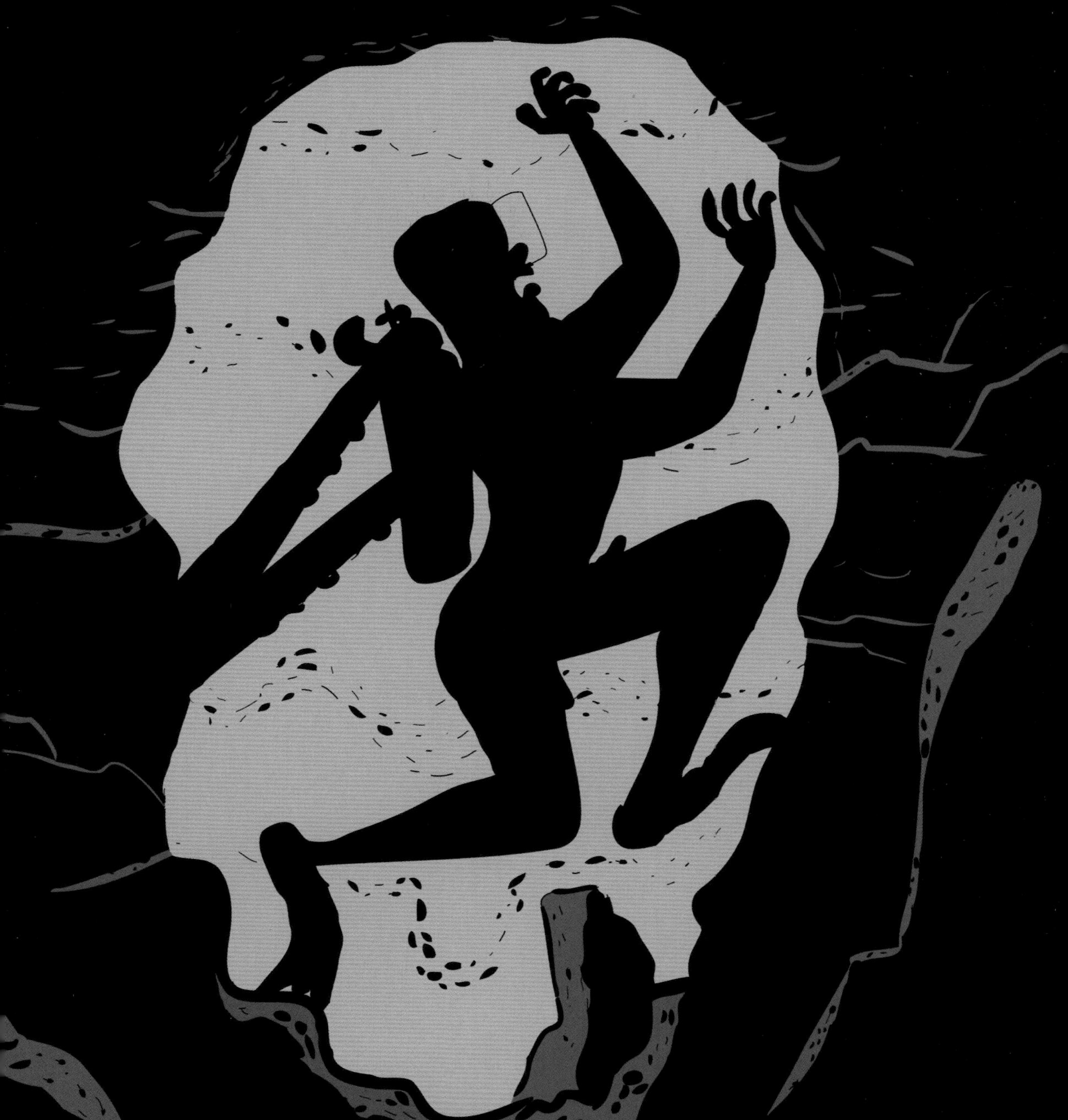

RIP HAYWIRE

AND THE CURSE OF TANGAROA!

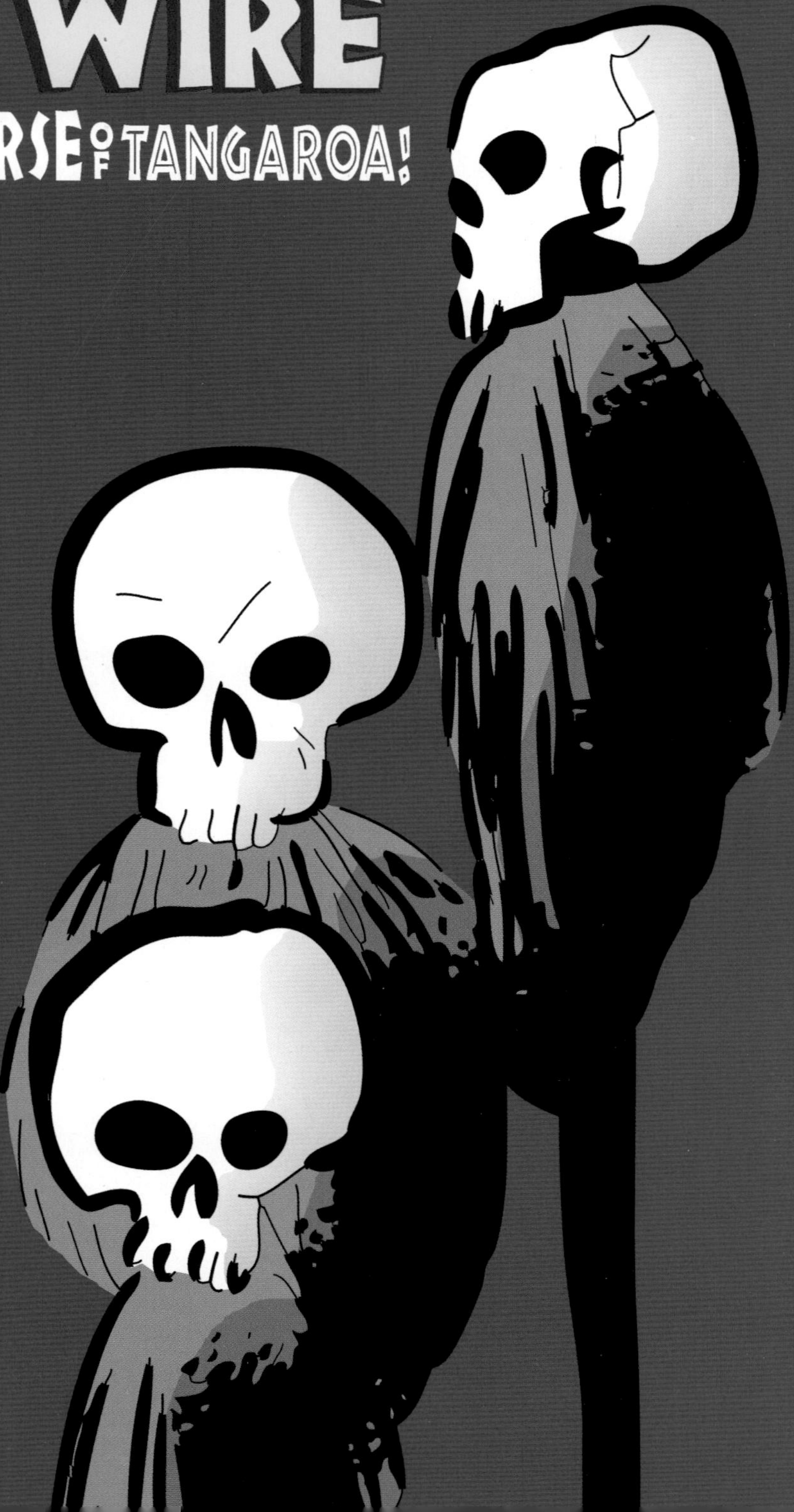